CW00544918

£8
JL

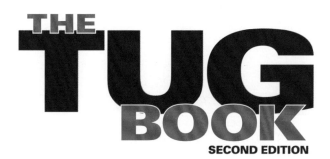

THE TUG BOOK

SECOND EDITION

THE TUG BOOK

SECOND EDITION

M.J. Gaston

Haynes Publishing

First published in 1991 as *Tugs and Towing*
New edition published as *The Tug Book* in 2002
This 2nd Revised Edition published in 2009

A catalogue record for this book is available
from the British Library

ISBN 978 1 84425 527 6

Library of Congress catalog card no 2008939601

Published by Haynes Publishing, Sparkford,
Yeovil, Somerset BA22 7JJ, UK.

Tel: 01963 442030 Fax: 01963 440001
Int. tel: +44 1963 442030
Int. fax: +44 1963 440001
E-mail: sales@haynes.co.uk
Website: www.haynes.co.uk

Haynes North America Inc.,
861 Lawrence Drive, Newbury Park,
California 91320, USA.

Printed and bound in Great Britain

Previous page: Apex, Phenix *and* Tenax, *operated by Solent Towage in the UK, were
built in Spain by Astilleros Gondan between 2006 and 2008 to the same Voith
tractor-tug design by Robert Allan. The tugs are highly sophisticated escort and
tanker-handling vessels of 6,850 bhp with a bollard pull of 67 tonnes. An advanced
hull form and skeg incorporating a Voith Turbo-fin enable the vessels to exert braking
and steering forces of 150 tons at 10 knots when operating in the escort role.*
(Author)

Contents

Foreword

Robert G. Allan, P. ENG., FRINA, FSNAME
President, Robert Allan Ltd.

In 2002, Captain Mike Banbury, writing the foreword to the preceding edition of Jack Gaston's *The Tug Book*, commented, 'The speed of change within the world's towage industry has continued to accelerate over the last decade.' It is unlikely at that time that he or anyone in this industry anticipated how that rate of change would take the further quantum leap that it has. The rate at which installed power in tugs has increased is dramatic; the rate of building is unprecedented in history, and the cost of new tugs has unfortunately risen dramatically as well.

In the last two years the industry has seen the advent of many new terminal tugs with 80–100 tonne bollard pull. The true 'Escort Tug' has become a highly refined vessel with the highest standards of safety and performance, proving that, when properly designed, the tugboat can indeed effect significant control over a disabled tanker. The 'Compact Tug' has become commonplace, with ever-increasing power. The market has seen broad acceptance of unique new design concepts such as the 'Rotor Tug' and the 'Z-Tech'. As the forum of tug operations expands, the industry has also recognised the need for serious research into tug performance, especially in heavy seas. Hence the current SAFETUG project at MARIN will bring much-needed science to the tasks of designing and predicting the performance of the next generation of high-performance tugs. It is both the most exciting and the most challenging of times to be in the tug industry.

Jack Gaston has, with his fourth book on this subject, done a great service to all of us interested in this genre, both the casual observer and the professional, by chronicling the dramatic changes and growth in the industry. By doing so at regular intervals, he has also ensured that the most recent developments are regularly and accurately reported. The industry is experiencing great volatility in oil prices, and pressure to reduce emissions at all levels. The first of a new generation of 'green' tugs is just emerging. Jack cannot rest on his laurels . . . a new volume will almost certainly be required very soon!

Introduction

This latest edition of *The Tug Book* attempts to portray in some detail the work of the marine towage industry and the wide variety of vessels it operates. With a history of approximately 180 years, the towage business is relatively young compared with the parent shipping industry. It has, however, evolved as one of the most interesting and technically advanced branches of shipping and one that continues to develop at an alarming rate. To many, the mention of a tug still conjures up a vision of a simple little vessel emitting vast quantities of smoke whilst assisting a large ship. In reality that image is several decades out of date and the present-day situation reflects a quite different picture. Large numbers of tugs continue to be employed to assist ships in the harbours of the world but also to carry out a multitude of other duties, as diverse as towing massive floating structures around the world, delivering fuel and supplies to Alaska, and supporting dredging and marine construction projects in developing nations.

Tug owners, regardless of the type of operation, are, and always have been, under constant pressure to provide an efficient and economical service and to meet the ever-changing requirements of their clients. For those providing ship-handling services the demands, from what is now a business with a large global dimension, have never been higher. There are, and probably always will be, ships which can only be handled safely in port with the aid of tugs and similarly there are harbours that are only accessible to ships of any size when tugs are on hand to assist them. This situation has been exacerbated by an increase in the size of container ships, a steep increase in the transportation of liquefied natural gas (LNG) by sea and the construction of terminals for oil, gas and bulk cargoes in locations with challenging weather and tidal conditions. Although 'state of the art' tugs are required to carry out this work, the use of 'tug assistance' still represents an unwelcome added cost to the ship owner.

The result of all those demands has been new generations of ship-handling tug, more powerful, fuel-efficient, exceptionally agile, and capable of safe operation with a very small crew. To meet these, often challenging, requirements designers and shipyards continue to use and explore every avenue in hull design, propulsion technology, towing gear, advanced electronics and computer technology.

Among the most recent demands placed upon the tug operator is the need to meet increasingly stringent environmental standards. In many parts of the world, port and local authorities are introducing limits on exhaust gas emissions, noise and other environmental conditions affecting all plant working in port areas and eventually the ships themselves. Meeting those requirements has generated a whole new area of research and development aimed at producing a future generation of 'hybrid' tugs that will not only meet present and future environmental conditions but address issues relating to fuel efficiency and the possible use of advanced new propulsion systems.

In ports and coastal areas frequented by ships carrying hazardous cargoes the provision of effective towage services is a crucial factor. Tugs working with oil and LNG tankers are built and operated to exacting specifications and the use of tugs with escort capability, fire-fighting and pollution-control equipment is now well established. The potential for serious incidents involving tankers, and other large ships carrying significant quantities of fuel oil, has become a serious issue for governments and environmentalists. When things go wrong it is frequently tugs and emergency response vessels that are first on the scene.

Salvage is still perceived by many as one of the more glamorous activities in which tugs and the towage industry become involved. It is in fact a highly competitive and increasingly sophisticated industry that now focuses much of its attention on pollution control and has been responsible for important technological advances in that area of expertise. Processes for removing oil and other pollutants from ships of all types, including tankers, under emergency conditions are now well established. Dedicated commercial salvage tugs are now rare but where they still exist they can be called upon to deal with some of the largest ships in the world, in all kinds of adverse weather conditions. Government-funded emergency towing vessels or emergency response vessels are growing in number and almost without exception they have a significant towing capability and are well equipped for fire-fighting, pollution control and casualty evacuation.

The towage of ships and large floating objects over long distances continues to be an important activity and a new generation of deep-sea tugs has emerged in recent years. Such vessels often have to compete with the growing number of powerful anchor-handling vessels from the offshore oil industry. Modern anchor-handling supply vessels operate increasingly in remote and extremely deep waters where enormous power is required to handle the very heavy anchors, wire and chain involved. The hazards are such that considerable effort has been expended to improve not only the vessels but the safety of crews working on deck.

The Tug Book attempts to describe the wide range of vessels employed by the towing industry, and the work that they do. A level of technical content has been chosen which will hopefully make this book a useful reference to those in the towing industry and of interest to enthusiasts and those with just a passing interest in tugs and towing. This second edition of *The Tug Book* has been made necessary by the sheer scale of change the industry has experienced over the past seven years and is published at a time when new vessels are entering service in greater numbers than ever before. The original format has been retained and the technical information expanded and revised where necessary. *The Tug Book* is not an instruction manual but it is intended to portray a broad view of a very specialised sector of the shipping industry and its vessels.

Chapter 1 describes the basic types of vessel currently in use and gives some insight into their design and construction. The chapters that follow deal with propulsion systems and the array of specialist equipment found aboard the modern tug and describe in more detail how the various types of tug are employed. Many oil-rig supply vessels have a very real towing capability and are included in this overview. Although the content of *The Tug Book* has a natural bias towards European vessels and their operation, considerable effort has gone into ensuring that examples are drawn from the industry world-wide.

No account of the towage industry would be complete without recognising the contribution made by the highly skilled tugmasters and crews. In spite of the advanced technology they have at their finger-tips, reduced crew numbers and increased regulation in the industry mean that the workload is high. In addition to traditional seamanship skills, many tug crews are expected to maintain sophisticated equipment, carry out management tasks, and achieve high levels of certification. By their very nature tugs are required to operate in all weather conditions, at all states of the tide, during the day or night, summer and winter. The illustrations in this book can be misleading, with many photographs taken during ideal conditions. In reality, crews are still required to manoeuvre tugs and handle ropes on deck in the worst possible conditions, and at the same time be responsible for assisting ships with cargoes worth many millions of pounds. A Canadian tugman* once described the life of a tugman as 'hours and hours of boredom interrupted by moments of sheer terror'. Many people in the towage industry will recognise the description. It is the business of designers, owners and tug crews to minimise those moments of terror, but wind, tide and unforeseen circumstances afloat will always be there to catch out the unwary.

M. J. G.

* Robb Douglas, in *Skookum Tugs*

Acknowledgements

This book is dedicated to my wife Ann and my family, who have endured my many hours, days and sometimes weeks of absence when I have been involved in my work with the towage industry.

I am deeply indebted to Robert Allan for his Foreword and kind words. As one of the world's most prominent naval architects specialising in tug design his contribution is much appreciated. As he so rightly states the rate of change in the towage industry and the important developments in design that have taken place over a very short period have surpassed all previous records. What he omitted to mention is that many of those new tugs and important developments were spawned on his drawing board.

I owe my sincere thanks to my many friends and acquaintances in the towage and salvage industries who continue to give me endless encouragement and support, without which this further edition of *The Tug Book* would not have been possible. For very many years my questions have been answered readily and with great patience. Whenever necessary, access has been granted to tugs, manu-facturers' facilities, and conferences, giving me first-hand contact with the towage business worldwide.

Special thanks are due to the staff and personnel of Damen Shipyards, Fairmount Marine, Fairplay Towage, International Transport Contractors, Klyne Tugs (Lowestoft) Ltd, Østensjø Rederi AS, POSH Semco, Smit International, Solent Towage, Svitzer Marine, Titan Maritime, and many other companies with whom I am in regular contact.

Once again, my grateful thanks are also due to my friend Captain David Brown who has always been a great source of encouragement and expertise. I am also indebted to the many companies and private individuals who have so readily supplied photographs and other material – all of which are acknowledged individually in the captions to the relevant illustrations. Help with line drawings has come from illustrator Tim Rolfe whose patience and expertise have been invaluable.

M. J. G.

Glossary

Amidships: A term referring to the centre portion of a vessel. Also used to describe the position of a vessel's rudder when set for 'straight ahead' movement.

Anchor-handling: The process of laying and retrieving the anchors for oil rigs, dredgers and similar pieces of offshore floating plant.

ASD: A common abbreviation for Azimuthing Stern Drive.

Bitts: Posts or similar fittings of heavy construction used to secure ropes for mooring or towing. Often mounted in pairs. See also *bollard*.

Bollard: A single post or similar fitting used to secure ropes for mooring or towing. See also *bitts*.

Bollard pull: The tractive effort produced by a tug or other towing vessel when pulling against a static object (a *bollard*). May be expressed in tons (imperial) or tonnes (metric).

Bow thruster: A means of providing directional thrust at the bow of a vessel to improve its handling characteristics whilst manoeuvring.

Brake horsepower (bhp): The actual power generated by a diesel engine under test conditions, when coupled to a dynamometer (brake).

Bridle: Two short lengths of wire rope or chain cable, assembled to form a 'Y', and used to make the connection between a vessel being towed and the tug's *towline*. The term is also used in some areas to describe a *gog rope*.

Bulwark: The side plating of a vessel above deck level.

Capstan: A vertical revolving drum used to assist in the hauling of ropes and towlines.

Chaser: An appliance used in anchor-handling to locate a buried anchor and provide a means of securing a *pennant* to heave it from the seabed.

Combi tug: A conventional screw tug with a steerable thruster unit located at the bow.

Dead ship: The term used by tug crews to describe a ship that is without its own means of propulsion and steering.

Deadweight: The weight of cargo, stores, fuel, passengers and crew carried by a ship when loaded to its maximum loadline.

Dwt: The abbreviation used for deadweight tonnes.

Dry towing: A method of transporting vessels that are unwieldy and difficult to tow by loading them on a specially designed barge.

Fairlead: A fitting attached to the deck or bulwarks of a vessel to act as a guide for ropes, to prevent chafing and other damage.

Fender: A pad of resilient material used to protect the tug's hull against damage from contact with other vessels and structures. When fitted to bow or stern the fender forms the interface between tug and ship or other vessel when pushing. Commonly manufactured from rubber, wood, rope or vehicle tyres.

Flanking rudders: Additional rudders located forward of the propeller(s).

Flying bridge: An open control position located above an enclosed wheelhouse.

Girding: A term used to describe a tug being capsized by the action of a ship or other vessel it is towing. Capsizing may occur when the *towline* is abeam of the tug (at 90 degrees to its centreline) and sufficient force is generated by the action of the tow to pull the tug over bodily. Also described as *girting* or *tripping*.

Gob rope: See *gog rope*.

Gog rope: A rope used in ship-handling work with European-style conventional screw tugs to control the position of the main towline as a precaution against *girding* (capsizing). Also known as *gob rope*, *stop rope* or *bridle*.

Gross tonnage: A volumetric measurement of the interior of the hull and other enclosed spaces. 100 cubic feet is equal to 1 gross ton. The formula used to measure a vessel can vary with the registration authority.

Ground tackle: An anchor and its associated tackle, used in salvage work to provide additional pulling power when refloating a vessel aground.

Gt or Grt: The abbreviation for *gross (register) tonnage*.

Handy: A term used to describe a vessel that is manoeuvrable and responds readily to the controls.

Heaving line: A light line or rope with a weighted end designed to be thrown by hand. Used when making a towing connection to haul across a *messenger* or *towline*.

Indicated horsepower (ihp): The calculated, theoretical power output of a steam or diesel engine.

MCR: A recognised abbreviation for maximum continuous rating in diesel engines.

Messenger: A small diameter rope used to haul a *towline* or rope of a larger size.

Molgoggers: See *norman pins*.

Norman pins: Pins or rollers which can be erected at the tug's after *bulwarks* to guide the *towline* and prevent it passing over the vessel's beam. Also known as *molgoggers* or *stop pins*.

Nozzle (propulsion): A device mounted around the propeller to augment thrust.

Pendant: A short length of steel wire or manmade-fibre rope attached to the end of a *towline* to resist wear and chafing. The word *pennant* is used in some regions to describe the same item.

Pennant: The steel wire rope used to lay and recover anchors. See also *pendant*.

Pitch (of a propeller): The theoretical distance the propeller will advance during one complete rotation.

Push knees: Structures fitted to the hull of a tug or multi-purpose vessel to enable it to push barges with a minimum risk of damage to either craft.

Rotor Tug™: A tractor tug design embodying three azimuthing propulsion units, two located forward and one aft. Trademark registered to Kotug.

Rubbing band: A band of resilient material fitted around the hull of a vessel as protection against impact damage.

SDM: Ship docking module, a tug design embodying two azimuthing propulsion units located fore and aft, introduced in the USA in 1999.

Ship-handling: Giving assistance to ships in confined waterways when they have insufficient manoeuvrability to proceed safely unaided.

Skeg: A fixed rudder-like fin fitted beneath the after hull of a tug to provide additional directional stability. Also a deep fin-like device fitted to tractor tugs, Z-Tech and stern-drive tugs to enhance the vessel's dynamic performance in the indirect towing mode. Also used on towed barges to improve their handling characteristics.

Splice: A method of joining two ropes or forming a permanent loop. Carried out by separating the strands of the rope and forming a connection by inter-weaving the free ends.

Spring: A section of rope forming part of a *towline* designed to introduce an element of elasticity, thus reducing the shock loads involved in towing. The term also describes a mooring rope intended to prevent fore and aft movement of a vessel.

Stern roller: A horizontal roller incorporated into the 'open stern' of tugs used for anchor-handling or laying protective booms for pollution control. Designed to prevent damage and enhance the passage of ropes, wires, anchors or other items passing to and from the deck.

Stern thruster: A device to provide transverse thrust at the stern of a vessel to enhance manoeuvrability.

Stop pins: See *norman pins*.

Stop rope: See *gog rope*.

Stopper: A device used to secure a *towline* temporarily while changes or repairs are carried out.

Superstructure: The wheelhouse, bridge accommodation and similar structures built above deck level.

Tackle: A combination of pulley blocks and ropes or lines used to provide a mechanical advantage when hauling or lifting.

Tow beams: Protective bars or tubular structures erected over the tug's after deck to prevent the *towline* fouling fittings or deck equipment. Sometimes passing over the entire deck from *bulwark* to *bulwark*.

Towline: A rope used in towing to connect the tug to its tow. May be of steel wire rope or manmade-fibre rope.

Tractor tug: A tug with its propellers or propulsion units located beneath the hull, forward of amidships, to pull rather than push the vessel along.

Turbo Fin™: The name of a specially enhanced skeg designed by Voith Hydro. Used on some high-performance Voith tractor tugs optimised to operate 'fin-first'. The leading edge of the skeg incorporates a rotating vertical roller to enhance water-flow and steering forces during indirect towing operations.

Wheelhouse: The main control position from which the tugmaster commands the vessel.

Winch: A mechanical device used to haul, control and store ropes during towing, lifting or hauling.

Z-Tech™: A unique development of the azimuthing stern-drive tug intended to combine the best operating characteristics of the stern-drive tug and tractor tug using similar propulsion systems.

Opposite: *The chart plots in very broad terms the evolution of the ship-handling tug and its propulsion systems in Europe, starting with the first commercial paddle vessel in 1830. By the 1900s screw and paddle designs were well established in a form that was to remain virtually unchanged until WWII. Development of the paddle effectively ceased with the introduction of eight diesel-electric tugs in Britain in 1958. By the 1950s diesel power was becoming common in screw-powered tugs and by the middle of the decade Voith Schneider propulsion and Kort nozzles were appearing in some numbers. By the 1980s azimuthing tractors, Voith tractors, conventional screw and a small number of stern-drive vessels of Japanese origin were in use in Europe. Development of escort tugs in the mid-1990s resulted in direct competition between Voith Schneider and stern-drive designs. By 1999 two new concepts had evolved, the 'Rotor Tug' and the 'Ship Docking Module', along with further developments in Voith tractor-tug design. A further notional milestone in 2005 saw yet more improvements to Voith escort-tug designs, further development of stern-drive tugs – including the arrival of new compact designs and the introduction of the new Z-Tech type.*

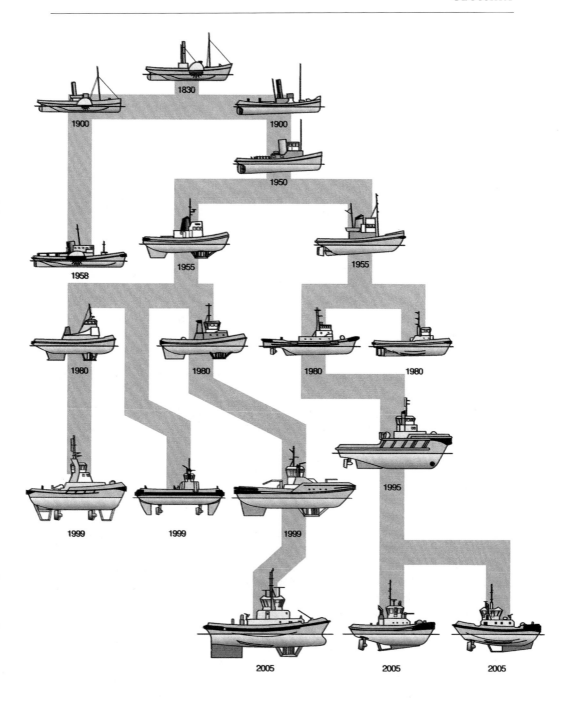

Romulo *is a stern-drive escort and tanker-handling tug built for Spanish operators* REPASA *of Tarragona in 2005. The 33.5 m vessel is powered by two MAN main engines of 6,470 bhp (total) coupled to Steerprop azimuthing propulsion units. This set up gives* Romulo *a bollard pull of 81 tonnes and maximum speed of 13.5 knots.* (Author)

CHAPTER 1

Tug Design and Construction

T he growing number of different tug designs and the way in which modern
propulsion systems are used have made tug design and construction one of
the most specialised subjects in the shipbuilding industry. In this chapter an
attempt is made to describe as simply as possible the different basic tug types and
show how the various modern propulsion systems have influenced hull
configuration. Also included are the features in tug design that set them apart from
other vessels. Many aspects of hull and superstructure construction differ
substantially from traditional ship design and the importance of these will be
highlighted. The propulsion systems employed in tugs are often installed and used
quite differently in various types of vessel. For this reason propulsion systems are
described separately and in some detail in Chapter 2.

From its inception in the 1830s, the tug developed rapidly for some sixty years.
The earliest vessels were driven by paddles but these were soon superseded in
many areas by those equipped with screw propellers. By the end of the nineteenth
century a basic configuration for propeller-driven tugs had emerged and was to
remain virtually unchanged for several decades. The majority of tugs retained
steam-powered machinery until the 1940s, and many of the long-established basic
principles of hull and superstructure design remain valid to this day in
conventional screw-driven vessels.

In the years following the Second World War, construction methods changed,
propulsion machinery was refined and eventually the diesel engine was universally
adopted by the industry at large. In spite of many experiments with engines,
propellers and nozzles to enhance thrust, the first radical departure in tug design
did not come until 1954. In that year the first ship-handling tug fitted with a Voith
Schneider cycloidal propeller was put into commercial use, bringing a whole new
concept to the industry. Known as 'tractor tugs' the first Voith-propelled vessels
set new standards for manoeuvrability in ship-handling tugs.

By the first years of the twentieth century the paddle tug was rapidly being superseded by tugs fitted with the screw propeller but several remained with tug fleets in Britain for more than half a century longer. President *is a typical example. Built in 1876, this vessel spent most of its working life on the rivers Tyne and Wear and remained in service until finally going for scrap in 1959.*

Demands for greater bollard pull combined with exceptional handling characteristics soon resulted in alternative advanced propulsion systems emerging from other manufacturers. Virtually all are based on the fully steerable, or azimuthing, propulsion unit employing a conventional propeller. Such propulsion systems have been used in a number of quite different tug designs, and their use has been responsible for the appearance of several new and highly innovative vessels in the past two decades. Even established concepts, such as the stern-drive tug, have been honed and refined to enhance their manoeuvrability and pulling power in very recent years.

Within the last decade two totally new tug designs have emerged, the 'Rotor Tug' and the 'Ship Docking Module' both invented by tug owners with a special interest in producing vessels with particular handling characteristics to satisfy the needs of their own business. The resulting vessels illustrate how, within a relatively short time and with a high level of persistence, an idea can become a working reality. Both concepts use azimuthing propulsion units but differ widely in approach and application.

One of the most prevalent developments, occurring since the start of the new millennium, is an almost universal demand to reduce the size of crew needed to operate harbour and ship-handling tugs. This reduction in manpower has resulted in a noticeable shift towards very small, extremely powerful and highly manoeuvrable vessels that can be operated safely and efficiently by a crew of two or three people.

Owners ordering new tugs now have a greater choice than ever before, requiring many complex decisions to be made regarding hull design, propulsion system and towing equipment. Obviously such decisions will centre primarily around the type of work the vessel will be expected to do and the environment in which it will operate. Later chapters will illustrate the wide range of duties undertaken by tugs of all shapes and sizes.

FUNDAMENTAL DESIGN PRINCIPLES

There are many established rules that govern the hull design of all ships and boats. Some of those rules have been in use since the days of the early steam ship and determine, for example, a direct relationship between a vessel's length, beam and speed. The underwater shape and size of a hull all play an important part in the vessel's performance and handling characteristics. Those principles apply to virtually any vessel that moves through the water and for the first century or so tug construction deviated very little from those basic rules.

The Dutch Furie *is one of a few surviving traditional steam tugs representative of the very large numbers once in use in mainland Europe and Britain. Built in Holland in 1916 by Bodewes, the tug was employed in Sweden as the* Holmen III *to tow log rafts across the Baltic Sea for the paper-making industry. The single-screw tug is 30 m in length with a beam of 6 m, powered by a triple-expansion engine of 459 ihp. After a long and varied career* Furie *was returned to the Netherlands and subsequently preserved as a working example in the Tug Museum at Maasluis.* (R. Wisse)

The introduction of novel propulsion systems, employing other than conventional screw propellers located beneath the vessel's stern, has complicated matters considerably. Additional space may be required to accommodate bulky propulsion units or the underwater shape of the hull may have to be modified to improve water flow to the propellers or to enhance a particular feature of the tug's performance.

In steam-driven vessels, where comparatively little power was available, tugmasters made good use of the weight and underwater shape of their vessels

3

when controlling a tow. Modern tugs, with much lighter machinery, have less actual weight but features are frequently built into the hull design to achieve improved performance by using similar dynamic effects. With enhanced performance often comes the need to maintain adequate stability under extreme conditions, necessitating changes to the underwater shape of the vessel. The following paragraphs describe the various types of tug and explain how designs have changed to satisfy particular roles and accommodate the propulsion systems currently installed.

BASIC TUG TYPES

Conventional Screw Tugs

The term conventional screw tug, in the context of this book, means a vessel propelled by one or more screw propellers fitted to rigid propeller shafts located at the stern. This type of propulsion is still regarded as the norm in the majority of ships and was standard in virtually all tugs prior to the 1950s. A great many tugs are still built using this form of propulsion but new types of propeller and the use of thrust-enhancing nozzles and sophisticated rudder systems have greatly increased in recent years. Although the vast majority of older tugs still in service around the world are driven by conventional screw propellers there are now fewer new vessels that employ a single, open-screw propeller without some form of

The motor tug Taucher O. Wulf 8 *is one of a diminishing number of single-screw motor tugs in use in Germany and elsewhere in Europe. Built in 1970 as a ship-handling tug escort, the vessel was purchased by Ottowulf Gmbh of Cuxhaven in 1994 and has been progressively modernised.* Taucher O. Wulf 8 *is 23.08 m in length fitted with a 1,012 bhp Cummins main engine and Kort nozzle.* (B. Dahlmann)

In the USA a number of tugs continue to be constructed to traditional twin-screw designs, but using modern techniques and machinery. Colonel, operated in this picture by Marine Towing of Tampa, was built in 1998. It is a 3,516 bhp vessel 29 m in length. (Author)

nozzle or steering device fitted. An exception is the single screw 'Combi' type of tug, mentioned later in this section.

Twin-screw designs are now common and widely seen in ship-handling tugs, coastal tugs, anchor-handling and deep-sea tugs, offshore supply vessels and small tug/workboats. In most modern applications, propulsion nozzles of the fixed type

The twin-screw tug Viking *was built by Gebr Kooiman in the Netherlands in 2008 for Dutch owner Koerts International Towing Service to provide coastal towing and on-site services to the marine civil engineering industry. Viking is 30.8 m in length and is powered by two Mitsubishi main engines producing a total of 3,040 bhp and a bollard pull of 65 tonnes. (Kooiman)*

are used, often with innovative rudder systems. Open propellers are rare in new European twin-screw vessels but are still preferred by a minority of operators in the United States of America and elsewhere. In terms of design, the hull form of a modern conventional screw tug has changed little from its predecessors. Length, breadth and hull configuration are chosen to suit the vessel's application. In some ports the dimensions of locks or other limiting features of a confined dock system may influence the size of ship-handling tugs that can be used effectively.

During the early post Second World War period diesel-powered tugs were built using a hull design known as 'Hydroconic'. The hull was of a double-chine configuration, built mainly from simple welded plates with little need for complex compound curves. Hulls of this type proved cheap to produce and had good performance characteristics while towing and running free. Modern designs frequently follow similar principles, adapted to accommodate recent advances in propulsion technology. In all cases the underwater shape is designed to provide unrestricted water flow around the rudders and propellers. A skeg, or extended keel, may be incorporated at the stern to give good directional stability. The shape of the tug hull in plan view is also of great importance to the master of a vessel working in close proximity to ships and other floating objects. For many years the traditional tug was built with a very rounded stern to assist when going alongside or leaving a ship's side, allowing it to turn away easily. With modern tugs, the use of twin screws and nozzles demand a stern shape that is less rounded to enable the steering gear to be accommodated and afford some protection to the propulsion equipment underwater. The eventual shape is almost certain to be a compromise between the need for some degree of roundness and the improved ability of a twin-screw vessel to manoeuvre at close quarters.

In larger, seagoing vessels the underwater shape of the bow may be given a bulbous configuration to enhance the vessel's free-running speed. The addition of a raised foredeck or a large fully enclosed forecastle is common in ship-handling tugs that may be required to work in exposed locations and essential in larger seagoing or coastal vessels to help reduce the amount of water on deck in heavy seas.

The hull of the small twin-screw tug Herbert Ballam *is typical of the double-chine construction found in many modern tugs. Built at Poole in 1996, it is a vessel of 18.25 m, powered by two Cummins main engines producing a total of 1,300 bhp. Note the lack of compound curves and the moulded rubber bow fender.* (Author)

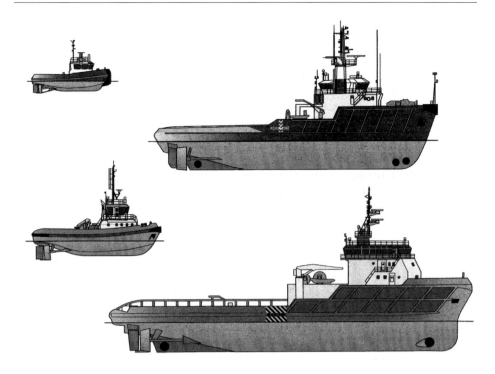

The diagram shows, to scale, four different modern vessels with conventional screw propulsion typical of those described in later pages. A tug/workboat of 16 m in length, a 26 m twin-screw harbour tug, a 54 m anchor-handling tug, and a deep-sea tug of 74 m.

An anchor-handling tug requires a large clear after deck and an open stern to enable anchors, buoys, chain and other equipment to be brought safely on board. Sufficient buoyancy is also needed to accommodate the increasingly large lifting forces involved in present day offshore anchor-handling operations. A new generation of smaller shallow-draft anchor-handlers is growing in popularity. This type of vessel is used extensively to support the construction of inshore oil production, wind-farms and other marine civil engineering projects.

Offshore supply vessels and anchor-handling supply vessels are invariably longer than a normal seagoing or anchor-handling tug and will have a significant cargo capacity. In such vessels cargo is accommodated in additional storage tanks, incorporated as part of the hull structure, and on a large clear expanse of open deck. The latter is used to transport containerised stores, drilling pipe, and other bulky items to oil rigs and other offshore installations. A hull form will be chosen that encompasses all of those needs. It must provide a good economical turn of speed, adequate towing characteristics and the ability to handle well when manoeuvring in close proximity to offshore installations.

There are a number of applications, usually where a high bollard pull is required from a shallow-draft vessel, for which a triple-screw system is adopted. Such vessels differ little in configuration or construction to a twin-screw tug. The major aim is to ensure the hull design allows a free flow of water to all three propellers.

A transverse bow-thrust unit is becoming an increasingly common feature in tugs of almost any size to improve manoeuvrability. They are virtually indispensable in large deep-sea tugs, anchor-handling tugs, and supply vessels working in the offshore oil industry. In the last it is common to find one or more transverse thrusters fitted at bow and stern, and in some cases an additional retractable, azimuthing, thruster in the bow.

Also covered by this book are vessels such as pusher tugs and multi-purpose work vessels that also incorporate conventional screw propulsion. These generally have a comparatively simple, barge-like, hull form. These and conventional tugs designed or adapted for pushing are described in more detail in later chapters.

Combi Tugs

There are a small number of operators, mainly in Europe and North America, that favour a ship-handling tug based on a conventional single-screw vessel but enhanced by the installation of a small azimuthing propulsion (thruster) unit located beneath the bow. This arrangement considerably improves the vessel's ability to manoeuvre and provides a modest amount (2–6 tonnes) of additional bollard pull. Tugs equipped in this way are known as 'combi tugs' and are particularly useful for ship-handling work in dock systems and other confined spaces.

A 'combi tug' is a conventional single-screw vessel fitted with a retractable azimuthing thruster unit beneath the bow. This example is a design introduced by the Belgian company U.R.S. in 1991.

In most instances the vessels concerned are existing single-screw tugs that have been fitted with a thruster at a later date, thus extending the useful life of an otherwise outdated tug. There are, however, examples of purpose-built combi tugs being put into service in Europe as late as 1993. Very little change is required to the tug's structure, apart from providing accommodation for the propulsion unit and its associated powerplant. A retractable thruster unit is the most common choice, with its machinery located in the forepeak and the steerable propeller extending through the hull plating when in use.

A new application for the combi tug principle is emerging with the introduction of a new and highly innovative towing system known as the Carrousel. The first vessels to use this new equipment, described in Chapter 3, are powerful single-screw tugs adopting the combi tug configuration with a fully azimuthing, non-retractable, thruster in the bow.

Stern-Drive Tugs

The nearest relative to the conventional screw tug in hull design is the stern-drive vessel. This is a vessel where normal propellers and shafts have been replaced by azimuthing propulsion units which enable the propeller and its associated nozzle to be rotated (or steered) about a vertical axis. Such vessels are invariably fitted with a pair of propulsion units, located in approximately the same position as the propellers of a twin-screw tug. Each propulsion unit is normally capable of being controlled independently, enabling thrust from each unit to be directed at any angle in relation to the hull. Manoeuvrability is improved dramatically when compared with a conventional screw tug. The vessel can be made to move forwards, backwards, sideways and turn in its own length with great precision in the hands of an experienced tugmaster.

SD Stingray *is one of four azimuthing stern-drive tugs built to the Robert Allan RAmparts 3200 design by Medmarine at Eregli, Turkey, for Kotug. It is 32 m long, powered by two Caterpillar main engines of 4,992 bhp (total) coupled to Schottel propulsion units, with controllable-pitch propellers, for a bollard pull of 65 tonnes.* (H. Hoffmann)

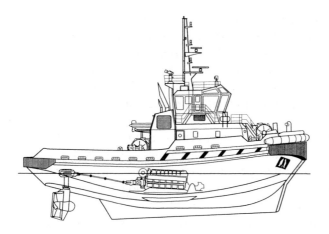

The drawing depicts the layout of a modern RAmparts 3200 azimuthing stern-drive tug, showing the relative positions of the vessel's engines, propulsion units, winches and other major items of equipment. (Sanmar)

Manoeuvrability, a relatively high bollard pull and no significant increase in the draft of the vessel have made the stern-drive tug a viable alternative to tractor tugs in many applications. Tugs of the stern-drive type are sometimes referred to as 'reverse tractors'. This term can and does cause confusion and has therefore been avoided in this book. Later chapters deal in more detail with azimuthing propulsion units, their controls and how stern-drive tugs are employed.

The stern-drive configuration is most commonly found in powerful ship-handling tugs and is particularly popular in applications where power and manoeuvrability of a very high order are a prime requirement, such as tanker-handling tugs and escort vessels. Stern-drive tugs were first introduced in Japan and elsewhere in Asia but in recent years vessels of this type have become the most popular choice for the majority of tug owners in the ship-handling business. This form of propulsion has also been chosen for larger specialist emergency response tugs used for pollution control where a high degree of manoeuvrability is essential.

In simple terms, the hull design used in tugs of this type differs very little from those employing conventional propellers. The main difference is that the underside of the stern must be of a suitable shape to accept the propulsion unit mountings and have sufficient structural strength to accommodate loadings quite different from those imposed by a conventional propeller and rudder system. In many vessels the propulsion units are accessible through removable plates in the after deck and may be lifted out vertically for repair, in some cases while the tug is still afloat.

Since the early days of stern-drive tugs considerable effort has been put into refining the underwater hull design, within the constraints previously mentioned. Much of this activity has been centred around the development of escort tugs and the increasing numbers of small, powerful, and very agile tugs that are appearing from American and Canadian designers. Among the operational requirements expected of a powerful stern-drive tug are a good performance when going astern and the ability to handle well when manoeuvring and towing in the indirect mode, that is when the dynamics of the tug's hull are being used to help control the tow.

Naval architects have approached these needs in different ways resulting in vessels with very similar specifications and performance but having quite different hull forms. The shape of the hull in the vicinity of the propulsion units is particularly important. Rotation of the units, with thrust produced in any direction, makes the need to maintain good water flow to the propellers and avoid any adverse interaction between the units a prime consideration in determining the underwater shape of the hull.

In most other respects the features of a stern-drive tug follow closely the rules that apply to a modern conventional screw tug. A raised foredeck is a feature frequently incorporated in tugs of this type and a complete forecastle is employed in vessels intended to operate at sea or in exposed locations. Stern-drive tugs employed in ship-handling work are almost invariably equipped with a towing winch on the foredeck or forecastle and are therefore strengthened accordingly. Another common feature is the installation of a transverse bow-thrust unit, to enhance manoeuvrability and station-keeping even further.

'Z-Tech' Tugs

The 'Z-Tech' is a recent and unique development intended to incorporate the best handling and operational characteristics of both azimuthing stern-drive vessels and azimuthing tractor tugs. This increasingly popular design was developed by the leading international firm of naval architects Robert Allan Limited expressly for PSA Marine of Singapore and is now available worldwide. The result is a new and distinctive design offering significant improvements in performance and safety, and almost uniform performance in either direction.

A 'Z-Tech' tug is a true 'double-ended' vessel with a unique hull form based on an azimuthing stern drive (ASD) configuration with a very deep keel (or skeg) beneath the bow. When ship-handling, the heavily fendered bow, with its low mounted towing winch and fairlead, becomes the 'business end' of the vessel

The drawing illustrates the unique configuration of the Z-Tech design, showing the heavily fendered bow and deep skeg. The propulsion units are beneath the stern which has an underwater shape optimised for running astern in tractor tug mode when required.

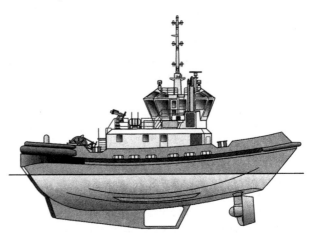

Star Emerald *is one of a growing number of 'Z-Tech' tugs built for the Port Authority of Singapore to a unique and specially commissioned design for a versatile ship-handling tug. This example was built by Cheoy Lee Shipyards in China in 2007 and is powered by Caterpillar main engines of 5,000 bhp to produce a bollard pull of 60 tonnes and a free-running speed of 12.5 knots in either direction.* (Author)

operating in much the same way as any other ASD tug. With the wheelhouse located aft of amidships this affords good overhead clearance and very stable towing characteristics. The vessel's stern incorporates a distinctive flare, enabling it to operate at sea in the same manner as an azimuthing tractor tug. In this configuration the tug tows from the same winch and has an equally good performance whilst towing or running free in this direction.

The first tug of this new design, designated a 'Z-Tech 2800', was completed in 2004. This first vessel, named *Indee*, was 27.4 m in length overall, with a beam of 11.5 m, powered by main engines generating a total of 5,000 horsepower. Since that date production of Z-Tech tugs has continued unabated, with a wide range of different sizes available to tug owners worldwide.

Voith Schneider Tractor Tugs

The introduction of the Voith Schneider tractor tug brought a whole new concept to the towing industry. The cycloidal propeller is a unique device, described in detail in Chapter 2, comprising a number of vertical blades that follow a circular orbit and produce thrust by means of their hydrodynamic profile and ability to change pitch at certain points in their circular path. Although this type of propulsion unit has many other applications, in ferries and other vessels where precise control is necessary the combination of the cycloidal propeller and the tractor concept produced a tug that was to revolutionise towing for many operators. The term tractor is used where the propulsion units are located in the forward part of the vessel.

The Voith Schneider tractor tug was originally introduced for ship-handling work and became popular largely due to its exceptional manoeuvrability and safety in operation, inherent in the tractor principle. Early designs had the disadvantage of being relatively low-powered and employing cycloidal propulsion units that were less efficient than screw propellers of the time. Improvements in the size and performance of the Voith propulsion units and sophistication of tractor designs has resulted in the concept spreading from Europe, where it was quickly adopted by many towage companies, to fleets throughout the world.

The hull of a Voith Schneider tractor has a number of essential features. In a modern vessel two propulsion units are located beneath the hull of the tug, in a position about one-third of its length from the bow. Very early designs incorporated just one unit but experience was soon to show that two such propellers, fitted side by side, dramatically improved the vessel's performance and

Zeus is a powerful Voith tractor tug built in Spain by Astilleros Armon for Italian owners in 2006 and chartered to a variety of operators in subsequent years. The tug is 34.5 m in length, with a beam of 11.6 m, draft of 6.4 m, and is fully equipped for fire-fighting and operation at oil or gas terminals. Two MAK 8 m25 main engines generating a total of 7,174 bhp drive a pair of Voith propulsion units with a blade orbit of 3.2 m. Zeus has a bollard pull of 74 tonnes and a maximum speed of 14 knots. (Author)

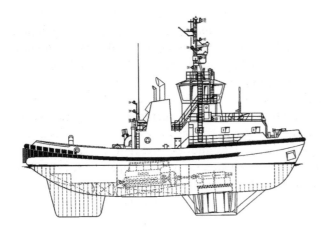

The drawing depicts the general arrangement of the German Voith Schneider tractor tug Weser *and illustrates the important relative positions of the engines, propulsion units and skeg in a basic ship-handling vessel.* (Voith)

agility. Another important feature is the large skeg, or vertical fin, located beneath the stern. The size and position of the skeg is critical and directly related to the position of the towing connection on the deck above. Located beneath the blades of the propulsion unit is a protection plate, held in position by a number of supporting struts. This has several functions: it affords some protection to the rotating blades when the vessel is working in shallow water and provides a supporting structure when the tug is placed in dry dock or on a slipway for repairs. The performance of the propulsion units is also affected by the protection plate which creates a nozzle effect in the water flow between the hull and plate with a resulting improvement in thrust.

In order to meet the constant demand for greater performance and the availability of more powerful engines the size of propulsion unit has increased considerably in recent years. This has resulted in the use of units with a blade orbit of well over 3 metres in diameter, and a larger number of blades of a highly

Bess *is one of a number of escort tractor tugs designed and owned by Buksér og Berging (formerly Bjergning), and intended to operate 'fin' (skeg) first. The 36 m tug has a Voith Schneider propulsion system, powered by two Ulstein Bergen main engines producing 5,455 bhp. Bess has a bollard pull of 72 tonnes and a free-running speed of 15 knots.* (Buksér og Berging)

developed shape. To accommodate two such units, side by side, in the hull of a powerful ship-handling tug of perhaps 5,000 bhp and 30 m in length, demands a hull with considerable beam and volume. The concept of the Voith tractor, combining the use of cycloidal propellers with the carefully developed hull configuration, is unique and gives vessels of this type an inherent ability to travel astern safely at relatively high speeds, push with the stern and tow in the indirect mode. The inherent ability to apply indirect towing methods, making full use of the vessel's large skeg, underwater shape and towing gear configuration, is a well recognised feature of this type of vessel. This and the ability to operate in a true 'push–pull' role is seen as a very great advantage by many operators, as will be seen in later chapters. Possible disadvantages are the vulnerability of the propulsion units, located beneath the hull, the resulting increase in draft, and relatively high capital cost.

Very recent designs incorporate hull forms that are very close to that of a true 'double-ended' vessel, with an enhanced ability to travel at high speed in either direction, yet able to carry out all the other functions required of a powerful ship-handling tug. The hull structure of a Voith tractor, as one would expect, incorporates many of the features common in tugs of all types. A suitable raised foredeck or forecastle is incorporated where necessary. In plan view the hull is invariably well rounded to give a sympathetic shape for working in close proximity with ships but the stern structure is frequently designed to provide a broad fendered area for pushing. A strengthened bow with extensive fendering is rarely necessary.

In the important role of tanker-escort tug the Voith Schneider propulsion system is in direct competition with vessels of the stern-drive type. At the time of writing Voith tractor tugs of over 45 m in length and 10,000 bhp are in service in this role. The design of such vessels is constantly being refined and improved to increase the line pull generated, while towing in the indirect mode, with tankers moving at up to 10 knots. Modern tanker-escort tugs capable of a bollard pull of 90 tonnes will produce a line pull in excess of 150 tonnes while towing on a moving tanker in the indirect mode. This performance can only be achieved with the aid of dynamic testing of models and full-sized vessels, and computer simulation.

Tug owners and naval architects are by no means unanimous in their approach to the design of high-performance escort tugs. The ability of tugs to achieve the high line pulls mentioned must go hand in hand with the need for a high degree of stability in the vessels concerned. The latter is attained by careful attention to hull design and the precise positioning of skeg and towing gear.

Tractor Tugs with Azimuthing Propulsion Units

Tractor tugs employing propulsion units of the azimuthing type, using steerable screw propellers, were first built in Europe in the early 1970s as a possible alternative to the Voith Schneider system, introduced some years earlier. The units are mounted in much the same way, side by side, under the forward part of the

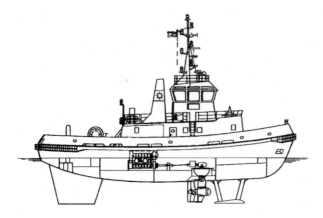

This general arrangement of the German tractor tug Fairplay VII *with azimuthing propulsion units, showing the important relative positions of the engines, propulsion units, skeg and winch.* (Schottel)

hull. With the exception of a few very small vessels used in the logging industry the units are always fitted in pairs.

Tugs of this type are designed to perform in much the same way as their Voith Schneider counterparts but some may be less suitable for towing in the indirect mode. Early vessels often had the advantages of improved performance (in terms of horsepower per tonne bollard pull), due to their use of azimuthing propulsion units embodying more efficient screw propellers, and a reduction in capital cost.

Svitzer Brunel *is a modern example of an azimuthing tractor tug of 29.5 metres in length and 59-tonne bollard pull and one of a series of four built for Svitzer in 2003 by Astilleros Zamakona in Spain. The tug is powered by two Niigata main engines producing a total of 4,400 bhp to drive a pair of Z-Peller fully azimuthing propulsion units.* (Author)

RT Claire *is one of a new generation of 'Rotor Tugs' to be designed and built by Dutch tug owners Kotug and their subsidiary KST. The 28.3 m vessel is powered by three Niigata main engines generating a total of 5,506 bhp, to drive three Z-Peller propulsion units.* RT Claire *has a bollard pull of 68–70 tonnes and a free-running speed of 12 knots.* (H. Hoffmann)

The subsequent development of new stern-drive vessels and greatly improved Voith Schneider cycloidal propellers tended to nullify those advantages. Consequently, the large-scale development of tractor tugs with azimuthing units has been substantially reduced.

The hull configuration incorporates a fixed skeg and a form of protection plate, similar to that of the Voith tractor. Protection plate design varies from a device fitted solely to protect the units and assist with docking to a more comprehensive structure intended to improve propulsion unit performance. A few tractors of this type have the propulsion units located in a shallow recess or tunnel beneath the hull in order to reduce the draft of the vessel. With this arrangement it is necessary to ensure that the effectiveness of the units is not seriously impaired by restricted water flow to the propellers.

The 'Rotor Tug'

The Rotor Tug is the result of radical forward thinking by Ton Kooren, president of the Dutch-based company Kotug. This design resulted from a personal quest for a powerful, versatile tug, capable of ship-handling, coastal towing, and a wide range of other duties. The main requirement was to have a highly agile vessel

This artist's impression shows the underwater shape of the 'Rotor Tug' hull and the position of the three propulsion units, two forward and one aft. (Kotug)

capable of moving and exerting all or most of its maximum bollard pull in any direction.

Rotor Tug is the registered trademark of this new concept which uses three fully azimuthing propulsion units. A basic azimuthing tractor design has been modified to incorporate a third propulsion unit at the stern, in place of the normal skeg. The hull form is of a hard chine type, almost flat on the underside, giving the best possible water flow to all three units. An important feature of this new design is the system installed to control all three propulsion units, which may be steered individually or in unison as required by the tugmaster. A more detailed description of the controls is included in Chapter 2.

The first four Rotor Tugs were introduced early in 1999 in Dutch and German ports served by Kotug fleets. Vessels of 31.43 m in length, with three engines producing a total of 6,300 bhp, the tugs have a bollard pull of 75 tonnes. The agility of this first generation of Rotor Tug is spectacular, with a high rate of turn, the ability to move rapidly sideways, and exert a high proportion of its bollard pull in any direction.

Since those early days the original tugs have proved their worth under a very wide range of operating conditions, in harbour, during coastal and short sea tows and even on salvage operations. This success resulted in the slow but positive acceptance of the Rotor Tug concept by other tug owners. By 2008 at least four more vessels had been introduced by Kotug and twenty others were under construction for other operators. Various Rotor Tug designs are available or under development, offering different sizes, bollard pulls, and equipment.

Ship Docking Module

Ship docking module (SDM) is the name of a tug design originally conceived by the chairman of the American towage group Hvide Marine (later Seabulk International), Erik Hvide. The title was chosen because the new vessel did not fit neatly into any existing tug category. This new concept was centred entirely around the company's need for a ship-handling tug that was not only extremely manoeuvrable, but could deliver *all* of its bollard pull in any direction, whether pulling or pushing. In his quest for a vessel to meet this requirement Hvide and his designers produced a relatively shallow-draft vessel with a very wide beam, incorporating a fully steerable azimuthing propulsion unit beneath each end. When the SDM first made an appearance it was quickly nicknamed by the media as the 'Floating Saucer'.

At this angle the SDM Endeavor *clearly shows its massive beam and unique towing gear with alternative fairleads.* Endeavor *is 27.43 m in length with a beam of 15.24 m and an almost elliptical planform. Owned by Marine Towing of Tampa, the tug is powered by two Wärtsilä main engines producing a total of 4,000 bhp. (Author)*

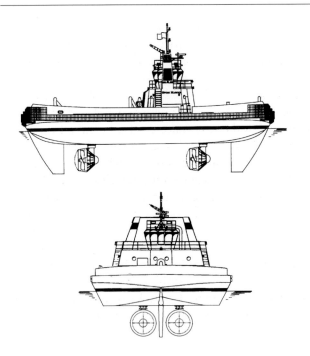

The most important features of the SDM are depicted in this drawing – an almost flat-bottomed hull and a fully azimuthing propulsion unit at each end. Note that the forward unit is offset to starboard of the centreline and the aft unit to port.

The hull is that of a true double-ended vessel with a small central skeg at each end. A unique feature of the SDM configuration is that each propulsion unit is offset, one to port and the other to starboard. This arrangement minimises flow interference between the units. The vessel's hull is heavily fendered all round, and the smallest possible superstructure is fitted to house a crew of up to three.

Construction of three Mk 1 vessels, powered by two main engines with a total of 4,000 bhp, commenced in 1997, with the first, *New River*, entering service at the end of the same year. Those were quickly followed by three more slightly larger vessels, designated Mk II and incorporating modifications to the superstructure, engines and towing gear. At the time of writing six ship docking modules are operating successfully in the USA with two separate companies. Two others have been built under licence, with various modifications, for local operators in Spain.

SPECIAL FEATURES OF TUG HULL DESIGN

Although tug construction employs normal shipyard practices, there are many features embodied in the design of a tug that have particular relevance in the towage industry. Many common items are designed or treated in a different way. Some of the more important items are described below.

Anchors and Anchor Pockets

Regulations governing the operation of vessels will require most tugs of any size to fit one or more anchors, either for use in an emergency or to enable the vessel to go to anchor as part of its normal operation. The type and number of anchors required may vary with the country and regulatory authorities concerned. The stowage of anchors when they are not in use often gives cause for concern among tug operators, particularly in ship-handling vessels and those operating in close proximity to other craft. By its nature an anchor is an unwieldy object, difficult to stow and capable of doing considerable damage if unrestrained. If the anchors are located in the bow, which is normal in the vast majority of tugs and oil-rig supply vessels, they are stowed in recesses in the hull shell plating often known as pockets. When an anchor is raised it is hauled into a pocket leaving little or nothing to protrude and possibly cause damage to other vessels or to foul ropes.

In some harbour tugs, only one anchor is required for occasional or emergency use. Where this is the case it is located in the bow or in a pocket beneath the stern. The latter arrangement is popular in tractor tugs where the propulsion units are located in the forepart of the vessel and therefore well away from the anchor and chain. The anchors are handled either by a separate windlass or by part of the towing winch mechanism. Modern stern-drive vessels, with a large towing winch on the foredeck, invariably use the latter option. Controls for an anchor windlass are now frequently located in the wheelhouse in easy reach of the tugmaster.

Bulwarks

The side plates above deck level, forming a protective barrier around the main working decks of the vessel, are known as the bulwarks. The bulwarks of a tug are generally of much heavier construction than those in other ships and are intended to provide protection from water coming on deck when working alongside other moving vessels. They also provide some physical security for personnel working on deck in difficult conditions. The height of bulwarks varies with the type of vessel and its employment but is subject to national regulations. Large tugs, including some ship-handling vessels, have hinged access doors on one or both sides of the tug. These are to enable personnel to move safely to and from another vessel without climbing high bulwarks. Similar openings may be fitted to allow anti-pollution equipment or divers to be deployed and maintenance tasks to be carried out on buoys or floating pipelines. An open stern, devoid of bulwarks, is a common feature in anchor-handling vessels and those engaged in pollution-control work.

Small tugs working on inland waterways may have very low bulwarks, or sections where the height is reduced, in order to prevent fouling or chafing towing gear. The bulwarks of all tugs have openings or freeing devices to ensure that any water taken on deck drains quickly overboard. In most tug designs the bulwarks slope in from deck level to the top rail, particularly around the stern and sides of the vessel. This is sometimes known as 'tumble home' and is intended to reduce the possibility of contact damage when the tug rolls whilst alongside another vessel. A similar remedy is to position the bulwarks in from the deck edge by up to half a metre, resulting in better clearance and a useful step for personnel. See also *Superstructure Design*, below.

A view of the afterdeck of the triple-screw tug Afon Cadnant *of the Holyhead Towing Company shows the open stern and roller, spacious work deck, winches and deck crane. The 35 m tug is powered by three Cummins main engines of 5,100 bhp (total) coupled to fixed-pitch propellers rotating in fixed nozzles. (H. Hoffmann)*

Decks

The working areas on the towing and after decks of tugs and oil-rig supply vessels are worthy of mention. These areas are frequently wet, taking a small amount of water on board when the vessels heel over whilst towing, and are susceptible to flooding in heavy weather. They remain, however, areas where crew-members must continue to work under the most difficult conditions. A non-skid surface, of special paint or compound, is normally applied to all exposed working decks.

There is also a need to protect the steel deck, in the case of anchor-handling tugs and vessels engaged in similar work, where heavy anchors, buoys, pipeline components and the like are hauled on board through an open stern. In these vessels a heavy timber sheathing is fitted over the working area to protect the deck from structural damage and provide a more suitable surface on which to handle these items. When the timber becomes seriously damaged it is easily replaced.

Fendering

One of the most distinctive features of almost any tug are the fenders used to protect the vessel from damage when it is working in close proximity to other craft. Most forms of towing must be regarded as a 'contact sport' where direct contact with the vessel being assisted is either essential or unavoidable. Throughout its history the towage industry has worked hard to find a suitable shock-absorbing medium to cushion the interface between tug and tow. In modern tugs a great deal of effort has gone into developing moulded rubber fendering and the structures needed to mount it on the tug satisfactorily. The resulting fender must be capable of absorbing the vast amounts of energy generated when two sizeable vessels repeatedly make contact with each other. This is particularly the case in ship-handling operations where the tug will almost certainly be required to push and pull. Under those circumstances fendering not only has to protect the vessel from unavoidable impact damage but must also survive the considerable abrasion encountered in everyday operation.

In high powered, ship-handling tugs the question of effective fendering is complex. The problem is not just a simple one of impact absorption. There have been many examples of damage to the hull plating of tankers and other ships. Hence the need to distribute the force over a reasonably wide area. Abrasion caused when the tug ranges up and down against another vessel in a swell may also have serious consequences for the life of the fender and its mountings. To

This spectacular bow shot of the Belgian stern-drive tug Union Diamond *shows in detail the two-stage fendering and additional protective tyres along the sides. The anchor pockets are also clearly visible along with the high bulwarks and massive towing fairlead. Note also that the lower wheelhouse windows are covered by temporary protective blanking plates denoting that the vessel is on a seagoing operation.* (H. Hoffmann)

combat this phenomenon some operators incorporate a water spray system to lubricate rubber bow or stern fenders when the tug is pushing. Others argue that some adhesion is essential to ensure that the tug can be held in position on the side of a ship under these circumstances.

Among the various solutions produced by designers are substantial rubber mouldings, of a tubular, 'D' and 'W' cross-section, applied to vulnerable parts of the hull, mainly at deck level. Bow and stern fenders are frequently constructed from one or more mouldings of that type. Many modern tugs employ a 'two-stage' fendering system for pushing on a ship's side. Such fenders usually comprise an upper tubular rubber element mounted to ensure that it absorbs the first impact, which will often serve to keep the tug's bow in place. The second stage is a more robust fender, made up in the form of a series of more complex moulded sections, that make contact when more pressure is applied.

In spite of the effort put into the design of suitable fendering systems there remains a place for the humble motor tyre. It is still quite common to see modern rubber fendering given the secondary protection of a layer of tyres. Discarded tyres from trucks, earthmoving vehicles and especially aircraft remain extremely effective in this role. Tyres used in this way are generally secured to the vessel's bulwarks by means of chains, steel wire strops or a high-strength fabric webbing. Fenders manufactured from rope were a traditional remedy employed by tug companies around the world for many decades as a substitute for, or in addition to, rubber fendering. This form of fender lacks the resilience of rubber and therefore is less suited to the high forces involved in modern tug operation, but is still used in some companies as secondary protection.

In North America and Europe scrap tyres are frequently used for tug fendering in a quite different way. Complete fendering systems are made up using sections cut from tyre treads, mounted in loops or 'end-on' so that the sections, form solid blocks of tough rubber. Many tugs rely completely on fendering systems of this type, which are claimed to be virtually indestructible but labour intensive and expensive to manufacture.

Tugs used for special purposes may have additional fendering. Those employed in naval yards to assist submarines for example are fitted with fenders that extend well below the waterline. In this way the tug may work close to the partly submerged pressure hull of a submarine without fear of causing damage. Vessels handling warships and cruise liners may also have fendering manufactured in a light colour rubber or use fabric covers to prevent damage to paintwork.

Deep-sea tugs and oil-rig supply vessels have less need for bow fenders but may have heavy strengthening around the stern and sides. This takes the form of heavy steel rubbing strakes, often faced with rubber or overlaid with heavy vehicle tyres.

Forecastles and Raised Foredecks

The purpose of incorporating a forecastle in a tug of any size is to improve its ability to work at sea or in exposed waters. By raising the deck at the bow improvements can be made to the shape of the forward hull, reducing the likelihood of the vessel taking water on board as it encounters heavy seas, or operates in a swell. This improves the handling of the tug and provides a safer, dryer, environment for those working on deck. It is common for the forecastle to be one whole deck higher than the main, or towing deck, enabling the space gained to be used for accommodation, additional machinery, or stores.

Smaller tugs, designed to work in more sheltered conditions, may be given a raised foredeck. This compromise gives the crew ready access when moving from one end of the vessel to the other but still affords some protection. The raised area may take the form of a steeply sloping deck or a foredeck raised by a metre or so.

The ship-handling tug V. B. Poder, *owned by the Spanish Boluda Group of companies, is a Voith tractor with a long high forecastle sheltering the afterdeck and allowing the vessel to operate in exposed locations and at sea. Any pushing is carried out using the stern, making a heavy bow fender unnecessary. V. B. Poder is 25.5 m in length, with a beam of 11 m, powered by Wärtsilä main engines of 5,500 bhp to achieve a bollard pull of 55 tonnes.* (Boluda)

Watertight Compartments and Subdivision

The hull of almost any vessel, from a small boat to a huge cargo ship, generally includes some means of subdividing the hull into a number of watertight compartments to minimise the danger of sinking if an accident occurs. A tug hull is treated in similar fashion but the problem of providing watertight compartments of a suitable size is particularly difficult in many vessels, due to the very large size of the engine-room in relation the rest of the hull. Any accident resulting in the penetration of the external hull plating in the engine-room area, or flooding of that compartment from any other cause, will seriously affect the vessel's ability to stay afloat. Many tugs have been lost through contact damage or capsizing, causing the engine-room to flood and the vessel to sink very quickly indeed.

There are several features that are often incorporated in the hull of a tug to improve the safety of the vessel in this respect. One common remedy is to ensure that fuel, oil, ballast and other storage tanks are located in the bottom and sides of the hull, reducing the areas where direct penetration of the large machinery spaces can occur. In the case of a tractor tug or stern-drive vessel the total volume of the combined machinery space can be enormous. This situation is sometimes improved by placing a transverse watertight bulkhead between the engines and the propulsion unit space but it is essential to seal the apertures where the rotating driveshafts pass through. Likewise, self-contained auxiliary machinery such as generators and pumps may be located in separate compartments. Carefully positioned storerooms and workshop areas are often fitted with watertight doors to afford additional subdivision in the event of an emergency.

SUPERSTRUCTURE DESIGN

Regional differences in the design of a tug's superstructure and deck layout are fast disappearing in the modern towage industry worldwide. In the past, the size, shape and position of the wheelhouse, upperworks, and funnels or exhaust uptakes were a major clue as to the type of vessel and often the part of the world it came from. Pronounced regional differences between European and American tugs still occur in conventional screw vessels. In North America, where such vessels are still built in substantial numbers, traditional deckhouse configurations still prevail. Early regulations in the USA, governing crew accommodation, resulted in the characteristic very long deckhouses, resulting in a towing connection much nearer the stern. Conventional screw tugs in Europe invariably have a long afterdeck with the towing connection made at a point very close to amidships to enhance manoeuvrability whilst towing.

The proliferation of modern tractor and stern-drive vessels and an increasing 'global dimension' in the towage industry has led to greater commonality. New propulsion systems and towing methods have imposed design constraints on particular types of vessel, whether produced in America, Asia or Europe. In terms of superstructure design, tugs have unique priorities, quite different from other vessels, where visibility, safe operation and crew accommodation are concerned. Some of the more important considerations are described below.

Clearance

The overall 'shape' of the superstructure is of prime importance if the tug is to work safely and efficiently. Almost every tug is required to work close alongside other vessels of one sort or another, often ones very much larger than the tug itself. Modern container ships, warships and the like have spectacularly flared bows and

The stern-drive harbour tug Smit Barbados *illustrates the measures that have been taken to provide 'clearance' while working alongside ships. Bulwarks are 'stepped in', the superstructure is heavily chamfered and the exhaust uptakes sloped inwards. Owned by Smit International,* Smit Barbados *is one of a large series of Damen ASD 2810 vessels of 4,930 bhp, with a bollard pull of 58 tonnes.* (Author)

areas around the stern that make it difficult for the ship-handling tug to approach safely. It is therefore necessary to ensure that no part of the tug's structure will make contact with the other vessel, particularly in conditions when either vessel rolls in heavy weather conditions or when the tug heels over while towing or pushing. To ensure that there is sufficient clearance under these circumstances the various portions of the superstructure are narrowed or 'set in' as shown in the photograph above. As previously mentioned, the bulwarks are similarly arranged to prevent contact damage. A profile that is designed to give adequate clearance often has the advantage of good lines of sight from the wheelhouse to the various working areas around the tug.

Superstructure Fendering

The need to fit fendering to the superstructure of tugs will seem bizarre, even to many people within the towage industry. There are, however, instances, mainly in North America, where this practice is still necessary. Conventional screw tugs that are required to work close alongside modern ships with a pronounced flare, such as car carriers and container vessels, are often fitted with soft rubber fendering to prevent damage to the wheelhouse and superstructure.

The Wheelhouse

The wheelhouse is the centre of operations on every modern tug. It is from there that the tug captain must effectively control the vessel and much of its equipment while towing and carrying out its various duties. Remotely operated controls and a wide range of navigational and other aids enable many functions to be carried out by the master that would once have been carried out by crew-members on deck or in the engine-room. As mentioned in later chapters, controls for the engines, propulsion system and much of the deck equipment are now located in the wheelhouse. Other equipment is provided for the safe navigation of the tug and to enable it to communicate with other shipping, its owners, port authorities and agents. For much of the time the wheelhouse of many smaller tugs will be occupied by just one person and considerable effort has gone into ensuring that controls and equipment are readily accessible and can be operated comfortably. The advent of tugs that are virtually double-ended has resulted in single, centrally located control positions where the tugmaster can face in either direction and the relevant controls still fall naturally to hand.

Smit Trafalgar, *a Voith tractor tug operating in the confines of Liverpool docks, demonstrates the excellent all-round vision possible in a powerful harbour tug. Note the short exhaust uptakes and the low profile of the deckhouse. The wheelhouse has a single centrally located control position for the tugmaster.* (Author)

It is around this working environment that the wheelhouse is configured and one of the most important considerations is good all-round visibility. The majority of tugs spend their working lives operating in very close proximity to other vessels and for much of the time the tugmaster is preoccupied with events happening astern of him or immediately alongside. In order to provide the best possible all-round vision wheelhouse designs have changed dramatically, from a simple rectangular structure at the forward end of the superstructure, to a prominent, fully glazed control position with clear all-round visibility. Wheelhouse windows are generally angled outward at the top and may also be tinted to reduce glare in bright conditions and reflections at night.

Not only is it essential to have good vision around the vessel but also overhead. When ship-handling tugs are at work beneath the overhanging bow or stern of a large ship, the tugmaster must be able to see what is happening above him, particularly when the towing connection is being made. Likewise the master of an anchor-handling tug will often operate in similar fashion adjacent to oil rigs and other tall offshore structures. To meet this need for good overhead vision the wheelhouses of most modern tugs are fitted with sloping windows around the periphery of the roof. In larger vessels the controls for the propulsion system, winches and other deck equipment may be duplicated on either side of the wheelhouse and if necessary at the rear, overlooking the stern. A stern-facing control position is common in anchor-handling tugs and oil-rig supply vessels where much of the vessel's work is carried out on the afterdeck.

Accommodation

The accommodation provided aboard a modern tug is generally of a very high standard but the size and scope of facilities provided depends largely on the type of vessel and its employment. At one end of the scale a small tug used mainly for harbour duties, and manned only for short periods, may only require very simple domestic facilities and very little sleeping accommodation. Conversely, a large deep-sea tug or supply vessel will have a crew of a dozen or so and be equipped to provide all their needs on voyages lasting several weeks, in a variety of climatic conditions. Between these extreme examples are a wide variety of needs met by individual operators when vessels are fitted out. The actual location, and basic standard of accommodation, is strictly regulated by the various maritime authorities and classification societies.

In modern vessels living accommodation is invariably located above the waterline, or even above main deck level, for safety reasons, and certain standards have to be met regarding access and emergency escape routes. The use of high-speed diesel engines and modern propulsion systems has increased the need to isolate living accommodation from the effects of noise and vibration by innovative design and the extensive use of insulation material. In some cases the accommodation is isolated from the main hull structure by special anti-vibration mountings.

The fire-fighting terminal tug Aeger *(now operating as the Danish* Asterix*) is one of a class of 32 m tanker-handling vessels designed to ensure that all of the crew accommodation is located above main deck level. This has resulted in a higher superstructure, good all-round vision and a high mounting location for the fire monitors.* (Author)

Where sleeping accommodation is required for regular use in modern vessels, a cabin is normally available for each crew-member and rarely do more than two have to share. Provision is also made for the preparation of food, dry and refrigerated storage, showers or bathing, and laundering clothes. Adequate facilities are also required for the important matter of drying and storing the foul weather clothing used by personnel working on deck in all weather conditions. Very large vessels will have additional accommodation for owner's staff, salvage personnel, divers and running crews. The latter term refers to the additional personnel required to man ships or similar vessels in tow. Air-conditioning systems are an essential requirement in tugs built for use in tropical regions and in vessels designed for long distance towing that may encounter a whole variety of climatic conditions.

The increased use of tugs and oil-rig supply vessels in sub-zero temperatures calls not only for comprehensive heating systems to be installed for accommodation and domestic use but also to ensure that all of the tug's machinery systems, on deck and elsewhere, remain operational and free of ice. In some vessels for service in locations such as Alaska, the decks themselves may be heated.

As with the hull, several aspects of the superstructure can affect the watertight integrity of the vessel. Doors, windows and portholes must all be capable of

The 78.3 m anchor-handling tug/supply vessel Far Sound, *operated by Farstad Shipping, has a large wheelhouse and superstructure positioned high above the bow and shaped to offer some protection in heavy seas. Exhaust uptakes from the main and auxiliary engines pass through a single duct with an outlet on the wheelhouse roof.* (Farstad)

remaining watertight in the environment in which the vessel will be expected to work. Seagoing vessels will have steel doors that can be sealed when conditions dictate. In some vessels regulations also require a watertight door or hatch to be fitted between the wheelhouse and the rest of the superstructure. This is to prevent serious flooding throughout the vessel in the rare event of the wheelhouse windows being broken by heavy seas.

Funnels and Exhaust Stacks

The continuing use of funnels remains an emotive subject in some tug companies. Since the demise of steam-powered vessels the need for a large prominent funnel of the traditional type has largely disappeared. However, the funnel provides a convenient surface for the operators to display their livery and act as a ready means of identification, a factor still extremely important to many owners. A major disadvantage of the traditional funnel, or even its streamlined successor, is that it invariably interferes with the all-round vision required from the wheelhouse.

The need to carry exhaust fumes away from the vessel remains a very real problem that has been tackled in a number of different ways. Exhaust outlets in the hull, usually in the stern, are not uncommon in small vessels but in tugs of any size there is a danger that personnel working on deck may be affected by noxious fumes. In many cases one or two slim vertical single, unclad, exhaust uptakes are used and located in positions designed to minimise interference with all-round vision from the wheelhouse. Exhaust silencers may form part of the vertical exhaust uptakes or be located separately below decks.

The 'compact' stern-drive tug Tiger Sun, *operating from Vancouver, is fitted with two slim exhaust uptakes with very little casing positioned to ensure they do not interfere with visibility from the wheelhouse. Such installations are becoming increasingly common, particularly in small tugs.* Tiger Sun *is 21.7 m in length, powered by Detroit diesels of 5,400 bhp and has a bollard pull of 70 tonnes* (Author)

TUG BUILDING

A large proportion of the world's tugs are built by shipbuilders specialising in the construction of smaller more complex vessels incorporating a high level of modern technology. Gone are the days when a whole host of shipyards was available to build vessels of any type using traditional shipbuilding methods. As the shipbuilding industry has decreased in size worldwide, a number of shipyards have emerged to specialise in building tugs, offshore vessels, survey craft and other vessels of a more complex nature.

Most of the mainstream shipyards that have survived have been forced to adopt modern manufacturing and quality-control methods in order to succeed in a highly competitive worldwide market. The geographic location of tug-building yards in today's global marketplace has become heavily dependent on labour costs. At the time of writing specialist shipbuilding facilities in Asia are becoming increasingly competitive in terms of price, delivery times and quality. Economies of scale have led to many specialist shipyards promoting series-built vessels which can be selected from a range and fitted out to the client's specification, or even in some cases purchased complete and virtually ready for use.

To undertake the construction of a new vessel is a major and extremely expensive project for any tug owner. For example the cost of building a 'state of the art' ship-handling tug for use in Britain in 2008 was in excess of £5 million.

The Design Process and Computer Simulation

When a tug is ordered the design work will be undertaken by the owner, an independent consultant, or the design department of the shipyard concerned. A mix of all three will often be used to achieve the result required by a particular owner. In these days of advanced propulsion technology, significant input may also come from the manufacturer of the propulsion system. Some major propulsion system manufacturers carry out extensive research and testing in order to offer designs tailored to suit their particular propulsion equipment and aimed at a particular aspect of the towage market.

Regardless of whether a new tug is to be specially designed or produced from an established design, the production of an accurate and comprehensive specification is extremely important. For a ship-handling vessel input is often encouraged from tugmasters and crew, ship's pilots, and port authorities. If the vessel is being built to satisfy the requirements of a specific contract, such as towage and other services at an oil or LNG terminal, the client will also be involved. Owners and operators of oil and gas terminals and shipowners using those facilities frequently have stringent requirements for the type of tug to be used, its performance, equipment and operation. Under those conditions, technical staff from the client will also be deeply involved in the choice of tug and its design.

Marine architects, design consultants, tug owners and in some cases their clients now rely heavily on computer simulation to test tug designs and establish the best possible methods of handling ships or other towage operations. Simulation programmes now in regular use can simulate wind and tidal conditions, a ship's handling characteristics and the power and position of each tug required to carry out a particular operation. From these studies considerable information can be established about the type of vessel required before an order is placed. This is particularly valuable if the operating environment or vessels to be handled are new and historical operating data is not available. In the case of high-performance escort tugs, and tugs of a completely new design, computer simulation is often taken one stage further, resulting in highly developed programmes used for training purposes. Simulation programmes of this type are used to train tugmasters, ship's pilots, and vessel traffic officers from the ports concerned.

If a completely new vessel is contemplated the hull form will be tested using scale models in a special test-tank facility. Tank testing with models provides data on how the new vessel will handle, its stability, performance and seagoing characteristics. Modern test tanks are capable of reproducing, to scale, wave conditions and many other factors a full-size vessel may encounter in operation. A form of computer modelling can also be used to determine the operating characteristics of a new hull and propulsion system design. Computer modelling may include the use of computational fluid dynamics (CFD), a computer based tool allowing the flow of water around the hull and propulsion equipment to be studied in great detail under a wide variety of circumstances. CFD allows hull designs to be optimised with respect to the vessel's speed, power requirements and handling characteristics under a whole range of conditions. The information obtained from tank testing will invariably be compared with data obtained from computer modelling and give rise to modifications to the tank-test model or the computer information. This process may well be repeated a number of times, as the design gradually evolves. Information derived in this way will also be used for comparison when the completed tug is eventually put through full-scale trials.

Once the basic configuration has been decided a computer-aided design (CAD) system is likely to be used to produce the general arrangement and detailed drawings that will eventually be necessary for the shipyard to proceed with construction. The strength of the vessel is particularly important in the design of a tug. Because of the work that they do, tugs of all sizes need to be rugged to withstand external forces on the hull and forces generated by the use of high-powered propulsion machinery, well above those experienced by cargo or passenger vessels. A tug must be capable of withstanding the rigours of working alongside other vessels and often the possibility of being 'squeezed' between barges or perhaps a ship and a quay wall. To avoid the possibility of serious damage, such considerations are taken into account in the design process. The strength of a tug's hull is largely determined by the thickness of the external plates and the spacing and size of internal frames and bulkheads. The broad and ancient term 'scantlings' is frequently used in ship construction to describe these features. Internally, the hull structure may be quite complex, particularly in the stern area

An engineer in the research and development department of Voith Hydro at Heidenheim in Germany works with a computational fluid dynamics computer-based modelling system that allows the flow of water around the hull and propulsion equipment to be studied in great detail. (Voith Hydro)

A model tractor tug is under test in the test tank in the Voith Hydro research centre where research and development on new tractor designs, modifications, and work on propulsion unit technology is carried out. (Voith Hydro)

where additional strength is achieved by carefully designed longitudinal and transverse stiffening. Much of the work of predicting the necessary structural strength and determining the design of the final structure will be carried out using the CAD system. Stress calculations that took many hours in the past are completed almost instantly by computer. Likewise, critical calculations concerning the finished vessel's stability in its various operating modes will be done using the computer system.

In some instances a sophisticated CAD system will have the ability to assist the owner and designer by showing graphically the effects of changes in the size and position of structures, equipment and accommodation. This is a considerable help in assessing, for example, the all-round visibility from various positions in the wheelhouse, checking that legal requirements are met for stability and accommodation, or simply validating the routes for pipework and so on. A great deal of thought is given to the positioning of the various controls and other pieces of equipment in the wheelhouse, to achieve an efficient operating layout. This too may be simulated by computer modelling, but a full scale 'mock up' is often constructed in wood to evaluate the ergonomics of the final design. When the design process is finished, general arrangement and individual component drawings are produced for the shipyard and work on the vessel can start.

Construction

The tug's hull is almost invariably a welded steel structure. In the majority of cases steel is also used in the superstructure and for other major structural items incorporated in the vessel's construction. Aluminium alloy is sometimes used in the construction of the superstructure, to reduce weight, but rarely in the hull and then only in relatively small vessels.

The steel plate used in construction is frequently cleaned and primed for painting before or after it arrives in the shipyard to reduce the growth of rust during the construction process. Alternatively, the finished structure will be shot blasted and primed at an early stage. In a modern shipyard the steel components for the main structure will be cut by a computer-controlled machine using plasma arc, gas or laser cutting equipment. The cutting machine will use information derived from the CAD system to produce accurate results with very little waste material. Component parts produced in this way fit accurately together ready for welding, often by a semi-automated electric arc-welding machine. Alternatively the parts may be cut by a specialist contractor and delivered to the shipyard in the form of a 'kit'.

Many modern shipyards have the ability to construct either the whole vessel or large parts of the structure under cover in huge workshops or covered dry docks. This has the advantage of ensuring that work continues unaffected by bad weather and reduces the adverse effects of rain on the partly built structure and the quality of its final painted finish. Both of these considerations have favourable economic connotations. The main components of the hull and superstructure are frequently built up in 'blocks' and welded together as construction proceeds.

The hull under construction at the shipyard of Foss Maritime, at Rainier, Oregon, is that of a 'Dolphin' class ship-handling tug designed by Robert Allan Ltd in Vancouver. All of the major steelwork was carried out using components cut precisely to size and shape by a computer-controlled cutting machine, using software generated as part of the design process. This particular vessel is the first of its type to be fitted with a 'Hybrid' propulsion system – see chapter 2. (Foss)

A completed hull is depicted being fitted out in a special hall at the Uzmar Shipyard in Turkey. Assembly and protective paint work are carried out in a dry protected environment. Note the first sections of a further hull being prepared for assembly astern of the almost completed vessel. (Uzmar)

To speed up the process some of these component parts may be sub-contracted to other shipyards or steel fabrication specialists. Economic considerations may involve the construction of complete hulls by yards located in areas where favourable labour rates prevail or international monetary exchange rates render some financial advantage. This has proved particularly relevant in the case of series-built vessels where large numbers of similar craft may be involved.

Standard Tugs and Series Production

As previously mentioned, the use, and advantages, of series production and standardised designs has had an important impact on the tug-building market. Because of their relatively small size, tugs have always lent themselves to production in large numbers with the economic benefits that result. This was amply demonstrated during both world wars when large numbers of tugs and other small vessels were constructed cheaply in a very short time. More recently, there has been a tendency for tug owners to build new vessels in small numbers, of two or more, in order to gain some financial advantage and achieve some commonality to aid maintenance and operation. A number of specialist shipbuilders in Europe, the USA and Asia have exploited these advantages vigorously and offer owners standard designs ranging from very small tug/ workboats to large and sophisticated oil-rig supply vessels. Tug builders in Holland, originally responsible for the introduction of small, mass-produced tugs, now provide vessels of all types and sizes to owners all round the world.

The standard designs offered by specialist builders and design consultants are widely researched and intended to satisfy the needs of a large cross-section of operators. Using standard hull designs, usually identified by overall length and propulsion configuration, owners are given a choice of engines and equipment. Deviations from the standard design can be made but will adversely affect the final

The stock hull for a large Damen Shoalbuster is stored afloat at the group's facility at Gorinchem in the Netherlands. Most hull and major steelwork for new tugs to be fitted out at the yard are fabricated at shipyards in Russia or Poland or elsewhere and towed to the Netherlands. (Author)

cost. A major advantage of adopting a standard tug design is the possibility of an incredibly quick delivery of the finished vessel. Large specialist companies often carry a stock of standard hulls or partially completed vessels that can be fitted out and completed to an owner's specification in a very short time. Similarly, stocks of other standard components, engines and propulsion equipment are maintained – adding the further benefit of a ready source of spare parts should they be necessary at a later date.

Series production is a process that has lent itself to further economies by sub-contracting the construction of hulls and all major steelwork to countries where labour costs are low but the necessary skills are still to be found. Major Dutch shipbuilders have used facilities in Poland, Romania and Russia, to build many dozens of hulls for many years. Once launched the vessels are towed to Holland, stored afloat until required, and then taken into an enclosed building hall to be fitted out and painted. As economic conditions have changed, however, many of those yards have become an integral part of the shipbuilders' own businesses along with further shipyards in China and elsewhere in the Far East. Those shipyards now also undertake the whole production process, building and fitting out completed tugs and other small ships. Rigorous quality control is exercised by the parent company and the end result is generally a high-quality product at a competitive price.

Another approach to series construction growing in popularity is where shipyards without their own comprehensive design facilities market and build

During the construction of a modern tug, the vessel is often almost complete when it goes into the water for the first time. In this picture the 32 m stern-drive tug Sanmar Eskort V *is fully painted and ready to be launched. Note the extensive fendering, the deep forward skeg and small bilge keels.* (Sanmar)

vessels to standard designs from one of a number of specialist naval architects and design consultants. Such 'design packages' are intended for production in any competent shipyard where the quality and performance of the end product can be assured. Tugs built under licence in that way now represent a very large proportion of vessels built each year worldwide.

Launching and Fitting Out

With relatively small ships, such as tugs, the vessel will be almost complete when it is put into the water. In the past, the hull would have been launched as soon as the main structure was complete and the machinery installed afterwards. More recently, it has become common practice to install virtually all of the major machinery components while the vessel is still on dry land. If the vessel is built under cover it is usual for the maximum amount of work to be completed while it is still unaffected by weather, including much of the detailed fitting out in the accommodation and engine-room. Whatever the facilities available, the tug still has to be launched by one means or another. Traditional launchings, where the vessel enters the water, stern first or sideways, making a spectacular splash, are becoming less common. More often than not the partially completed tug will be moved from the construction shed to a slipway or lift and lowered gently into the water. In some yards, where vessels are built in a covered dry dock, the dock is flooded and the tug floated out. Smaller craft may be lifted into the water by crane.

Whatever the method of launching there are various tasks which cannot be undertaken until the vessel is in the water. A major consideration is the final lining up of engines, gearboxes, propulsion units and other major items of machinery. This important work is not generally carried out until the tug is afloat and the hull is supported by the water, due to the possibility of minute structural changes taking place during the launching process. A representative of the owners may be constantly in attendance at the shipyard during the final stages of construction and the fitting-out process. This is usually a senior member of the company's engineering staff or the chief engineer designated to serve on the new vessel. This ensures that decisions regarding minor changes and quality standards can be made without undue delay and that owner's staff rapidly become familiar with their new equipment.

As previously mentioned the amount of fitting-out work still to be done will vary, often depending on the facilities available at the site where the hull was constructed. Whatever the level of completion, the remaining work to finish and equip the vessel will be done afloat in the yard's fitting-out berth. Electrical wiring

Many different methods are used to launch tugs, some highly spectacular and others slow and sedate. In this Malaysian shipyard the anchor-handler Surya Wira 15 *is coaxed gently into the water on inflatable rubber rollers, an unusual but effective method on a gradually sloping shoreline. (S. L. Shipbuilding)*

will be completed and the installation of navigational aids will be carried out. Some of this equipment, such as radar sets and radios, is hired or leased by tug owners and will be installed by the supplier or a specialist, fairly late in the fitting-out process.

The matter of painting is also worthy of mention. In the present financial climate the paint finish on a new vessel is an important factor and taken very seriously by most owners. A new tug will be painted with great care, using advanced paint and protective finish technology, not only to ensure that it will look good when delivered but to reduce the need for maintenance in the long term. With reduced manning levels and improved utilisation the crew of a modern tug has much less time to spend on repainting than did their predecessors. Prior to launch the hull will have been treated below the waterline with an anti-fouling preparation that is impervious to the corrosive action of sea water and will resist the accumulation of marine growth, which quickly affects a vessel's performance. The superstructure and decks will be painted appropriately and attention will be given to the paint finish throughout the trials and pre-delivery period.

Trials

Before any new vessel is delivered it is subjected to exhaustive trials to ensure that it does actually meet the owner's specification. The trials are normally conducted by the shipbuilder and attended by representatives from the owners, design consultants and specialists from the engine, propulsion and other equipment suppliers. Such trials cover not only the performance of the propulsion and steering systems but many other aspects of the vessel and its equipment. Testing and commissioning equipment and systems aboard a new vessel starts well before the actual sea trials, to ensure that the deck machinery, fire-fighting installations, life-saving equipment and a whole host of other systems are operating correctly. Basin trials will be conducted, with the tug still at its moorings, to check that the engines and propulsion machinery operate correctly and react properly to the controls in the wheelhouse.

One of the trials to be carried out before the tug leaves the quay is likely to be an inclining test, to check that the vessel's stability characteristics are within the expected parameters. This is done by moving large weights, of known values, from one side of the vessel to the other and recording various measurements to enable the centre of balance (known as GM) to be calculated. The GM is related to the vessel's metacentric height and is affected by draft, the vessel's loading, weight distribution and other variables. The whole question of stability is a particularly serious and complex matter in tug design and beyond the scope of this book.

Trials to confirm the handling characteristics of the new vessel will vary with the type of tug and the work that it is designed to do. Tests will be carried out to measure the tug's turning circle, going ahead and astern, response to varying degrees of helm, and stopping distances from different speeds. All control systems have an inherent time delay. These response times are important, particularly in

Once completed all tugs undergo extensive handling and manoeuvrability trials. Sanmar Eskort V demonstrates its agility and control whilst going astern, an essential requirement for any ship-handling tug. The tug, built for Italian operators, is powered by two Wärtsilä main engines of 5,500 bhp coupled to a pair of Rolls-Royce fully azimuthing propulsion units embodying controllable pitch propellers to achieve a bollard pull of over 65 tonnes. (Sanmar)

ship-handling vessels, and are the subject of a great deal of attention during trials. From the bystander's point of view the crash stop is the most spectacular test. The vessel is brought to a stop from full speed by instantly going full astern. Any undesirable deviation from a satisfactory course during this procedure may be cause for concern. Tugs built to undertake other duties such as fire-fighting, pollution-control work, anchor-handling and perhaps pushing will all have specific trials carried out to confirm that those roles can be satisfactorily carried out safely and efficiently.

The free-running speed of a tug is measured in the time-honoured fashion using a 'measured mile' or electronically using the vessel's navigational equipment. A number of 'runs' are made over the measured distance, in each direction, to compensate for wind and tidal conditions. With some vessels, the speed achieved when running astern is also important and is measured in exactly the same way. The results are a calculated average speed expressed in knots.

Bollard-Pull Trials

Last and by no means least is the bollard-pull trial. The bollard-pull rating for a tug has become a vital factor and in most cases the one most likely to be scrutinised by a potential client. Due to the variety of propulsion systems now in use, it is no longer possible to judge the power of a tug by the horsepower of its engines alone. Therefore it has become necessary to adopt a bollard-pull test that can be universally accepted as a measure of a vessel's ability to tow. Bollard pull is simply the amount of static pull the vessel can exert when tethered to a measuring device. The figure obtained is usually expressed in tonnes.

Bollard pull trials are normally conducted under strict conditions laid down by the classification society or authority that will ultimately certify the results. These conditions include specific requirements concerning the location for the trial and the condition of the vessel. A large stretch of water is required, unaffected by tides and of suitable depth. Depth of water can be critical, especially in the case of powerful deep-draft tugs, the performance of which is affected by a phenomenon known as 'ground effect'. A depth of water of not less than 20 metres is typical but not always easy to achieve at a suitable site. A bollard of adequate strength and proportions is also essential. A modern harbour tug will often produce a bollard pull of between 60 and 80 tonnes and a very powerful anchor-handling supply vessel well over 200 tonnes. It has been known for a dockside mooring bollard to be pulled bodily from its foundations during such a trial.

The tug's towline is shackled to the bollard with a measuring device inserted in the line. For many years a mechanical device, in the form of a very large spring balance known as a 'clock', was used. More recently, modern electronic 'load cell' devices have become more popular and have the advantage of being lighter and capable of producing a graphical record and tables of results automatically. It is also possible to monitor the results remotely, either ashore or on board the vessel under test. The towline length is also a critical factor. A minimum length of 300 metres is typical, to avoid misleading results because of waves reflecting from dock walls. With the tug pulling against the measuring device in this way, readings are

This photograph was taken from the deck of the anchor-handling tug Al Wassay *during a bollard-pull trial carried out in deep water at Europort in the Netherlands. An electronic 'load cell' is shackled into the very long towline and readings are immediately available to trials staff aboard the tug via the cable just visible beneath the shackles.* (Author)

taken at various predetermined power settings for set periods of time. The most important result will be the maximum steady bollard pull achieved with the engines at their maximum continuous power setting. In most cases, particularly with ship-handling tugs, the trials will include the vessel pulling both ahead and astern, the astern pull being equally important in many applications. From the readings obtained tables of results are compiled for analysis.

Dynamic Towing Trials

Escort tugs and similar vessels, where indirect towing with large ships under way is an important factor in the tug's performance, will usually have special trials carried out once the vessel is in service. It is not uncommon for line-pull figures exceeding 150 tonnes to be recorded by an escort tug towing on a tanker at speeds of, for example, 10 knots. In order to carry out such tests special arrangements are made with the owners of a suitable ship, the ship's captain, the pilot on board at the time, and the port authority. Tests may then be carried out to determine the tug's ability to stop or steer the ship under specified conditions with a towline connected to the ship's stern. The towing winch aboard the tug will have been calibrated beforehand to enable the line pull exerted on the ship and the towline length used during the operation to be recorded. Further information on escort tugs and indirect towing will be found in later chapters.

The 'Rotor Tug' RT Magic is engaged in dynamic towing trials with a large tanker under way to determine the line pull achieved when towing in the indirect (escort) mode of operation. The tug is using its three azimuthing propulsion units to control the vessel's angle in relation to the towline and increase the pull available by using its own hull characteristics. (Kotug)

CHAPTER 2

Propulsion Systems

The most important feature of any tug is the propulsion system. For the purposes of this book the 'propulsion system' refers to the entire assembly of engine, propellers or propulsion units, and any associated gearboxes, clutches, drive shafts and steering gear. A tug's propulsion system must enable the vessel to tow or push effectively and at the same time manoeuvre quickly and precisely. Unlike almost any other type of vessel, the propulsion system in a tug can vary from a single engine driving a screw propeller to a number of highly sophisticated propulsion units powered by separate engines and operated under computer control.

In keeping with almost every other transport related industry, tug operators are becoming increasingly aware of the need to improve fuel economy and reduce exhaust emissions to meet new environmental standards. To that end considerable effort is being expended on improving diesel engine performance and develop new hybrid diesel-electric propulsion systems.

This chapter describes in more detail the propulsion systems mentioned, with the basic types of tug, in Chapter 1. Modern marine engines are generally compatible with a wide range of propulsion systems. The various types of propeller and propulsion unit may be used in several very different configurations, dependent on the basic tug design. The control systems favoured by various manufacturers and owners also vary widely with the type of tug and its employment. Therefore examples have been chosen to give the simplest explanation of what are often quite complex systems. The operation of the different types of vessel will be dealt with in later chapters.

THE MAIN ENGINE(S)

The term main engine is used in marine circles to differentiate between an engine used to drive the main propulsion system and engines installed to provide power for other purposes – power-generation, pumping, and driving other auxiliary equipment. In modern tugs diesel engines are invariably the primary source of

*One of a pair of Rolls-Royce Bergen C25:33L8P diesel main engines installed in the
Voith Schneider tractor tug* Velox. *Each of the 8-cylinder, turbo-charged engines
develops 3,265 bhp (2,400 kW) running at 1,000 rev/minute (MCR).* (Author)

power for both propulsion and auxiliary use. Whatever the choice of propulsion
system – conventional propeller, azimuthing propulsion unit or Voith Schneider
cycloidal propeller – the main engine will remain basically the same. The type of
engine will be chosen to satisfy requirements such as power output, suitable
operating speed ranges, power-to-weight ratio, fuel consumption and, increasingly,
the ability to meet local and/or national environmental regulations.

Since the diesel engine was first used in tugs, prior to the Second World War, the
approach to its use has changed considerably. The large slow running diesel
engines, coupled directly to the propeller shaft, popular for several decades, are
rapidly disappearing. A noticeable feature of the modern tug's engine-room is the
relatively small size of the engines. Not only are the engines smaller, they have a
much improved power-to-weight/size ratio. Modern marine diesel engines have
highly developed combustion systems and tend to run at higher speeds than their
predecessors. Improved materials, a careful choice of cylinder configuration, and
advanced electronic engine-control systems have all contributed to increased
efficiency. There remains stiff competition among rival engine manufacturers to
meet the demands of their customers in a cost-effective manner. Particular engines
meeting the needs of the towage industry at a given time tend to become

'fashionable' for a number of years, and there are regional preferences for particular engine types, often based on the type of vessel, reliability, and the availability of spare parts.

A typical modern diesel engine, used widely by the towage industry in a ship-handling tug, will be turbo-charged and may have 8–16 cylinders arranged in-line or in a 'V' configuration. Modern diesel engines are broadly divided into two categories 'medium' and 'high speed'. Medium-speed diesels in common use will produce their maximum power at between 750 and 1,000 revolutions per minute (rpm). A 'high-speed' engine of similar horsepower will typically be running at 1,600–1,800 rpm. A common example of an engine used in a modern harbour tug will produce in the order of 2,000–2,500 bhp.

The ratings given for each engine are generally quoted giving the horsepower and the revolutions per minute at its maximum continuous rating (MCR). This is the maximum power recommended for prolonged use. Other maximum power ratings may be quoted, such as a horsepower figure allowable for 1 hour – known as a 1-hour rating.

The various horsepower figures quoted by towage companies are often confusing. The output of modern diesel engines is usually expressed in brake horsepower or, increasingly, in kilowatts. Where possible brake horsepower (bhp) figures are used throughout this book for consistency and to aid comparison. Brake horsepower is a figure derived from tests on the engine under load and in carefully controlled conditions in a test facility. Indicated horsepower is still occasionally quoted by operators in publicity material and was the normal means of rating engines in the days of steam. This is a calculated figure that gives a rating approximately 13 per cent higher than brake horsepower.

A feature of diesel engine design receiving serious consideration by engine manufacturers is the subject of smoke emission and other exhaust gas pollutants such as nitrogen oxide and particulates. In many parts of the world, including some North American ports, authorities are laying down regulations governing acceptable emissions from vessels working within their boundaries. Unfortunately, in earlier generations of marine diesel engine, it was common for large amounts of black smoke to be emitted at various power settings. Improved combustion technology, electronic engine-management systems, and other significant advances have dramatically reduced not only visible smoke but also the emission of other more harmful but less visible pollutants.

Fuel consumed by the modern diesel engine varies in grade but is generally of the light or gas oil type. The necessity to address 'green' issues has encouraged many tug owners to use 'low sulphur' diesel fuels to meet increasingly rigorous emission standards. In a similar vein, research is being carried out into the use of liquid natural gas in tugs to achieve much lower exhaust emissions. Diesel engines used in some ferries and other vessels are already operating on this fuel but difficulties related to the storage and use of LNG under carefully controlled cryogenic conditions, and possibly higher fuel consumption in high-power engines, leave much to be addressed. Once those issues are resolved LNG may prove an attractive alternative fuel offering an almost total lack of noxious emissions.

In large seagoing tugs involved in long voyages considerable attention has been given to improving fuel economy. Some large vessels of this type have been equipped to use cheaper, very much heavier, fuel oil which would normally only be used in larger ships and steam boilers. The equipment installed to enable this fuel to be used normally comprises special heaters and a filtration plant to lower the viscosity of the oil, so that it can be burnt by the diesel engine in the usual manner.

Many owners try to introduce some commonality among engines installed in a tug fleet. The adoption of engines of a given type or manufacture brings a number of benefits. Purchasing and holding spare parts is made easier and more cost-effective, and maintenance and crew training are simplified.

In many smaller tugs and tug/workboats the engines are cooled by means of a self-contained 'keel cooling' system. On this Damen 1605 tug/workboat, shown whilst fitting out, the cooling ducts welded to the bottom of the hull are clearly visible. (Author)

Cooling Systems

All diesel engines employed in tugs or any other type of vessel require efficient cooling systems to maintain optimum engine temperatures regardless of the operating environment. In large vessels and the majority of coastal and harbour tugs the engines will be water-cooled using a cooling system comprising primary and secondary elements. In such an arrangement cooling water is circulated by pumps through the engine and a series of coolers in the 'primary' continuous loop system. In the secondary element of the system water is pumped from outside the vessel's hull through the coolers and discharged overboard. In this way seawater, or contaminated water from outside the vessel cannot come into contact with the engine or its components causing damage and excessive corrosion.

In many modern tugs cooling water in the 'primary' system passes through 'box coolers', large radiator-like components that are located in 'box' compartments open to the sea. Usually located in the side of the hull plating, with grilles allowing a free flow of seawater, the box coolers are continually immersed and no secondary pumped water supply is necessary. The size of the coolers is carefully calculated to provide the necessary temperature control. In some vessels the 'box coolers' have separate additional elements used to cool auxiliary engines, gearbox and hydraulic oil systems.

Smaller tugs and multi-purpose work vessels used in shallow water may be fitted with 'keel cooling' systems that use channels attached to the bottom plating of the hull as coolers. This system ensures that there is no contact whatever between the engine cooling water and the river or seawater in which the vessel is operating.

Engine Installations and Gearboxes

To enable the modern diesel engine to be used effectively it is necessary to provide a means of transmitting the power to the propeller or propulsion unit at a suitable rotational speed. In the case of the conventional screw propeller this is usually achieved by using a gearbox or some alternative means of power transmission such as a diesel-electric or hydraulic drive system. Azimuthing or Voith Schneider propulsion units are inherently 'self-contained' and any speed reduction required is generally carried out by an integral gear train.

The engine (or engines) used to power most conventional screw-propeller systems is mounted with the drive coupling located at the after end. The gearbox is located immediately behind the engine and designed to transmit power from the engine to the propeller at a speed calculated to give the most efficient results. Generally, the gearbox has a fixed reduction ratio of somewhere between 3:1 and 7:1, thus lowering the output speed to the propeller by the same proportion. The gearbox may incorporate a reverse gear and automatically operated clutch. A reverse gear may be unnecessary when controllable-pitch propellers are used, as will be explained later. In most installations the gearbox and clutch controls are operated hydraulically and interconnected to the engine speed controls. A brake may be incorporated in the gearbox or on the propeller shaft to control the movement of the propeller automatically when the vessel is manoeuvring. A high degree of automation is normal in the transmission system in order to protect the engine and gearbox from damage and simplify the controls in the wheelhouse.

In a relatively simple installation a single engine drives one propeller through a gearbox, via a rigid steel shaft. It is not uncommon, however, particularly in deep-

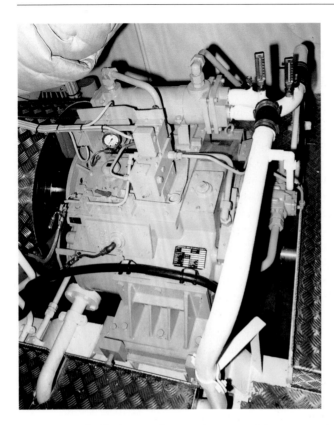

Each main engine on the twin-screw tug Regain *drives its propeller via a reverse reduction gearbox as shown. The gearbox is a Reintjes WAF 541 giving a reduction of 4.45:1. The engine drive shaft can be seen on the left and the output to the propeller on the right.* (Author

sea tugs and oil-rig supply vessels, to couple two engines to one propeller shaft. This is achieved by using a twin-input, single-output gearbox. The small size of modern diesel engines makes this a practical proposition, and a four-engine installation driving twin propellers can provide an economical powerplant in a seagoing vessel. This arrangement enables an engine to be shut down for repair or maintenance while the tug is under way, and when necessary the vessel can proceed more economically on only two engines (one coupled to each propeller) while running light without a tow.

The manner in which main engines and gearboxes are mounted in a tug, or any other vessel, is now an important issue. In order to minimise noise and vibration, to improve the living conditions for the crew, and meet the requirements of regulatory authorities particular attention is given to the engine and gearbox mounting and the couplings between engine, gearbox and propulsion system. It is now common practice to use high-tech flexible mountings to support engines and where necessary gearboxes to reduce the transmission of noise and vibration through the vessel's structure. Likewise, highly developed rubber-based flexible couplings are also used in the drive-line between the engines and propeller shafts of the propulsion units.

The main engines in stern-drive and tractor tugs and are located in a fore and aft configuration in much the same way as in a conventional screw vessel but the means of connecting them to the propulsion units varies considerably. A brief description of the drive arrangement is included in the relevant sections that follow.

Diesel-Electric and Diesel-Hydraulic Propulsion Systems

The use of diesel-electric propulsion systems was more popular in the early days of the diesel engine, when it was quite difficult to attain good control and power at slow speeds. A diesel-electric system is one where the main engine is coupled directly to a generator. The current produced powers an electric motor, which in turn drives the propeller shaft, giving precise control in a relatively simple manner via electrical switchgear. A number of diesel engines may be used to generate power for one or more propulsion motors. Such systems are, however, expensive to manufacture and under most circumstances can no longer compete with the modern high-speed diesel engine and gearbox installation in most towage applications. But see also *Hybrid Propulsion Systems* below.

Diesel-electric transmission systems are widely used to power bow and stern thrusters in large tugs and offshore support vessels.

Diesel-hydraulic systems operate on a similar principle. The diesel engine drives a hydraulic pump and a hydraulic motor provides power at the propeller shaft. The connection between the two can be by means of pipes or hoses, giving greater choice in the location of engines and other matters. These systems are expensive to manufacture and are generally unsuited to high-powered installations. Diesel-hydraulic transmission systems are generally restricted to very small tugs and also to transmit power to bow thrust units in larger vessels.

Hybrid Propulsion Systems

As public and political concerns for the environment grow, tug owners are actively pursuing a number of options to produce a 'green' vessel that will significantly reduce harmful nitrogen oxide, particulate matter, sulphur dioxide, carbon and other emissions. Such a vessel should also consume less fuel and be quieter than its conventional predecessors.

The result is a number of proposals for 'hybrid propulsion systems' the majority of which have not advanced beyond the concept stage. In the main these proposals centre around advanced diesel-electric concepts involving various combinations of diesel engines, diesel generators, batteries and even hydrogen based fuel cells. Other options include a combination of multi-fuel diesel engines, running on liquid natural gas or diesel oil in a system incorporating a diesel-electric drive. Virtually all of the proposals incorporating electric drives involve complex, state-of-the-art power-management systems to provide automatic but precise control during every conceivable operational situation. At present it is obvious that considerable development is inevitable before anything resembling a universally acceptable system emerges. In simple terms the towage industry is attempting to achieve something approaching the now established automotive hybrids

Carolyn Dorothy *is the world's first tug powered by a true 'hybrid' diesel-electric propulsion system optimised to reduce exhaust emissions, fuel consumption, and noise. The 23.77 m stern-drive tug with a bollard pull of 65 tonnes was built by Foss Maritime and entered service early in 2009.* (Foss)

employing internal combustion engines and battery-electric drives but in a much more complex operating environment.

What is claimed to be the first true hybrid tug entered service in 2009. American tug owner Foss Maritime commissioned the vessel, a ship-handling tug of 5,000 horsepower based on a well-established modern azimuthing stern-drive design known as the 'Dolphin' class.

At the heart of this new concept is a unique diesel-battery-electric propulsion system. Two fully azimuthing propulsion units are powered by batteries coupled to diesel generators and feature a modified engine-room accommodating two battery packs, producing the equivalent of 670 horsepower, and two 335 horsepower diesel generators. In its various modes of operation the new tug will employ battery power for low speeds and light running, with battery and generators for medium-power operation. When full power is required the main diesel engines will be coupled to the drive system in addition to the electric motors. Any surplus power will be used to recharge the battery packs. Although the main engines in the hybrid tug have a lower horsepower rating than those of existing tugs of the same type, the same total horsepower will be available.

The Foss hybrid tug project was encouraged and partly financed by the Californian ports where the tug will operate and where enormous efforts are being expended to control emissions in every aspect of port operation from land-based plant to tugboats. Among the environmental and health-related benefits quoted for this hybrid tug are reduced emissions (nitrogen oxide, particulate, sulphur dioxide and carbon) due to design efficiencies and lower fuel consumption. The Foss hybrid tug design minimises fuel consumption by using a power management system to match the power required to the most efficient combination of batteries, generators and main engines for any particular demand.

Overall, the hybrid tug is much quieter than traditional vessels, running on battery power in standby mode and only bringing the generators and main engines online when higher power is required. This reduction in noise levels will protect crews from hearing loss and generally reduce ambient noise pollution.

Step-Up Gearboxes

In vessels where fire-fighting pumps, and/or hydraulic pumps, are driven by the main engine an additional gearbox is sometimes fitted to provide a mechanical drive at the required speed. Known as 'step-up' gearboxes, they are normally coupled to the front (opposite end to the flywheel) end of the engine. The purpose of such gearboxes is to enable pumps to be driven at speeds faster than normal engine revolutions. Some step-up gearboxes have provision for more than one output coupling and may be used to power fire-fighting pumps and the hydraulic pumps used to supply bow thrusters, towing winches and other deck machinery.

Engine Controls

Engine controls have become increasingly sophisticated in recent years and with the anticipated introduction of hybrid propulsion systems will become even more complex. The days when the various engine controls were manipulated by an

The engine control room on board the emergency towing vessel Abeille Liberté *contains the monitoring and alarm systems and controls for four main engines, auxiliaries and the twin-screw propulsion system. The two computer displays show the various systems in diagrammatic form. In the background are the electrical switchboards.* (Author)

Machinery data monitoring and alarm panels are frequently installed on modern tugs of all sizes. This multi-function display is one of several installed in the engine control room, ship's office, wheelhouse and chief engineer's cabin on board the emergency towing vessel Anglian Sovereign. *(Author)*

engineer in the engine-room and communication with the wheelhouse took place via the telegraph have virtually disappeared from the present-day tug fleet. Modern remote-control systems give the tugmaster direct and precise control of engine speed, and where necessary direction of rotation of the propeller, via the gearbox controls or controls associated with Voith Schneider or azimuthing propulsion units.

In most modern tugs the engineer is provided with a control station, often in a soundproof cubicle, in the engine-room from which he can monitor and if necessary start and operate all of the major items of machinery. Once the tug is ready to get under way the captain has full control of the main engine and steering systems. In most small or highly automated vessels main engine starting and shutdown may also be controlled from the wheelhouse along with some of the auxiliary machinery. Even in very large vessels, highly automated engine-rooms may be left unattended for long periods. Alarm systems are installed to warn of potentially serious or dangerous faults developing in propulsion or auxiliary machinery in what are often designated as 'unmanned machinery spaces' (UMS) for certain periods. Where this is the case alarm panels are provided in the wheelhouse and the crew accommodation during the periods when the engine-room or control-room are unmanned.

A comprehensive machinery monitoring system is often installed in modern tugs of all sizes. These computer-based systems are used to monitor, record and display a wide range of functions. The most common functions covered are various engine temperatures and pressures, cooling and fuel system performance, and the liquid levels in fuel, water, ballast and other storage tanks. Critical functions can be programmed with pre-set parameters to activate alarms should a malfunction occur. In most systems the information is displayed on a computer screen in the engine-room control cubicle and some or all of the data relayed to a similar, duplicate, display in the wheelhouse. The data recorded in this way are available for analysis by the owner's engineering staff and are often capable of being transmitted ashore via the vessel's communications equipment.

PROPELLERS

Conventional Screw-Propeller Systems

The traditional screw propeller, used in one form or another, remains the principal means of propulsion for the great majority of tugs. In modern tugs the conventional screw propeller is invariably used in conjunction with a nozzle and, increasingly, embodied in a sophisticated fully steerable azimuthing propulsion unit. The most common application remains that which employs one or more propellers located in the traditional position under the vessel's stern, and used with or without some form of nozzle or thrust-augmenting device. As mentioned in Chapter 1, the arrangement without a nozzle is often referred to as an 'open' propeller. These are usually found in older vessels, still continuing to give good service, or which for operational reasons remain most suitable for the local conditions in which they work.

Propeller design for any ship is a compromise, but in the tug there are a number of conflicting demands that make the designer's choice more difficult. For example, in a ship-handling tug there is a need to produce good towing characteristics at very slow speeds; at the same time the vessel must have the ability to travel quickly between tasks, and indeed be able to keep up with the ships it may be assisting. The basic factors to be considered are propeller diameter, pitch and rotational speed, and power. The diameter will be governed by the hull

The single-screw ship-handling tug Sun Kent *(now the Portuguese* Montado) *is fitted with a steerable Kort nozzle and a controllable-pitch propeller.* (Kort Propulsion)

design, operating draft, and the power to be absorbed from the powerplant. Pitch can be defined as the theoretical distance the propeller will travel in one complete rotation. There are inherent inefficiency factors affecting propeller design that are too complex to be addressed here in any great detail. Propeller pitch is interrelated to diameter and speed of rotation and is frequently chosen as the most convenient variable when reaching a compromise between pulling power and speed. In simple terms, for towing purposes a large propeller with a fine pitch and slow rotation produces the best results. A smaller, faster-rotating propeller with a coarser pitch would be chosen where the vessel's speed was a more important feature. In order to operate efficiently the propeller must, ideally, be deeply immersed and have a free passage for water from around the hull. As we have seen previously several of these factors have a profound influence on the design of a tug hull.

Propellers may have three, four, or even five blades depending on their application. The shape of the blades varies widely in advanced propeller designs. Propellers intended to operate in conjunction with propulsion nozzles may have broad blades with tips that follow the interior diameter of the nozzle with very little clearance. Or, alternatively, faster-rotating propellers may have a large number of blades of a streamlined 'skewed' shape. In each case the intention is to improve efficiency by avoiding the phenomena known as 'slip' and 'cavitation'. The former is often the result of a mis-match in speed, pitch or blade design and the latter a condition which causes air bubbles to be generated in the waterflow through the propeller, causing problems with noise and vibration. The choice of materials also varies, with various bronze alloys and stainless steel the most popular.

The number of propellers installed on a tug depends very much on the type of vessel and its draft. Two propellers are frequently used where one cannot efficiently absorb the necessary power without adversely affecting the hull design and draft. A twin-screw arrangement, where each propeller is normally controlled separately, may also be chosen to enhance manoeuvrability. Three or four propellers are often used where the vessel is designed for operation in very shallow waters. Powerful pusher tugs and some multi-purpose vessels employ multiple-screw propulsion systems in order to use high-power main engines efficiently and keep the vessel's draft to a minimum. In order to reach an optimum arrangement for shallow-draft vessels the propellers are often located in tunnels formed in the underside of the hull.

Controllable-Pitch Propellers

The controllable-pitch propeller has proved to be an effective means of overcoming much of the need for compromise in propeller design. With this type of propeller the pitch of the blades can be controlled while the vessel is under way, to suit the work in hand. This has the following advantages:

(a) Propeller pitch can be changed automatically by a system that matches pitch to engine revolutions, giving the most efficient setting for the power available.

(b)   The propeller can be used to provide astern power without the need for a clutch or reverse gear in the gearbox.

c)   Very fine adjustments in pitch are possible, giving precise control of thrust both forward and astern, which is particularly important when manoeuvring and taking up the slack in a towline.

The pitch actuating mechanism is generally hydraulically operated and controlled directly from the wheelhouse. The pitch and engine-speed controls are frequently combined and operated by a single lever. A disadvantage of the controllable-pitch propeller is its relatively high capital cost. In some working conditions it can also be vulnerable to damage and consequently expensive to repair. Controllable-pitch propellers are frequently used in deep-sea tugs and offshore vessels with wide operating parameters and powerful harbour tugs equipped with thrust-enhancing nozzles.

PROPULSION NOZZLES

The propulsion nozzle was produced in Germany in 1932 by Ludwig Kort and was intended originally as a device to reduce the effects of propeller wash from tugs that were causing erosion damage to the banks of German canals. It was soon apparent that the fixed tubular shroud fitted around the propeller not only had the desired effect but also considerably improved the tug's performance. Known as the 'Kort nozzle', the original device was soon adopted by towage concerns elsewhere in Europe and Britain. The nozzle has been developed considerably since its inception and is now capable of producing significant improvements in performance.

To quantify the benefits of a nozzle exactly is not simple since each tug design has differing characteristics, but generally an improvement in bollard pull of

The diagram shows the flow of water through a typical Kort nozzle of the steerable type. Additional thrust generated by the action of the nozzle is shown by the arrows adjacent to the top and bottom pivot points. In a fixed nozzle thrust is transmitted to the hull through the supporting structure.

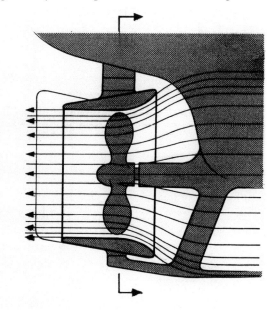

between 30 and 40 per cent would be expected, when compared with an open propeller. The nozzle is basically a tube within which the propeller rotates. In cross-section the tube is tapered with an aerofoil shape on the interior. The effect of the nozzle is to cause a differential pressure between the outside and front inside surfaces, inducing additional forward thrust from the nozzle. This additional thrust is transmitted through the nozzle mountings to the vessel's hull.

Propulsion nozzles are also used in conjunction with many propulsion units of the azimuthing type covered later in this chapter. The nozzle structure forms an integral part of the steerable propeller unit but the principles involved are identical to those described below.

Fixed and Steerable Nozzles

Two forms of nozzle are commonly in use with conventional screw-propeller systems: the fixed nozzle, which is part of the hull structure, and the steerable nozzle. The latter incorporates a rudder and is mounted on pintles in much the same way as a conventional rudder. When a steerable nozzle is used, the propeller shaft and its stern tube are extended to give the nozzle sufficient space to turn about the propeller, without fouling the hull. The use of a steerable nozzle requires a particularly powerful steering mechanism to cope with the weight of the nozzle

This twin-screw installation on a 16 m Damen tug/workboat is typical of many employing fixed propulsion nozzles. Similar systems, with twin nozzles and rudders, are fitted to tugs of all sizes. Note the protective anodes around the nozzles and attached to the rudders. (Author)

structure and the forces involved. Such an arrangement was most common in single-screw ship-handling and coastal tugs but has fallen from favour in recent years with the development of highly efficient fixed nozzle and rudder systems.

The fixed nozzle is one that encloses the propeller in the same way but is attached firmly to the hull. This arrangement allows the use of modern rudder systems that require less powerful and less robust steering gear and is easier to incorporate in a shallow-draft vessel. Fixed-nozzle systems are frequently used in modern twin-screw tugs and are almost certain to be the choice for very large deep-sea tugs and oil-rig supply vessels. Single or multiple conventional rudders may be used, or special rudders designed to reduce the vessel's turning circle.

A particular problem encountered in many nozzle systems is that of electrolytic erosion of propeller blades, nozzle, and hull plating caused by the use of dissimilar metals, for example a bronze propeller rotating in close proximity to a steel nozzle. In order to combat this problem zinc blocks known as anodes, working on a sacrificial principle, are fitted to the exterior of the nozzle(s) and surrounding hull structure. Stainless steel is often used for the internal surface of the nozzle to resist erosion and wear caused by sand and other particles in the water flowing through the nozzle.

RUDDERS

The choice of rudder or rudders is an important feature of any tug employing conventional screw propellers. With traditional open-screw systems a single conventional rudder located aft of each propeller is still most common. With manoeuvrability high on the tug designer's list of priorities, a great deal of development has gone into producing rudders of suitable size, area, shape and cross-section. The position of the rudder's pivot point and its cross-sectional shape are chosen to provide the best possible steering characteristics when the vessel is moving forward or going astern. Location of the pivot point on the rudder blade is also used to determine rudder balance, which to some extent determines the amount of power required to actuate the rudder.

There are a number of patented rudder designs used in tugs; some have unique cross-sectional shapes and others additional movable blades at the trailing edge to change their cross-section progressively as helm is applied. All are intended to improve the tug's turning circle and handling characteristics.

Perhaps the most important aspect of a tug's steering system is its ability to act quickly and positively. To achieve this, the actuating mechanism is generally faster and more powerful than in many other craft and gives greater angular movement.

Rudders are usually supported at the bottom by a pintle (hinge pin) to give added strength. Those without a lower pintle are known as the 'spade' type and may be more vulnerable to damage in shallow water. In many tug designs more than one rudder is fitted. Twin rudders are sometimes used to give a single-screw tug improved steering and are the norm in twin-screw vessels. The use of propulsion nozzles also influences rudder design, as will be seen later. In North

The 25.4 m twin-screw 'Dogancay' class tug has two rudders mounted on each nozzle. With two main engines of 1,500 bhp each, the tug is highly manoeuvrable and has a bollard pull of over 40 tonnes. Note the double-chine hull design. (Sanmar)

America, additional rudders, known as 'flanking rudders', are sometimes fitted ahead of the propeller(s) to improve handling. Flanking rudders are common in large pusher tugs – a typical triple-screw European vessel may well have nine rudders, one aft and two forward of each propeller.

Enhanced Nozzle and Rudder Systems

Development of the Kort and similar nozzle systems continues and various enhancements are available to suit particular vessels and conditions. One such development that emerged some years ago and continues to be fitted in some parts of the world is the British Towmaster system. Used on a variety of tug types, from harbour tugs to oceangoing vessels, the system is based on a type of fixed nozzle not unlike the Kort design. The main difference is in the rudder system used. Rudders, described as shutter rudders, are positioned ahead and astern of the nozzle. Often three rudders are located astern of the nozzle and two (flanking rudders) ahead. The shutter rudders closely control the flow of water through the

This Towmaster nozzle and multiple rudder system is typical of those fitted to many ship-handling tugs. In this installation three rudders are fitted aft of the nozzles and two forward. Note the specially shaped rudder blades. (Burness, Corlett and Partners)

propeller and nozzle, improving both pulling performance and manoeuvrability.

Another well-known manufacturer of high-performance nozzle, propeller and rudder systems is the American company Nautican. Like Towmaster, Nautican and other similar propulsion systems are fitted not only to new tugs but also retrofitted to existing vessels to enhance performance. There are many examples where older tugs have been given a significant new lease of life when upgraded in this way.

PROPULSION CONTROLS IN CONVENTIONAL TUGS

To complete this section on conventional tug propulsion systems mention must be made of the engine and steering controls located in the wheelhouse. The actual controls fitted vary in detail with the type of tug and the owner's specific preferences but the following equipment is found in the majority of vessels.

For tugs with a fixed-pitch propeller and gearbox, engine speed and gearbox forward and reverse gears are commonly controlled by a single lever with a central neutral position. The lever is moved forward to move ahead and backwards to go astern. In twin-screw tugs the two controls are normally mounted side by side, enabling the propellers to be controlled independently and precisely.

A similar arrangement is also used when controllable-pitch propellers are fitted. A single lever is used to control engine speed and propeller pitch, thus enabling speed and forward and astern movement to be controlled with great accuracy. The relationship between pitch and engine speed can often be adjusted, to suit operating conditions, by push-button switches or some similar means. The lever is moved progressively forward, to move the tug ahead, and backwards to go astern, with the same fine degree of control available in either direction.

Tugs with conventional screw-propulsion and rudders are steered either by a wheel, a small lever, or even a pair of push-buttons. In conventional tugs of any size steering wheels are frequently fitted for emergency use only. Small steering levers, often described as 'jog levers' are most common and a number may be installed, conveniently located with engine and other controls at strategic positions

The control console aboard the twin-screw tug/workboat Helmut *follows the layout common to all of the smaller vessels from Damen Shipyards. Control levers for the main engines and gear-boxes are to the right of the wheel. The tug can be steered by the wheel or the small 'jog' lever on the extreme right.* (Author)

in the wheelhouse and sometimes at vantage points outside. For the same reason, steering and engine controls are sometimes fitted to a small portable hand unit, connected by an electric cable to the control systems, to enable captains to position themselves in full view of the work in hand.

AZIMUTHING PROPULSION UNITS

The 'azimuthing propulsion unit' is an unwieldy but universal title given to a great many propulsion units of a similar type and produced by a number of manufacturers. The terms 'fully steerable propulsion unit', 'rudder propeller' and 'Z drive unit' are also used. The trade names Aquamaster (now Rolls-Royce), Duckpeller, Z-Peller, Schottel, and Compass all apply to units of a similar type that are widely used in the towage industry.

Azimuthing propulsion units are used in tugs for main propulsion or as bow thrusters. As previously described, twin units are installed beneath the stern of the vessel in the stern-drive configuration or in the forward part of the hull in a tractor tug. Propulsion units of the same type are used in Z-Tech, Rotor Tugs and ship

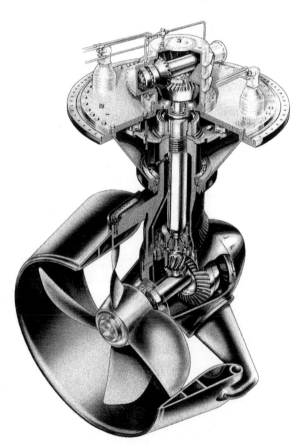

A cutaway view of a typical fully azimuthing propulsion unit clearly shows the 'Z drive' configuration. The propeller rotates within an integral nozzle and is driven via two sets of spiral bevel gears. A further geared mechanism in the upper gear casing enables the entire underwater portion of the unit to be steered by the two hydraulic motors visible on the mounting plate. (Schottel Propulsion)

docking modules. When employed as a bow thruster the unit is generally fitted with a retracting mechanism to enable it to be housed within the hull when not in use.

An azimuthing propulsion unit is basically a conventional screw propeller that is driven through a system of gears in such a way that the entire propeller and its shaft can be rotated about a vertical axis – in much the same way as an outboard motor. Most units can be turned through a full 360 degrees, enabling thrust from the propeller to be used to propel and steer the vessel in any desired direction. The majority of units incorporate a thrust-enhancing nozzle and fixed-pitch propellers. All units incorporate a gear train to enable propeller speed to be matched to the pitch of the propeller and produce the required performance.

Each propulsion unit is self-contained. An upper gearbox casing bolts into the hull of the tug and contains not only gears to drive the propeller but also the steering mechanism and a lubrication system. A drive shaft connects the unit to the engine and the only other services required are electrical or hydraulic to control the steering gear.

In high-powered tug units with fixed-pitch propellers precise control can be difficult at very slow speeds – when taking up the slack in a towline, for example. To improve this aspect of performance either a controllable-pitch propeller is used, or more commonly a device is fitted in the drive system to enable the propeller to turn very slowly. This may be a fluid drive or a slipping clutch. The slipping clutch is controlled automatically and programmed to operate in conjunction with the speed of the engine and load on the propeller. Slipping clutches are either mounted as a separate unit in the drive between the engine and the propulsion unit or, in some more recent examples, as an integral part of the azimuthing unit itself.

Azimuthing Propulsion Units in Stern-Drive Tugs

In a stern-drive tug twin azimuthing propulsion units are invariably employed and located beneath the vessel's stern. The position of the units, with the gearboxes located high in the hull, sometimes requires complex shafting to transmit power from the engines, which for the purposes of weight distribution and stability must remain low in the structure. The drive shafts are fitted with large flexible joints in order to accommodate the differing heights of engine and propulsion unit. Great care is taken with the design and installation of the drive shafts in order to avoid problems with excessive noise and vibration. In a number of very recent designs the engines are located on flexible mounts and the drive shafting incorporates at least one flexible rubber coupling. The weight of drive shafting has also become an issue, resulting in some designers specifying light-weight carbon-fibre shafts to reduce the effects of weight and inertia.

One of the main advantages of the stern-drive configuration is that a very high bollard pull can be attained, coupled with impressive handling characteristics, yet without greatly increasing the draft of the vessel. Properly handled, the stern-drive tug can move ahead, astern or sideways and turn within its own length. To achieve these manoeuvres the units are turned, in unison or individually, to a whole range

This pre-launch view of the Sanmar Eskort V *shows the location of a pair of fully azimuthing propulsion units beneath the stern. The Rolls-Royce units are fitted with high performance controllable-pitch propellers with blades and high-performance nozzles. Note the double-chine hull construction and grilles in the side plates giving water access to the box coolers.* (Sanmar)

of positions designed to produce the correct thrust for the evolution required. The diagram above right shows the relative positions of the units for basic manoeuvres.

One of the most important features of a stern-drive tug of this type is that its bollard pull when towing astern is almost equal to that produced going ahead. This is of great significance in a ship-handling and escort tug and a feature that is impossible to reproduce in a conventional screw vessel.

Controls in Stern-drive Tugs

Control of the azimuthing units in stern-drive tugs is a complex process, and one that has led propulsion unit manufacturers to devise ingenious control systems to simplify matters for the tugmaster. An electro-hydraulic system is generally used to control the steering movements of each unit and the rotational speed of the propeller. In the wheelhouse, controls vary from a complicated array of individual engine and steering controls for each unit to computer-controlled systems that enable a single lever to be used to manoeuvre the vessel. Some operators and crews

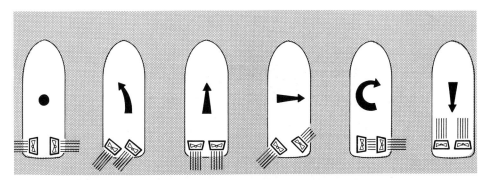

The diagram illustrates the relative positions of the propulsion units in a stern-drive tug to accomplish the basic manoeuvres indicated by the arrows. The same basic techniques apply to a tractor tug fitted with azimuthing units.

prefer separate individual controls, which appear daunting to the outsider. There is usually a single handle, incorporating a speed control, that is used to 'steer' each unit individually. In the controls of most tugs using azimuthing propulsion units there is no neutral or reverse position for propeller rotation. When the vessel is at rest the propellers continue to rotate but are turned outboard as shown in the diagram. To move forward the units are progressively turned to direct thrust towards the stern. Moving astern is accomplished by turning the units through 180 degrees, directing the thrust forward. Each unit can be rotated using a separate lever. Indicators show the position of each unit in relation to the hull. More complex manoeuvres are carried out by moving the units as shown and applying differing amounts of power. In some systems a small steering wheel is used to steer a course in the normal way with the units turning in unison, either ahead or astern.

When a single-lever control system is installed an electronic microprocessor controls all of the required functions. The lever is simply moved in the direction the tug is required to travel. In some systems the engine speed control is separate; in others it is incorporated in the lever mechanism. Whatever the control system,

The control console of a modern 28 m stern-drive tug from Damen Shipyards contains the main controls and indicators for the azimuthing propulsion system and towing winch. A hand-controller on each side controls both propeller speed and steering for one unit. Foot switches control the VHF radios. (Author)

the speed and precision with which the units can be rotated through the full 360-degree steering arc is most important.

Azimuthing Propulsion Systems in Tractor Tugs

The azimuthing propulsion units used in tractor and Z-Tech tugs are of the same basic design as those previously described in stern-drive tugs. Their location beneath the forward hull in a tractor simplifies to some degree the installation of units and engines and reduces the need for very long and complex drive shafting. The Z-Tech type has a similar layout to a stern-drive tug.

Hybrid tractor tugs such as the Rotor Tug and the Ship Docking Module have propulsion system installations that are quite different from those in tractors where two azimuthing units are mounted in the forward part of the vessel. In the case of the Rotor Tug a third engine is located between those driving the forward units. The additional engine is mounted on the centreline and has the 'drive end' at the rear, enabling the drive shaft to transmit power to an azimuthing unit in the stern of the vessel. In the SDM the engines are mounted diagonally across the vessel, enabling one engine to power the forward azimuthing unit and the other to drive the unit located in the stern. Each propulsion unit is positioned off the centreline, a feature that enables the engines and drive shafting to form a very neat installation.

Other factors relating to the design of tractors with azimuthing and Voith Schneider propulsion units are covered in Chapter 1.

Controls in Tractor Tugs with Two Azimuthing Units Forward

Similar principles apply to the control of the azimuthing unit tractor as those previously described for the stern-drive type of vessel. The propulsion units are rotated to much the same positions, in relation to each other and the hull, to

The azimuthing tractor tug Montali *is steered using the joystick in the centre of the console. Both propulsion units are automatically turned to the appropriate positions to achieve the desired manoeuvre. Engine speed is controlled by the levers at right. The propulsion units may also be steered independently using the two large knobs on the panel. (Author)*

achieve similar manoeuvres. Handling characteristics will be different due to the presence of the large skeg but the azimuthing unit position diagram remains valid for the tractor configuration.

Controls in the wheelhouse also follow much the same basic pattern, with various manufacturers using the same systems regardless of whether the vessel is a tractor or stern-drive tug.

Controls in the Rotor Tug

Control of the three azimuthing propulsion units in the Rotor Tug is even more complex than the tractor and stern-drive systems previously mentioned. The individual controls for each unit are the same as those installed in any vessel using, in this case, a Schottel propulsion system. Three individual control units are fitted but a computerised system enables any combination of the two forward- and one stern-mounted unit to be controlled at the same time via a fourth 'master controller'. The tugmaster may therefore choose to control the tug using the master controller coupled to all three units, or control any or all of the units using its own individual control handle.

Controlling the propulsion units aboard a Rotor Tug can be a complex matter. Three separate controllers on either side of the tugmaster's chair can be used to control the units individually. The fourth (larger) controller operates all three or any desired combination of units in unison. Note the three indicators on the forward end of the consoles, showing the orientation of each unit. (Author)

Controls in the Ship Docking Module

In the SDM the propulsion units are operated in quite a simple manner. Each unit has its own individual hand controller, incorporating steering and propeller speed. The tugmaster works from a split console with one controller in each hand and faces in the direction the tug is heading. The control handles are positioned in such a way that the controller for the forward unit is always in his right hand. Thrust is directed in a logical manner, to enable the vessel to travel forwards, astern or sideways.

The anchor-handling tug Sidney Candies *is one of a number of American vessels to have a unique triple-screw propulsion system. Two fully azimuthing propulsion units are fitted and one single conventional propeller. A high-performance propeller and nozzle are fitted on the centreline to enhance bollard pull but the vessel is steered entirely by the azimuthing units.* (Rice Propellers)

Azimuthing and Conventional Propeller – Triple-Screw System

A unique American design of anchor-handling tug makes use of a single screw and two azimuthing propulsion units located at the stern. This arrangement has been adopted in order to combine a high bollard pull with exceptional manoeuvrability. In this configuration a powerful single propeller and nozzle is fitted on the vessel's centreline without rudders. A pair of azimuthing propulsion units are fitted, one on either side of the conventional propeller. For steering and normal cruising the vessel is controlled in the same way as a normal stern-drive vessel. When making a fast passage, or towing and anchor-handling when a high bollard pull is required the conventional screw is used, with engine speed controlled in the normal way.

Voith Schneider Propulsion Units

The present-day Voith Schneider propulsion unit is based on the unique cycloidal propeller invented by Ernst Schneider and the J. M. Voith company in 1928. The propeller is unlike any conventional screw propeller or paddle mechanism. Although Voith Schneider propulsion units have many applications in ferries and several other types of vessel, in the towage industry they are almost exclusively

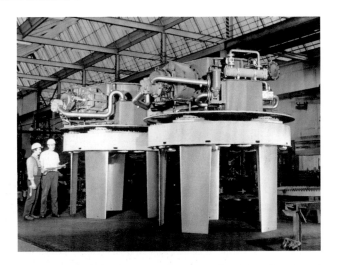

Two five-blade Voith Schneider cycloidal propulsion units are shown assembled and ready for installation in a tractor tug. Each unit is completely self contained with its own hydraulic system. (Voith Hydro)

fitted to tugs of the tractor type. The tractor tug originally evolved hand in hand with the Voith Schneider system. As mentioned in Chapter 1, most of the early development took place Germany, but the Voith tractor tug soon became popular in other European countries. Acceptance of this type of propulsion took some time to spread elsewhere, but examples are now in use in ports throughout the world. With the exception of very small tugs, and a number of earlier vessels, most modern tractors are fitted with two propulsion units, side by side.

Each propulsion unit has a series of blades, pointing downwards, attached to a hub which rotates about a vertical axis. Each blade has a hydrofoil cross-section.

This very much simplified diagram of a Voith Schneider propulsion unit shows the principal components of the cycloidal propeller and its control mechanism. The cut-away section depicts the kinematic linkage that controls the pitch of each blade as the assembly rotates. In the centre is the control rod, connected at the top to its two servo actuators. The input shaft enters from the left and, through bevel gearing, drives the entire rotor assembly.

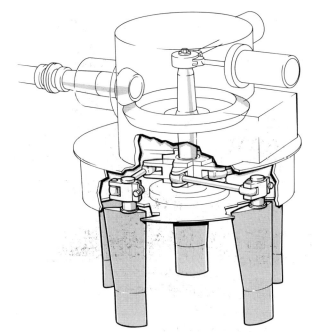

At a predetermined position in the blades' circular path, a change of pitch occurs producing propulsive thrust. The action is not unlike the sculling action of an oar but uses circular rather than the more complex oscillating motion. The circular path around which the blades travel is known as a cycloid – hence the name cycloidal propeller. The point in the blades' path at which the change of pitch takes place is controlled by a mechanical linkage, comprising levers and cranks known as the 'kinematics', located inside the hub (or rotor) of the propeller. At the centre of the linkage is a control rod which determines the position where the change in blade pitch occurs and the magnitude of that change. In this way thrust can be vectored in any chosen direction in relation to the hull and its force controlled with great precision. The diagram on page 73 shows a simplified blade arrangement and the way thrust is generated and directed. In practice, the number of blades used and the diameter of the blade path, or orbit, is chosen to match the power available and the size of vessel. The thrust available when going ahead or astern is almost identical and changes very little throughout the 360-degree steering circle, The Voith system affords a degree of control superior to most others, but in terms of propeller efficiency the cycloidal unit compares unfavourably with those using a screw propeller.

A view of the high performance escort tug Velox *prior to launching at the Gondan shipyard in Spain shows the complex hull form, protection plate, bilge keels and skeg aft. The blades of the Voith Schneider propulsion units are visible above the protection plate and its supporting struts. (Gondan)*

Modern Voith propulsion units are normally fitted with five or six blades. When specifying propulsion units the main criteria used are the diameter of the blade orbit, and the number and length of the blades.

Each propulsion unit is self-contained. The main casing embodies a mounting flange to secure the unit to the hull structure. The casing encloses the main gear train to drive the hub of the propeller and the necessary lubrication system. Located in the top of the casing is the hydraulic servo-mechanism used to operate the control rod. Originally, the wheelhouse controls were invariably connected to this servo-mechanism by means of a mechanical linkage but more recently electronic control systems have been developed that offer greater flexibility.

The installation of the units and main engines is similar to that of the azimuthing tractor, with the engines low in the hull and a simple shaft drive to the units. The hull design also incorporates a large skeg at the stern and a protection plated fitted below the propellers as described in Chapter 1. This plate is sometimes referred to as the 'nozzle plate'. It was discovered early in the development of the Voith tractor that the plate could be given a certain hydrodynamic cross-sectional shape and used to improve the flow of water through the propeller blades and consequently thrust. The effect is similar to that of the nozzle surrounding a conventional screw propeller. In common with other tractor-tug designs, the Voith Schneider-propelled vessel tends to have a relatively deep draft.

The operating characteristics of the propulsion units allow the main engines of a Voith tractor tug to run at constant, preset speeds. Once the engines are started and the propellers rotating, all further control can be carried out using the units' pitch controls. A useful by-product of having a constant engine speed is that auxiliary machinery can be driven directly from either engine. In fire-fighting tugs this is particularly advantageous, enabling high-capacity fire pumps to be driven from the main engines, yet leaving enough power available to manoeuvre the tug.

Controls in Voith Schneider Tractor Tugs

The controls of a Voith Schneider tractor tug are extremely simple and always take the same basic form. In the wheelhouse the captain is provided with a steering wheel and pitch levers. The number of pitch levers depends on whether the vessel has one or two propulsion units. One pitch lever is used to control each unit. In the most basic installations the controls are located on what is known as a control stand. One central control stand is fitted in the most modern ship-handling tractors but a second or third can be found in some larger vessels to give the tug captain a choice of operating position. In the later generations of escort tug, the controls are arranged on either side of the captain's chair, with the wheel on one side and the pitch levers on the other.

In very simple terms, the steering wheel controls transverse thrust and the pitch levers longitudinal thrust. The pitch levers have a central neutral position and as they are moved forward or backwards pitch is progressively increased in the ahead

The central control console on board the Lady Sarah *is typical of those on Voith tractor tugs used for ship-handling. The levers on the right of the wheel control the pitch of the propeller blades. Two rows of buttons on the left control engine speed. The panel on the extreme right contains the towing winch controls.* (Author)

or astern direction respectively. Movement of the steering wheel vectors thrust to either side as required to steer the vessel. Small movements of the wheel produce changes in heading similar to any other steering systems, but as more wheel is applied increasing sideways thrust is produced. With the wheel turned to its full extent, in either direction, only sideways thrust is produced by the propulsion units.

The two pitch levers fitted in twin-unit tractors are generally located side by side and enable the longitudinal pitch component produced by each unit to be controlled separately. In modern control stands the levers may be manipulated independently or in unison without restriction. This gives extremely precise control when manoeuvring and enables the tug to turn in little more than its own length. Early versions of the control stand incorporated a simple latch to allow the levers to be locked together and moved as one when required.

A device is also fitted to most pitch controls to limit the maximum movement of the pitch levers under certain conditions. This takes the form of a small

Voith controls installed on board the escort tug Velox *are designed to enable the tugmaster to remain comfortably seated for long periods during escort operations. The wheel is on the left of the seat and the pitch controls on the right. All other necessary controls and instruments are also within easy reach.* (Author)

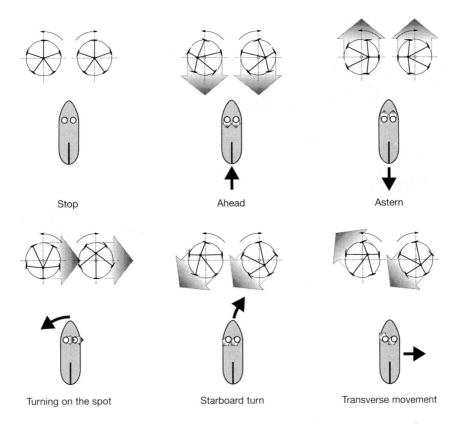

Stop   Ahead   Astern

Turning on the spot   Starboard turn   Transverse movement

The diagram illustrates the propulsion units of a twin-unit Voith tractor tug, showing where changes of pitch occur in the blade orbit and the direction of the resulting thrust in relation to the hull. Control positions have been chosen to illustrate the direction of thrust required to perform the basic manoeuvres indicated.

additional lever or simple limiting flaps on the lever quadrant. The purpose of this device is to prevent maximum pitch being selected under circumstances that might overload the main engine(s). For example; in the modern fire-fighting tractor a lever marked 'Free Running', 'Towing' and 'Fire-fighting', allows units to be used at maximum pitch when the vessel is running light between operations and subject to some restriction when towing. During fire-fighting operations maximum pitch is restricted still further to enable power from the main engines to be used to drive the fire pumps but with sufficient in hand to manoeuvre the vessel.

As mentioned, the propulsion units are designed to operate at a constant engine speed. The most common arrangement is to provide the tugmaster with a number of preset speed ranges that can be selected by means of push buttons, located on or adjacent to the control stand. Typically, four buttons are provided for each engine and annotated MIN; 75%; 85%; MAX. The annotations are self-explanatory and indicate the engine speed range to be selected – to suit the conditions under which the vessel is operating.

This photograph of the bow of a large oil-rig support vessel shows the installation of two transverse bow thrusters and a retractable azimuthing thruster. The azimuthing thruster is shown partly retracted; when fully deployed it can be steered through a full 360 degrees. (Brunvoll)

BOW AND STERN THRUSTERS

The term 'bow thruster' is a familiar one in shipping circles. Various forms of bow thruster are used in ships of all sizes as a means of improving their handling characteristics in port. In fact the installation of such units in large numbers of medium-sized ships has contributed greatly to a reduction in demand for ship-handling tugs. Bow thrusters are used in tugs for two reasons. The simple transverse thruster has become increasingly popular in tugs of all types, with the exception of tractors, to improve handling and station-keeping in difficult conditions. More sophisticated, retractable azimuthing propulsion units may also be fitted in the bow of conventional screw ship-handling tugs and offshore support vessels to enhance their manoeuvrability.

Transverse Thrusters

The most common form of transverse thruster found in a tug comprises a simple tube passing through the bow of the vessel. A conventional screw propeller installed in the tube provides thrust at 90 degrees to the vessel's centreline. The direction of thrust to port or starboard is controlled by changing either the rotational direction of the propeller or the pitch of the blades. Power to drive the propeller is produced either by an electric motor, a hydraulic motor, or a diesel engine. In deep-sea tugs the bow thruster may be quite a powerful unit driven by a powerplant of 900 bhp or more. Very large vessels may have one or two transverse thrusters fitted in the bow and one or two further units located aft, usually just forward of the propellers.

Bow thrusters generally derive their power from auxiliary machinery in the engine-room. A diesel engine coupled directly to the thruster may also be used but requires considerably more space in the normally cramped forecastle of the tug.

Transverse thrusters are controlled directly from the bridge by a simple lever, mounted athwartships, adjacent to the normal steering and propulsion controls. The lever is moved to port or starboard in the direction the bow of the vessel is required to move. Multiple thrusters, fitted in the bow and stern of large offshore tugs, may be controlled separately or as part of an integrated manoeuvring system.

The Azimuthing Bow Thruster

The azimuthing thruster used in this application is identical in design to those used as main propulsion units, but smaller and lighter. Thrusters of this type are sometimes installed in single-screw tugs to fit them for a particular task and possibly extend their useful life. As described in Chapter 1 the term 'combi-tug' is frequently used to describe a vessel equipped in this way. This type of unit is also popular in very large anchor-handling offshore support vessels, where it may be used as part of an integrated control system. The thruster unit is installed in the forward part of the hull, near the bow. Most units are retractable and housed within the hull when not in use. This has the added advantage of enabling the vessel to return to its original draft when necessary, thus preventing possible damage in shallow water.

An azimuthing thruster of this type may be driven by a separate diesel engine or an electric or hydraulic motor. A powerplant of between 400 and 650 bhp is common. In a harbour tug space is at a premium in the forward part of the vessel and crew accommodation is often sacrificed to make room for the unit, its retracting mechanism, and powerplant. Where a separate diesel engine is used to drive the unit, a mechanism is incorporated in the power transmission system to disconnect the thruster from the engine as it retracts.

A single-lever controller in the wheelhouse is normally used to control the azimuthing bow thrusters. The controller enables the unit to be 'steered' through 360 degrees and propeller revolutions to be adjusted as required. In most cases the control lever is very similar to those used in stern-drive vessels to control individual propulsion units.

INTEGRATED CONTROL SYSTEMS

Many large tugs and offshore support vessels make extensive use of an 'integrated' control system, to enable the vessel to be manoeuvred simply and precisely by means of a single lever. Such systems reduce the tugmaster's workload enormously,

This view of the aft control console aboard the anchor-handling tug Anglian Monarch *shows the main propulsion controls and to the right of the wheel a portable integrated control unit. The single lever gives precise control for manoeuvring. Whilst under single-lever control the tug's heading is maintained via the auto-pilot.* (Author)

particularly when station-keeping during offshore operations or connecting a towline at sea.

The single-lever control system in this context enables the vessel's rudders, propellers, bow and stern thrusters to be operated in unison under the control of a microprocessor. This obviates the need for the tugmaster to co-ordinate the use of separate controls for each of those functions when carrying out precise manoeuvres. Using a lever often referred to as a 'joystick', the vessel moves precisely, forward, astern, to port or starboard and bodily sideways by simply moving the lever in the desired direction of travel. Most systems also make use of inputs from the gyro compass or automatic pilot to control the vessel's heading, an important advantage to the master of a relatively large vessel manoeuvring in offshore locations. In order to be fully effective the computer control system is programmed to suit the individual vessel, taking into account the response and power output of each element of the propulsion system and the handling characteristics of the ship.

Where offshore support vessels are required to work with even greater precision, to assist in cable- and pipeline-laying operations or working with remotely operated vehicles, a full dynamic positioning system is installed. A dynamic positioning system works on very similar principles to an integrated control system but receives additional information from the vessel's global positioning system (GPS) or other highly accurate navigation system. By using the ship's propulsion system controls, as previously described, the dynamic positioning system is capable of holding the vessel's position above a fixed point on the seabed to tolerances of less than one metre. Various standards of dynamic positioning are employed, each requiring special certification and crew training.

CHAPTER 3

Towing Gear and Deck Equipment

A ny tug is only as effective as the towing connection it makes with its tow. The more powerful and more manoeuvrable the tug becomes, the greater the emphasis on an adequate towing connection. Demands placed upon towing gear by the current generation of tugs are higher than ever before. Modern escort tugs are a good example of those increased demands; the loads placed upon the towing gear in such vessels now far exceeds the tug's static bollard pull. Every element in that vital link between tug and tow, the towline, winches, fairleads and bitts, must all be designed to withstand those loads and continue to operate effectively. Similar demands exist in the offshore oil industry where anchor-handling tugs are required to deal with rig anchors in greater water depths than ever before, and where the weight of the gear to be handled continues to grow.

In spite of its long history the industry has failed to dispense with the towrope as the primary means of connecting tug and tow. The types of ropes used and the gear to handle them are continually changing but many old established principles remain valid. In ship-handling commercial pressures demand that the work must be done quickly, safely and with the smallest acceptable crew. This has placed greater emphasis on new lightweight towing gear and advanced deck equipment.

Alternative methods of establishing a towing connection appear from time to time but none have succeeded in replacing the humble towline. In ship-handling, several remedies have been tried to simplify the process of making a towing connection, including giant suction pads connected to the tug by hydraulically-controlled arms and capable of firmly attaching themselves to a ship's side, but none have been adopted by the towage industry worldwide. Specially adapted hydraulic cranes to assist in passing the towline to the ship were also used for a while in some tugs fleets in North America but were found to offer little advantage. More recently the industry has concentrated on developing lighter and more flexible towlines that can be readily handled by the crews of both tugs and ships.

Even the majority of pusher tugs rely to some degree on the equipment described in this chapter. Securing wires, winches and emergency towlines all have a place in the various vessels in the pusher-tug category. Pusher tugs and pushing are dealt with in Chapter 9.

In spite of many decades of research and development the towline remains the vital link between the tug and its tow. This photograph shows the 'compact' stern-drive tug Adsteam Harty *(now* Svitzer Harty*) assisting a container ship, working bow-to-bow from its forward winch and towing hard stern first. The 24 m tug has a bollard pull of 68 tonnes and the towlines used are capable of sustaining transient loads of close to 200 tonnes.* (Author)

TOWING GEAR

The Towrope

The terms towrope or towline are frequently applied to both fibre and steel wire ropes used for towing. A modern fibre towrope is a very different piece of equipment from that used in tugs sixty years ago. Before the introduction of synthetic textiles in rope production the towing industry relied entirely on natural materials such as manila and hemp. Ropes made from these materials were heavy and very difficult to handle when wet. Once waterlogged they sank rapidly, presenting a hazard to the tug with a high probability of fouling its propeller. The size of rope required by a powerful tug of the day was enormous, often as large as 300 mm (1 ft) in diameter.

Modern manmade-fibre ropes are manufactured using a variety of materials and often complex construction methods to produce operating characteristics tailored exactly to meet the needs of the tug owner. Polypropylene, polyester, nylon, aramid and high modulus polyethylene (HMPE) synthetic fibres are among the more commonly used basic materials now used for towrope manufacture. The last is a modern ultra-high-strength material, marketed around the world bearing the names Dyneema and Spectra. Each material has different attributes, such as strength, elasticity, buoyancy and resistance to wear.

The term construction describes the manner in which ropes are spun, plaited, or laid up, and this varies considerably, with new methods continuing to appear. Methods of construction affect the flexibility of the finished rope, its strength, weight, buoyancy, and again resistance to chafing and wear. The towline used by a powerful ship-handling or escort tug may well be subjected to loads in excess of 200 tonnes, yet must be light and flexible enough to be manhandled on board the tug and the vessel to be towed. Most of the modern generation of synthetic-fibre towropes are buoyant and impervious to the likely forms of contamination encountered on board tugs but still need to be used with care. In many types of rope considerable internal friction is generated under extreme loads, particularly on winch drums, where they pass through fairleads, around bollards and in knots. The heat generated inside the ropes under these circumstances can cause the strands to melt and the rope to fail.

Many modern ropes are no longer spun in the traditional manner but incorporate various methods of plaiting and multiple plaiting. In some recent products, known generically as 'jacketed towline', the internal strands of the rope are only slightly twisted and not plaited in any way. The strands are kept tightly secured by a strong woven outer sheath that maintains the shape of the rope and protects the load-bearing strands from external damage. Several examples of this type of construction use HMPE fibres and are intended to replicate, as far as possible, the strength and operating characteristics of a steel wire towline but with a vast reduction in weight, and much improved handling characteristics. Such ropes must be capable of operating successfully on modern towing winches and, because of their relatively high cost, must have a long working life.

Nylon was the first synthetic material to be used in the towing industry. It had many advantages over early natural fibres but also had several disadvantages. Nylon ropes stretch considerably in use and are extremely elastic. Both of these features make them difficult to use in many towage applications, particularly in ship-handling. The material still has special uses, where those characteristics are advantageous. In deep-sea towing its elasticity is exploited by connecting short lengths of large diameter nylon rope into steel towlines to act as 'springs'.

Steel wire towropes, or hawsers, have been in use for many decades in offshore operations and for all types of long-distance towing. This type of rope is also used in many harbour tugs where a towing winch is used. The ropes are manufactured from high-grade, cold-drawn steel wire, and spun in the traditional manner. Recent advances in the production of steel wire rope are the use of more sophisticated grades of steel and the protective treatments applied. During manufacture, and in use, the ropes are treated with advanced synthetic lubricants designed to reduce internal friction and resist damage from salt water.

A modern towline has to withstand not only the high tensile loads of a towing operation but also the effects of friction from contact with towing fairleads and other fittings and the pressures incurred when wound on the towing winch. The towline in use in this ship-handling operation is a HMPE fibre-jacketed rope. (Author)

The length and type of rope usually used for towing operations varies enormously with the vessel concerned and its employment. As a rough guide, a modern ship-handling tug using a towing winch will have towlines for harbour work of some 100–120 metres in length. These will be manmade-fibre, or steel wire ropes. A similar vessel carrying out coastal and short sea towing will carry on its after winch at least one towline of approximately 600 metres of steel wire rope. Oceangoing tugs and vessels working in the offshore oil industry are normally equipped with steel wire towlines in the order of 1,200–1,800 metres in length.

Pendants

Both steel and manmade-fibre towlines are frequently used in conjunction with a shorter length of rope of another material, connected to its outer end.

This is known as the pendant, or sometimes pennant, and is used to resist the loads and chafing that occur where the towline passes through the fairleads and around the bits on board the tow. Short lengths of fibre rope are used in conjunction with steel towropes to provide a degree of elasticity and flexibility and to simplify making a connection aboard the ship or other vessel to be towed.

In this photograph the seagoing tug Braveheart *is shown towing a large pontoon barge with its steel wire towline connected to a heavy chain bridle. The chain bridle is resistant to chafing and wear and the weight, with that of the steel towline, provides a damping effect when the tug and tow are at sea.* (H. Hoffmann)

Where modern synthetic-fibre towlines are used it is also common practice to incorporate a pendant manufactured from a synthetic material of a different type. The pendant material will be chosen to afford more elasticity, better wear resistance, or simply to provide an easily replaceable element at the end of an expensive towline.

Chain cable is rarely used as part of the main towline due to the difficulty in handling this material and its weight. It is, however, often incorporated in the pendant between the towline and tow. Chafing is the main enemy to all towlines particularly at the point at which they are secured to the tow. In long-distance towing a single length of chain cable or a 'Y' shaped bridle is used to make the connection aboard a tow such as a ship or large barge. The weight of chain in the bridle also acts as a shock absorber, reducing the effects of snatching in bad weather.

Towing Bollards

In many earlier tugs and smaller vessels, particularly in Holland and the USA, the primary means of securing the towrope aboard the tug is by using towing bollards. These take the form of large 'H'-shape bollards on which the rope is secured in a particular way. The method of 'turning the rope up' on the bollards varies from country to country and port to port and is intended to give a crew member on deck the means quickly to secure the rope at the appropriate length. Where American towing methods are used, towing bollards will be fitted on the foredeck and on the towing deck aft. This method of securing the inboard end of a towrope is still used in many tugs, but with modern high-powered vessels it is impractical and unsafe. Many of the modern synthetic fibre ropes previously mentioned do not lend themselves to this method of towing without damage if high bollard pulls are involved. Towing bollards are, however, convenient in some applications and are often incorporated in the fairlead of a towing winch or the mounting of a towing hook as a secondary means of securing a rope end.

Towing bollards are used by many operators of small and relatively low-powered tugs as a convenient means of securing the towline aboard the tug. Here, the 500 bhp tug Dixie *from the Fremont Tugboat Company of Seattle assists a large trawler with a towline 'turned up' on bollards in a manner that will allow it to be released quickly in an emergency.* (M. Freeman)

Towing Hooks

A common method of securing the inboard end of a towrope is a towing hook. This method is universal in most British and European tugs, when a towing winch is not fitted. Even when the towline is normally handled by a winch a tow hook is frequently provided as a secondary means of securing a towline. The main

A typical quick-release towing hook, shown in the closed position. To release the rope in an emergency, the lanyard visible above the hook is used to trip a release mechanism – causing the circular portion of the hook to rotate and release the rope. (Author)

advantage of the tow hook is its ease of use and the ability to release the tow instantly in an emergency.

There are many types of quick-release tow hook, all of which are designed to enable the towline to be released easily and quickly if the tug is endangered by capsizing or any similar hazard. To release the towline, the hook is generally designed to open or swing down, letting the rope slip away. This mechanism must be capable of operating even under the extreme loads imposed on the towline when the tug is towing or being dragged at full power. In early designs the release mechanism was a simple one, normally activated manually by a large hammer wielded by a member of the crew. Present-day hooks are normally released by remote control – a much safer procedure obviating the need for someone to approach the hook and towline in a dangerous situation. The release mechanism may be operated via a pneumatic or hydraulic system, or by a cable, with controls duplicated in the wheelhouse and on deck.

Many tugs, particularly conventional screw vessels, have their tow hook located on a 'righting arm'. With this type of mounting the hook is fitted on a long radial arm, which is free to pivot on the centre-line of the vessel to allow the hook to swing through an arc to either side – effectively moving the 'point of tow' closer to the deck edge. A semi-circular track is usually fitted to guide the righting arm and hook. This arrangement is a safety feature, designed to reduce the likelihood of the vessel being accidentally capsized when the towline is directly abeam of the tug.

Dynamic Towing Systems

The principle of the 'righting arm' has been carried much further by two competing 'dynamic towing systems' both originally conceived and developed in the Netherlands by Dr Marcus van der Laan working closely with tug owners and towing-gear specialists. The towing systems are similar in concept and aim to achieve a 'radial' towage connection on a conventional style tug that is safe, effective and flexible.

There are tugs now in service that incorporate, the Carrousel system, marketed by Novatug, and the Dynamic Oval Towing (DOT) system introduced by towing gear manufacturer Mampaey. The systems are similar in basic principle, comprising a 360-degree all-around towing system offering safety, controllability and flexibility, to enable the tug to manoeuvre in any direction in a safe and controlled manner irrespective of the heading of the assisted vessel. Full power can be used in any direction and the line pull available can be enhanced dramatically using indirect-towing methods. In both systems, when the tug is at 90 degrees to the towline, the 'towing point' is moved away from the tug's centreline to the 'deck edge' making it virtually impossible to capsize (girt) the tug.

The Carrousel towing system, first introduced on the prototype vessel *Multratug 12*, a converted combi tug owned by Multraship of Terneuzen in the Netherlands in 2002. This system uses a circular rail around the tug's superstructure that supports a free-moving carriage incorporating a towing hook, and later a winch, that allows the towline to be deployed and remain connected regardless of the tug's heading as previously described. Trials proved highly

A 'Carrousel' towing system was first fitted to the adapted prototype combi tug Multratug 12. *This photograph shows the circular ring, carrying a small specially designed winch that allows the tug to tow with the towline at any angle (through a full 360 degrees) in relation to its own centreline.* (Novatug)

The small tug/workboat Ugie Runner *of Peterhead Port Authority shows off the Mampaey Dynamic Oval Towing (DOT) system. Using the quick-release tow hook the vessel can operate safely at any angle in relation to the towline and has proved to be highly effective using the indirect method of towing and while working in confined spaces.* (Author)

successful and the tug was still operating at the time of writing. Multraship, led by Kees Muller, enthusiastically supported the project from its inception and the associate company Novatug was formed. Two purpose-built combi tugs, of 80-tonne bollard pull, equipped with the Carrousel and a specially designed winch are due to enter service during 2009.

Mampaey has taken a different approach and uses an 'oval' track having a natural bias when towing over the bow or stern and thus offering slightly different handling characteristics. The first system was fitted to the *Ugie Runner*, a 13 m twin-screw tug/workboat with 9-tonne bollard pull, which entered service with the Peterhead Port Authority in Scotland in 2008. A Mampaey quick-release tow hook is mounted directly on the carriage and can be operated in an emergency via a wireless link from the wheelhouse. Again the system has proved most successful and has been ordered for a number of other new vessels.

TOWING WINCHES

The towing winch has become an essential piece of equipment on most modern tugs of any size. Winches were first introduced in tugs to handle the very long towropes used in ocean towing. Such towing gear was extremely heavy and there was a need to find a means of shortening and retrieving the towline quickly and safely. The basic function of the towing winch has changed very little but in most modern tugs winches are fitted to ease the workload on board and allow the tug captain to control the towline remotely and precisely from the wheelhouse. The winches currently in use are predominantly of the traditional drum type but examples of an alternative 'friction winch' are still to be found.

Drum Winches

The drum winch is by far the most common type of winch used in the towage industry. It is basically a power-driven drum, or barrel, on which the towline is wound. This type of winch is produced in many sizes and with one or more drums in a variety of configurations.

In modern ship-handling tugs a typical towing winch is likely to be fitted with one or two drums, driven by an electric or hydraulic motor. Forward and reverse controls for the winch and a powerful brake are normally located in the wheelhouse, and duplicated on deck. The winch will be sufficiently powerful to retrieve the towline and, with the brake applied, withstand a pull well in excess of the tug's bollard pull. However, even a modern ship-handling tug may not necessarily be equipped with a winch powerful enough to shorten the towline with the vessel at full power. A typical vessel of this type will have a winch installed capable of a maximum line pull of 35 tonnes and a brake holding load of 150 tonnes. Two-speed winches are popular with some operators, and enable the crew to choose the most appropriate setting for shortening the towline whilst the tug is connected to a ship, or rapidly retrieve the towline once a job is finished. The winch will accommodate either a steel wire towrope or one made of synthetic fibres.

Tugs of the azimuthing stern-drive type will conduct most ship-handling duties from a drum winch on the foredeck. A winch designed for this purpose may have

The single 'split-drum' towing winch on the azimuthing tractor Svitzer Bristol *is typical of many used on ship-handling tugs. In this example the two sections each carry a different type of towline, a steel wire towline on one portion of the drum and a manmade-fibre towline on the other. The drumhead on the end of the winch shaft is used as a capstan in conjunction with the roller fairlead in the foreground.* (Author)

The diagram depicts the layout aboard a tug using a single winch to deploy a towline over the bow during ship-handling operations or over the stern for other work when required.

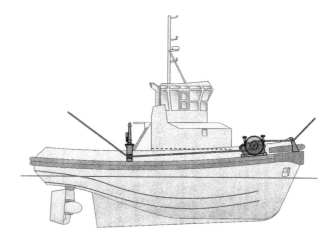

two separate drums, driven independently, or a single drum partitioned to enable two towlines of different characteristics to be carried and be available for immediate use. The latter is known as a 'split drum'. A forward-mounted winch may also incorporate a windlass to handle the vessel's anchors. Stern-drive tugs are frequently equipped with a second towing winch aft, for use when towing over the stern, in harbour or at sea.

Tractor tugs and the Z-Tech type require only one winch. In a number of modern stern-drive tugs, particularly 'compact' vessels, a single winch is installed either forward or aft in a manner enabling the towline to be deployed at either end of the vessel via a tunnel beneath the superstructure. If the winch is fitted on the foredeck, when necessary, the towline passes from the winch via a tunnel to a fairlead located on the after deck in the normal position. In some cases a double drum winch is installed and a towline from each deployed – one forward and one aft. This application of a single winch reduces building costs and is particularly suitable if a second winch is only required for occasional use.

Drum winches installed aboard modern escort tugs are becoming extremely sophisticated machines capable of handling very high loads under difficult circumstances. Such winches will be equipped with high-performance manmade-fibre towlines capable of dealing with transient loads of over 200 tonnes. The winch will have a brake-holding capacity of well in excess of that figure and be capable of a very high line pull. Devices are fitted to monitor the length of the towline in use and the load it is subjected to. Winch controls can also be preset to limit the load on the towline, allowing the towline to pay out automatically. When the load is reduced the winch recovers sufficient rope to bring the towline to its original preset length. This type of winch is often controlled via a microprocessor and a touch-screen display, allowing the tugmaster to monitor the towline forces and length and preset the operating parameters.

Drum winches fitted in tugs designed for coastal and deep-sea towing will have the power and brake-holding capacity in keeping with the vessels' bollard pull and type of operation and are likely to have more than one drum. Two or even three drums, side-by-side on a single shaft and controlled independently, are common. The drums will contain either identical towlines or towlines of different dimensions, to be used for different purposes. Winches installed in large deep-sea tugs may also incorporate a device to limit and control the tension on the towline. When in use the winch will pay out or wind in automatically to compensate for abnormal shock loads but keep the towline at approximately the required length. The winches will be located on the towing deck aft and may be totally or partially enclosed within the superstructure to afford some protection from the elements.

A winch known as the 'waterfall' type has two or more drums mounted in tandem, with each drum a little higher than its neighbour. Winches with two or three drums are used extensively in anchor-handling tugs of various sizes and anchor-handling oil-rig supply vessels. One drum of the winch will accommodate a special wire rope and have sufficient power to handle the anchors used by oil drilling rigs and similar floating plant. Winches of this type fitted to the latest vessels employed by the offshore oil industry will typically have a brake holding load of over 400 tonnes and a line pull in excess of 300 tonnes.

A good example of a compact 'Waterfall' winch is shown aboard the Rotor Tug Pioneer. The top drum, used for towing at sea, can hold 650 metres of steel wire rope. Two lower drums carry 200-metre towlines for ship-handling. A pennant of manmade-fibre rope is used on each of the three . Note the quick-release tow hook, stowed for emergency use. (Author)

Most drum winches used with long lengths of steel wire rope are fitted with 'spooling gear'. This is a mechanical device to guide the rope onto the drum in neat orderly layers, with the turns of rope lying neatly alongside each other. The main purpose of spooling gear is to prevent the rope becoming damaged by successive layers being wound onto the drum in a haphazard manner.

With any drum winch the turns of rope nearest to the centre of the drum become compressed by the outer layers, particularly where very high bollard pulls are involved. Crushing of this kind can be more pronounced with drum winches using long lengths of manmade-fibre rope. Spooling gear is normally fitted only where very long fibre towlines are used. Winches fitted to most ship-handling tugs and using relatively short fibre ropes are not fitted with spooling gear.

Friction Winches

The friction winch, sometimes known as a twin-drum capstan winch, was introduced to the towage industry some fifty years ago in very powerful deep-sea tugs and some ship-handling vessels to overcome some of the deficiencies of the drum winch. This type of winch employs two, grooved, friction drums arranged parallel to each other (*see diagram*) and driven in unison. The towline passes around both drums about five times. A third drum, simply a large reel, acts as a storage drum for the inboard end of the rope. The storage drum applies a small load to the inboard end of the rope, keeping tension on the turns around the friction drums. In this way the rope is wound in or out using the capstan principle, relying on the friction between the drum grooves and the rope.

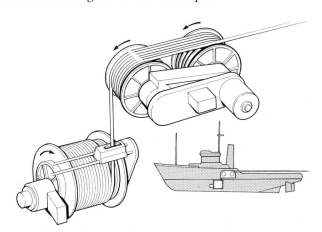

A friction winch, of the type used in large ocean-going tugs, uses two grooved drums to impart motion to the towline in much the same manner as a capstan. The lower storage drum is generally located well below decks and contains the bulk of what is often a very long steel wire rope.

There are a number of significant advantages in this system, perhaps the most important being that no crushing or deformation of the rope occurs. The winch in a large seagoing tug is generally located inside the superstructure and fully protected from the weather. With the friction winch, the twin drums can be placed in the most practical position, from a towing point of view, and the storage drum located well below decks. This enables the great weight of the steel towlines to be kept low in the vessel, thus contributing to the tug's stability. A tug of this type may have well over 2,000 metres of towline on board, including spare material.

The friction winch was also used in Britain and elsewhere to handle synthetic-fibre towropes in ship-handling tugs, using exactly the same principle as those designed for steel wire towlines. With improvements in drum winch design and continuing developments in towline technology, the friction winch has fallen from favour in most applications.

Tugger Winches

The term 'tugger winch' is common in the salvage and offshore oil industry and refers to a small auxiliary drum winch used extensively aboard deep-sea tugs and anchor-handling vessels. Such winches are commonly fitted on either side of the main towing deck and sometimes on a higher level at the after end of the superstructure.

Tugger winches are used to provide a ready means of handling the outer ends of the main towlines on the tug's afterdeck, and for many other purposes. In many cases the towlines are too large and heavy to be manhandled or manipulated by means of a capstan. Large pieces of towing gear such as chain bridles and equipment used in anchor-handling will be moved around the deck using the wires from one or more tugger winches. Tugger winches are usually controlled locally from a convenient position near the winch. In some vessels a tugger winch may be used to control a gog rope used to secure the main towline – see *Gog Ropes* below.

LINE-HANDLING DEVICES AND DECK EQUIPMENT
Gog Ropes

Gog rope is a British term referring to a rope used to control the movement of the main towline in ship-handling and deep-sea tugs. The term 'gob rope' and 'bridle' are also commonly used in some localities for the same item. Bridle is also a name commonly used to describe a 'Y' shaped towing connection used between a towline and tow.

Conventional screw ship-handling tugs, working with a ship in difficult conditions, may use the gog rope to hold the towrope down, at a position close to its stern, thus effectively moving the towing connection aft. This procedure gives the tug captain better control of his tow and prevents the towline from being taken across the tug's beam, thus subjecting it to the danger of being capsized. Likewise, a deep-sea tug may secure its tow in a similar manner also to prevent a long heavy towrope from passing over the bulwarks amidships, to port or starboard. A deep-sea tug or anchor-handling tug may also use its hydraulically operated line-handling equipment to secure the towline, with similar results.

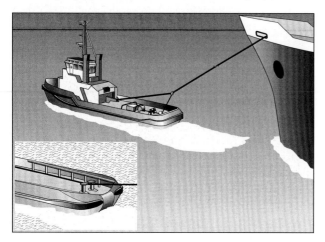

When a gog rope is used the point at which the towline is secured aboard the tug is effectively moved to a location much further aft. The length of the gog rope is often controlled by a small winch or by a capstan. The inset shows an alternative method of securing a towline using hydraulically controlled line-handling gear.

Tugs using gog ropes are fitted with a large steel eye or fairlead on deck, in a position a little forward of the rudder post(s). The gog rope passes through this eye and is looped over the towline or attached by a free-running shackle. The inner end of the rope is controlled by a small winch fitted for the purpose, a capstan, or simply by securing it to bollards.

Towing Fairleads

The towline on all modern tractor tugs and stern-drive vessels will pass through a very large, specially designed fairlead. Sometimes referred to as a 'staple', the most common form of towing fairlead is a large inverted 'U'-shaped structure of tubular steel. Such fairleads are fitted adjacent to the towing winch to guide the towline and determine a fixed 'point of tow' from which the towline is effective.

The after deck of the Voith tractor tug Lady Sarah *is fitted with a single-drum towing winch, carrying a manmade-fibre towline that passes through a large towing fairlead (staple).* (Author)

This view of the after deck of the anchor-handling tug Anglian Earl *with a tanker in tow during a salvage operation, shows the use of a restraining chain strop on the towline to prevent girting. The towline is also held by the retractable line-handling pins, just forward of the stern roller.* (D. McCall)

In a tractor tug the fairlead is precisely located on the after deck above the underwater skeg. This has the effect of controlling the 'point of tow' in relation to a predetermined point above the skeg. In tractor tugs used for escort towing the position of the fairlead is critical and a second alternative fairlead may be installed further aft, usually in the bulwarks above the trailing edge of the skeg (the leading edge when going astern). The latter provides greater course stability when the tug is being towed stern first by a ship under escort.

A similar fairlead, sometimes in the form of a heavy tubular 'H', is fitted on the foredeck of stern-drive tugs and located just forward of the winch. Alternatively, a heavy steel fairlead is built into the centre of the forward bulwarks. Again the purpose is to provide an accurate 'point of tow' and avoid chafing of the towline near the winch drum.

Whatever the design and position of the towing fairlead, it is important to avoid any damage to the towline, particularly expensive manmade-fibre ropes. To this end the interior surfaces of the fairlead are frequently lined with stainless steel and well finished to avoid rough surfaces and sharp edges.

Stop Pins and Specialist Line-handling Equipment

Stop pins, sometimes known in the past as 'Norman pins' or 'molgoggers', are vertical pins that can be fitted in the tug's after bulwark rail, one on each quarter.

They are often used in the conventional tug to prevent the towline passing over the sides of the vessel, particularly when the rope is being retrieved and there is a danger of the rope end fouling the propeller. The pins take a number of forms, the simplest being solid or tubular pins inserted in sockets in the after rail. In larger vessels they may be supported in hinged brackets, allowing them to be erected when required. Most modern tugs will have hydraulically-operated pins controlled remotely from the wheelhouse to rise vertically from the after bulwarks when required.

Tugs employed in specialist duties, such as anchor-handling for the offshore oil industry, are frequently fitted with stop pins in addition to more sophisticated devices – enabling work to be carried out safely under extremely hazardous conditions. In these vessels the crews are faced with handling heavy anchors, their chains and massive wire-rope pendants, in heavy weather and sometimes extremes of temperature. In order to assist with these tasks various patented devices have been developed to mechanise much of the work carried out on the exposed afterdeck of these vessels. The more common consist of retractable 'jaws', 'stoppers', and clamping devices that can be raised from the deck to control the chains and wires used in anchor-handling operations. When not required they are lowered, flush with the deck. They are operated remotely along with the controls for the winches, stop pins and other deck equipment. This type of equipment, in a simpler form, is increasingly used in powerful ship-handling tugs and escort vessels to control towing gear over the stern and in some cases obviate the need for the gog rope. Further information is included in the section on anchor-handling tugs and oil-rig supply vessels.

The Karm Fork and line-handling equipment is fitted to many anchor-handling vessels. The forks rise vertically from the deck to grip or control the wires or chains used in anchor-handling or towing. The associated stop pins can be raised, lowered or rotated to produce a form of closed or open fairlead.
(Karmoy Winch)

Stern Rollers

To enable anchor-handling operations to take place easily, and with minimum damage to the tug, the stern is left devoid of bulwarks and the extreme end of the after deck is heavily rounded and fitted with a large roller. The roller is recessed into the deck edge and has sufficient strength to allow very large anchors, buoys, chain and other mooring equipment to be hauled safely on deck. In most cases the rollers are parallel cylinders, with sufficient strength to resist impact damage, and intended to rotate freely when heavy objects pass over them. The stern of the vessel, around the ends of the roller, is generally shaped to avoid sharp corners and give free passage through the stern opening without wires or ropes becoming trapped.

Stern rollers have become increasingly popular, with tugs of all sizes being called upon to handle mooring lines and hoses at offshore moorings, deploy anti-pollution booms and support civil engineering and dredging work. In almost every case the stern roller is able to bear a safe working load commensurate with the power of the winches installed in the vessel and the loads likely to be hauled on to the deck.

Bitts and Bollards

In common with all ships and smaller craft, tugs have an obvious need for the usual mooring bitts, or bollards. These are generally considerably stronger in construction than in many other vessels because in some roles the tug is called upon to perform they may be used to help secure the tow. Many tugs are fitted with a large 'stem post' in the bow and similar 'shoulder posts' on the port and starboard quarters. These, likewise, have multiple uses in mooring and towing, particularly when the tug is towing with a barge or other vessel secured alongside.

The Capstan

Possibly one of the oldest pieces of mechanised deck equipment in the shipping industry, the capstan is still alive and well in many present-day tugs. The basic concept remains unchanged – a power-driven vertical barrel with a concave outer surface used to heave and control ropes. The modern capstan is usually driven either by an electric or hydraulic motor and operated by a simple control, conveniently located in easy reach of the user.

In tugs where no towing winch is fitted, the capstan is the most common means of retrieving or shortening a synthetic-rope towline. Two or three turns of the rope around the capstan give the crew on deck assistance in getting the rope aboard easily and with a high degree of control. Where the rope is too large to pass conveniently around the capstan a lighter 'messenger' rope may be used to haul the towline on board in stages. The capstan is sometimes used in conjunction with a gog rope to control the towline, as an aid during mooring, and for many other purposes.

A common alternative is to have a drum-head fitted to the anchor windlass or towing winch, which is used in the same way as a capstan. These horizontal drums are found in all types of tug and again have a wide range of uses. Many vessels, particularly in Europe, have separate powered drums located horizontally in convenient positions on the after superstructure.

The afterdeck of the former Belgian ship-handling tug Burcht *has tow beams or protective rails over several deck fittings to prevent fouling. Its towing winch is located adjacent to the superstructure. A small winch for the gob rope is sited in the centre of the deck with a hinged sheave for the rope near the after bulwarks.* (Author)

Tow Beams

Tow beams are an item of equipment found less and less in modern tugs. This is the name given to the beams or guards used to prevent the towline from fouling or becoming entangled with items of equipment and fittings on the tug's after deck. These usually take the form of guards located over individual parts of the vessel or beams extending from bulwark to bulwark.

On some American tugs intended for coastal and deep-sea operation, tow beams are fitted that incorporate a rotating bobbin or sheave to accept the towline and prevent damage from chafing. The bobbin rotates freely on a cylindrical section of the tow beam, allowing towline and bobbin to move from side to side.

Deck Cranes

Some form of crane or simple lifting derrick has always been an important item of equipment on tugs involved in salvage or offshore work, where the movement of heavy equipment and spares can be an everyday chore. The traditional derrick has been almost entirely replaced by the much more convenient deck crane. Such cranes are usually operated electrically or hydraulically and range in power from about 2 to over 20 tonnes lifting capacity.

In other types of tug, smaller crews and the need to employ vessels more effectively have resulted in small hydraulic cranes being fitted on the majority of new vessels and many older ones. The crane is used for the transfer of stores, maintaining towing gear, launching workboats, and to assist in the maintenance of harbour facilities. Vessels involved in anti-pollution duties are likely to have a crane suitable to lift and manipulate protective booms and possibly skimming equipment. The cranes generally have telescopic jibs and when not in use can be folded or stowed to minimise the space they occupy.

The powerful deck crane shown on the Tarka *of Herman Snr BV is typical of many fitted to vessels of a similar size and type working in the dredging and marine civil engineering sector. Shown partially stowed, the crane is hydraulically operated, has a telescopic jib and can be remotely controlled.* (Author)

In Europe and the UK, where there has been a massive increase in powerful tugs and multi-purpose work vessels to support the dredging and marine civil engineering industries, the size of deck cranes has grown enormously. Versatile, hydraulically powered cranes are now being fitted to relatively small vessels of less than 30 metres in length with lifting capacities of over 200 tonnes/metre (a common method of designating the capacity of cranes of this type). That figure is heavily dependent on the length to which the telescopic jib is extended– for example a crane rated at 180 tonnes/metre might lift approximately 32 tonnes at an outreach of 5 metres or 10 tonnes with the jib extended to 16 metres.

In order to improve safety aboard some high-powered anchor-handling tugs, a variety of mechanical handling equipment is being installed to assist crew-members working with heavy anchor-handling equipment on the exposed after deck. Latest developments include travelling hydraulic cranes mounted above the bulwarks on either side and retractable cranes that fold into a chamber beneath the deck adjacent to the towing pins and line-handling equipment.

CHAPTER 4

Ancillary Equipment

his chapter might well have been entitled 'everything else that goes to make an operational tug'. And there are a great many systems and items of equipment that go into a tug, apart from its propulsion system and towing gear, even in a vessel of the simplest type. Every vessel is required to carry out its duties efficiently and safely, and with due regard to the needs of the crew and operating company. This requires suitable services on board, good communications, and all the facilities required by the client, whether it be a ship in tow or a casualty requiring salvage assistance.

The term 'ancillary' certainly does not mean that the items mentioned are unimportant. Much of the equipment covered is to be found in virtually any small ship but in tugs certain items of marine equipment are often of particular importance. Other more specialised features are fitted to improve the tug's versatility or fit it for a particular role.

The facilities required on board vary from that of a simple tug/workboat, crewed by a couple of people for daytime shifts, to a very large deep-sea tug carrying out tows of many thousands of miles with a crew of perhaps twenty-five. Navigational and communications systems will also reflect the vessel's role, with the most sophisticated vessels bristling with advanced systems allowing them to be virtually self-sufficient from a vessel-management point of view.

ON BOARD SERVICES

Electrical Power

Every tug is fitted with an electrical system of some kind. At the very simplest level, a small tug/workboat will require electrical power for engine starting, lighting, and possibly basic domestic facilities and items of deck machinery. At the other end of the scale, the large deep-sea tug or anchor-handler will have an electrical system capable of supplying a small village.

In the very simple tug/workboat example it is likely that a generator(s) on the main engine(s) will be the main source of electrical power. This type of electrical

Abeille Liberté *is one of a pair of highly sophisticated emergency towing vessels operating in the English Channel and Western Approaches. These vessels embody state-of-the-art navigational and communications equipment, a formidable fire-fighting system and many other systems described in this chapter.* (Author)

system will include a substantial battery pack that will be charged while the engine(s) is running. In the very simplest example the lighting and power supply on board will comprise a low voltage, direct current (DC) system, operating at 24 volts.

As the size of vessel increases so does the need for a more substantial electrical system, which will include a 100–110 or a 240-volt alternating current (AC) supply. The voltage of mains equipment will vary geographically, with the lower voltages to be found in some vessels in North and South America and the Far East, and 220–240 volts in Europe.

For example, in a modern European harbour tug the main electrical power supply will be produced by one or two diesel-driven auxiliary generating sets. These will be self-contained units with a diesel engine coupled directly to an alternator. The output of each unit will range from 80–200 kVA depending on system requirements, giving a 50 Hz AC, 3-phase supply at 380 volts. Power from generators of this type is controlled by the vessel's main switchboard, and distributed to various parts of the vessel as required – at the appropriate voltage and current. Major items of deck and engine-room equipment will use a 3-phase supply and domestic equipment will use a 220–240 volt supply similar to shore-based equivalents. In such a vessel navigational and communications equipment will be provided with a 24-volt DC supply.

The generating sets will be housed either in convenient locations in the engine-room, or in a separate compartment. Where two generating sets of equal capacity are installed it is likely that each will have sufficient capacity to meet the normal demands of the entire electrical system. In this situation the generators will under normal circumstances be run alternately for set periods of time. If a generator fails or demand for power is increased the second unit will be started. In most modern systems the generators will be monitored and controlled automatically from the main switchboard.

It is not unusual for tugs of most types to be fitted with a smaller self-contained diesel-driven generating set for use when the vessel is in harbour with most of the machinery and systems closed down. Commonly referred to as a 'harbour set', the generator will have a much lower capacity, of perhaps 60 kVA, and supply basic lighting and battery-charging circuits and a few domestic services. In smaller vessels where crew members may sleep aboard when the tug is not in use, the 'harbour set' is often housed in a sound-proofed casing or positioned in a separate compartment away from the main accommodation.

In much larger tugs and offshore support vessels with heavy demands for electrical power, from equipment such as electrically operated bow and stern thrusters and/or deck machinery, additional diesel generators are installed or generators driven from the main propulsion system. Large alternators of this type, known as 'shaft generators', are coupled to specially provided power-takeoffs on the main propulsion gearboxes.

Many tugs, including those involved in salvage, are equipped to supply external electrical power to other vessels if required in an emergency. During salvage operations electrical supplies may be required for lighting, portable salvage pumps, welding, and to power the casualty's own electrical equipment.

Hydraulic Power

Hydraulic power is required aboard many modern tugs to operate the deck machinery, towing winches and bow or stern thrusters. Hydraulic systems are less sensitive to water contamination than similar high-power electrical equipment

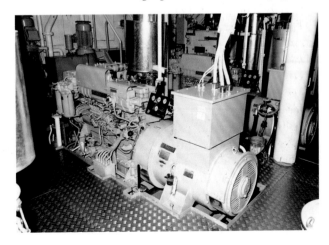

The electrical system aboard the anchor-handling tug Anglian Monarch *is typical of many large offshore tugs. Power is supplied by three Taiyo generators located in the main engine-room. Each 350 KvA generator (shown) is powered by a 414 bhp Yanmar diesel engine. A further 'harbour set' is rated at 200 kVA.* (Author)

and frequently more efficient, with none of the power losses and difficulties associated with long lengths of cabling. To provide power for hydraulically operated machinery it is usual for the necessary hydraulic pumps to be driven either by the main engines, by separate diesel engines or in some cases electric motors. In some designs hydraulic pumps may also be coupled to diesel-driven auxiliary generators.

Where a single hydraulic system supplies power for a number of items of deck equipment the pump, or pumps, will be supplied with oil from a large reservoir tank. The system, known as a 'power-pack', will be fitted with all the necessary pressure control valves, filters and monitoring instruments. Steel pipes carry the hydraulic fluid, usually a special high-grade oil, to individual pieces of equipment and their associated controls. The fluid provides power for the hydraulic motors and/or rams embodied in thrusters, winches, capstans, cranes and line-handling equipment.

System pressures vary considerably with the age of the vessel and often the part of the world from which it originates. Many owners prefer what are regarded as 'low-pressure' systems, operating at approximately 30–50 bars, for ease of maintenance, reduced noise, and for safety reasons. High-pressure systems, with operating pressures in the order of 150–250 bars, are also in use on many vessels.

Typical of many tugs of its type, Fairplay 26 *is a modern stern-drive tug of 5,500 bhp completed in 2000. The vessel relies heavily on its hydraulic system to power a bow thruster, towing winches fore and aft, spare rope reels, retractable tow pins and a deck crane.* (B. Dahlmann)

The multi-purpose tug Marineco Toomai, *built in 2007, is equipped with dedicated tanks and high capacity transfer pumps to enable it to supply fresh water and fuel oil to other vessels and floating plant.* Marineco Toomai *is also fitted with a powerful hydraulic deck crane and a towing and anchor-handling winch.* (Author)

Where a hydraulic system is required to operate a single or isolated piece of equipment, such as a deck crane, a small hydraulic power-pack may be installed on or adjacent to the item. Relatively small power-packs of this type incorporate all of the components necessary to operate the equipment. including an oil reservoir, and power is usually derived from an electrically driven pump.

Compressed Air

Λ supply of compressed air is also a necessity aboard many tugs. Air pressure is frequently the medium used to start the main engines in tugs ranging from large harbour tugs to deep-sea salvage vessels. Pneumatically operated systems are also used as a safe and reliable means of controlling the brakes and clutches associated with winches. Compressed air is generated by diesel or electrically powered compressors, and stored at a predetermined pressure in specially manufactured air cylinders.

In salvage tugs a compressed-air supply may be needed to assist ships and other vessels in trouble. Pneumatic power tools and pumps are also widely used, being much safer to operate than electrically driven equipment in a marine environment. In case it is impractical to supply compressed air from the tug's own systems, larger seagoing salvage tugs will normally carry portable diesel-powered compressors as part of their salvage equipment.

Where tugs are called upon to assist steam-driven ships with boiler or other machinery problems, a supply of compressed air may be required as a substitute for steam. The winches, anchor windlass, and other steam-driven deck machinery can often be operated effectively in this way.

Fresh Water

A fresh water supply is obviously needed aboard every tug for domestic purposes. Most tugs of any size are equipped with relatively large internal tanks, specially treated and dedicated to accommodating fresh water, suitable for human consumption. Such tanks can also be used to transport water for use by other vessels, or floating plant. This is a common service provided by tugs, from small contracting tugs employed on marine civil engineering projects to large oil-rig support vessels. Where this type of service is anticipated the tug is usually equipped with high-capacity pumps to enable water to be transferred rapidly to the recipient.

NAVIGATIONAL EQUIPMENT

The choice of navigational equipment fitted in tugs depends very much on their employment and operational environment. The availability of a wide range of advanced and relatively inexpensive electronic aids has resulted in even very small vessels being fitted with quite sophisticated equipment.

Compasses and Position-Finding Equipment

A compass is fitted in almost every type of tug. Magnetic compasses suffice in small locally based craft and instruments of increasing sophistication are installed in coastal and deep-sea tugs. In seagoing vessels the equipment fitted differs little from that of a normal seagoing ship and is frequently superior. Gyro compasses may be connected to an 'auto-pilot' system even in small harbour craft and multi-purpose vessels. This enables a course to be steered automatically during long passages, once the vessel's directional heading has been set.

Position-finding is a very important matter in most aspects of towage. Accurate navigation for route planning is not the only consideration. In salvage and long-range towing it may be necessary to rendezvous with a casualty or another tug well away from coastal stations and local navigational aids. The offshore oil industry also requires great accuracy when positioning oil drilling rigs, pipelines and other equipment. Traditional navigational methods and many established radio position-finding systems relying on coastal stations have been replaced or supplemented by modern satellite navigation equipment. Global positioning systems (GPS) have been in use at sea for many years, using signals from space satellites to provide extremely accurate positional information, usually in the form of straightforward longitude and latitude figures. Such technology has advanced rapidly, hand in hand with equipment miniaturisation, to produce GPS equipment suitable for all types of vessel. The equipment is generally very small and easily installed. In addition to displays of longitude and latitude, a typical unit will give the vessel's speed over the ground and its heading, and make other calculations automatically. For more specialised use, systems known as 'differential global positioning systems' (DGPS) have been introduced in most parts of the world to give positional accuracy down to just a few metres. DGPS relies on additional land-based stations to enhance the accuracy of the satellite data.

Hopetoun is a well equipped 10,000 bhp tanker-handling and escort tug operated by BP in Scotland. The tug is fitted with a host of modern navigational and communications systems to enable it to work safely at sea and within the confines of the Forth estuary. Note the high visibility wheelhouse, fire monitors, and inflatable rescue boat. (Author)

Electronic Charting

An innovation that quickly found an important place aboard many tugs and similar craft is electronic charting. Navigational and hydrographic charts of specific areas are now widely available in electronic form and can be displayed on a visual display unit (VDU) and can be integrated with other information, usually from the vessel's GPS and/or radar. This enables the tug's position to be shown accurately on the VDU screen in real time on a detailed chart of the operational area. Additional information, such as shipping channels or search areas and the tracks of other vessels in the vicinity, can be superimposed on the chart to assist the tugmaster. Electronic charts are stored on magnetic tape, magnetic or optical discs, or on memory cards and may be updated regularly.

A comprehensive type-approved electronic charting system, is known as ECDIS (electronic chart display and information system) and requires specialist crew training and regulation. In general, maritime regulations only allow electronic charting systems to replace traditional paper charts for navigational purposes under strictly controlled conditions. To comply with those conditions there must be a number of safeguards in place to satisfy international standards. The full detail of those safeguards and regulations is outside the scope of this book.

Echo Sounder

Accurate measurement of water depth is an important requirement in every tug. Because of the nature of their work, tugs probably spend more time in coastal waters than most other vessels. They are often required to work close inshore on civil engineering projects or manoeuvre to assist ships aground, operations that demand an accurate knowledge of the depth of water and the profile of the seabed or river bottom. Practically every tug is equipped with at least one echo sounder, using sound waves to measure the distance between the keel of the tug and the ground. This is a universal method of depth measurement used throughout the shipping industry. Modern equipment is available which can read depth to within a few centimetres. Many tugs and oil-rig supply vessels are fitted with instruments which show the information on a colour graphic display and produce a recording of the depth measurements and seabed profile in the form of a chart.

Radar

Radar is now regarded as an essential tool in any tug, where it may have several different roles. The most obvious application is in navigation in the dark and in poor weather conditions, particularly in congested port areas, coastal waters and busy shipping lanes. In this role it is possible accurately to locate other vessels and various features of the shoreline. In common with many similar pieces of electronic equipment the modern radar set has advanced enormously in recent years. A typical modern radar, installed in a harbour or coastal tug, will have a high definition colour display screen and many features enabling range to be measured and possible hazards to be plotted automatically. The range will be adjustable, depending on the type of set, between perhaps 0.5 and 36 nautical miles, with a maximum range of 72 miles. Two and even three separate radars may be fitted in larger tugs. This enables, for example, one set to be used at very short range – to monitor possible hazards nearby and another to be adjusted to a longer range for navigational purposes. In the most sophisticated radar sets incorporating ARPA (automatic radar plotting aid) other vessels under way can be plotted along with their course and speed, enabling decisions to be made regarding collision avoidance and similar safety issues. As previously mentioned, data from a radar set may be integrated with an electronic chart display to superimpose additional information, such as the position of other vessels, onto the electronic chart.

The tugmaster's chair aboard Hopetoun *is surrounded by consoles containing VHF communications equipment, a high definition radar, and electronic charting, in addition to the controls for its propulsion system, winches, and other machinery.* (Author)

In salvage work the radar set has transformed the whole business of locating ships in trouble. Used in conjunction with modern navigational aids and communications equipment, searching is no longer the lengthy, tedious procedure it was in the days before radar was invented. If a towline breaks in very bad weather conditions, providing there is no hazardous shoreline nearby, the tug may well make no attempt to reconnect until conditions improve. The tow will be monitored at a safe distance using radar and, if necessary, warnings broadcast to prevent collisions with other shipping.

Communications Equipment

The subject of marine communications equipment continues to become wider and more complex. Advances in communications technology and the increased use of space satellites in particular have completely changed many aspects of radio communication between ships and ship-to-shore links. Facilities now available, even to very small vessels, have a profound effect on the way that tugs can be operated and managed.

Even the smallest tug and workboat is equipped with a VHF (very high frequency) radio telephone to enable the vessel to communicate easily with its owners, port authorities, and other shipping. In virtually all ports around the world the VHF radio telephone has replaced whistle signals and hooters as the main means of communication between tug captains, ship's masters, and pilots during ship-handling operations. The use of synthesized electronic channel selection circuitry has made such radio equipment extremely versatile. A very small radio set will often be capable of operating on all 80 channels in the international VHF marine band. This frequency band is intended for relatively short-range use. Depending on the equipment and local geographical conditions, 20–30 miles is normally regarded as the maximum range. Radios of this kind are standard equipment on all larger tugs for 'ship-to-ship' and 'ship-to-shore' use. Very often two or more sets are fitted to enable several functions to be carried out at the same time. A common facility on this type of radio telephone is known as 'dual watch', which allows the international distress and calling channel, channel 16, or other pre-set channels, to be monitored regardless of other activities.

For longer-range use, standard HF (high frequency) and MF (medium frequency) radios are used, operating in the international marine bands. Radio equipment of this type is fitted in most seagoing tugs and has for many years been the standard method of communication between ships, owners and agents, often working through the national coastal radio stations The HF band also has designated distress frequencies. These are monitored not only by the various rescue authorities and shipping in general but also by towage and salvage concerns.

A large proportion of the communications traffic, between ships, tugs and other craft, their owners and other land-based agencies, now passes over satellite radio communications systems. As with other shipborne electronics equipment, such systems are now within the means of most operators of seagoing vessels. The main advantage offered by radio systems of this kind is the worldwide coverage possible, via the satellite link, without the need for complicated land-based relay arrangements. This is of particular value when the vessel is operating in remote

Under GMDSS regulations a tug is required to carry communication equipment to a certain standard (depending on size and its area of operations), including portable VHF radios for immediate emergency use and a ship's VHF radio incorporating digital selective calling (DSC) on distress frequencies. The fixed radios in the harbour tug Redbridge *are Sailor VHF sets, shown above a sound-powered telephone used for internal communication.* (Author)

Part of the safety equipment carried by virtually all tugs is the EPIRB located in a special mounting on the exterior of the superstructure. The sealed tube beside it carries a plan of the vessel's interior intended to assist the emergency services in case of fire or similar incident. (Author)

parts of the world or involved in long ocean voyages. The facilities offered by satellite communications systems such as Inmarsat-A & B are direct dial voice telephone, facsimile, telex and data transmission. The smaller, lightweight Inmarsat-C equipment provides 'non-voice' text and data transmission. Vessels equipped with satellite communications equipment are fitted with a dome or conical shaped antenna, located on the mast or high above the wheelhouse.

Such systems have become an important ingredient in initiatives to improve maritime safety. The Global Maritime Distress and Safety System (GMDSS), developed by the International Maritime Organisation (IMO) is now well established and recognised worldwide. International regulations required the installation of GMDSS equipment on all vessels over 300 gross tons by 2005. The GMDSS system requires a vessel to carry communications equipment capable of meeting certain standards for the sea area in which it will operate, with respect to radio communications and search and rescue facilities. In addition to various radio communications equipment of the types previously mentioned, vessels are also required to carry 'Emergency Position Indicating Radio Beacons' (EPIRBs) and 'Search and Rescue Radar Transponders' (SARTs). EPIRBs are radio beacons carried aboard the parent vessel and in lifeboats or rafts that, when activated, alert the satellite communications system to the vessel's current position. One form of EPIRB is incorporated in a buoy that floats free from a sinking vessel, remains

The control console of the tug Tarka *includes three main display screens, one for radar (centre) and two which can be used to display charts, GPS data, or information from the vessel's other systems. Above the VDU screens are the compass repeater, echo sounder, intercom, and other instruments.* (Author)

tethered and continues to transmit a signal to mark the position of the casualty. A SART is an active radar transponder which operates in much the same manner to enhance the signal received by the radar aboard a searching vessel, giving a clearer indication of the position of the casualty, wreck or liferaft.

A further mandatory requirement for vessels over 300 gross tons is the installation of NAVTEX equipment. NAVTEX is generally described as, 'receiving, automatically, maritime safety information on 518 kHz, by narrow band direct printing'. The equipment is rather like a very small facsimile machine. A variety of information is received automatically at regular intervals, depending on the requirements of the operator, but always includes regular weather reports for the area of operations. Other available information can include ice reports, maritime distress warnings and notices to mariners regarding known potential hazards.

Another recent introduction to the communications outfit on many tugs is an Automatic Identification System (AIS). AIS is used by ships and Vessel Traffic Services (VTS) principally for the identification and location of vessels. AIS provides a means for ships automatically to exchange ship data electronically including: name, callsign, position, course, and speed, with other nearby vessels and VTS stations. This information can be displayed on a VDU screen or an ECDIS display. AIS is intended to assist the vessel's watch-keeping officers and allow maritime authorities to track and monitor vessel movements. AIS works by using a standardised VHF transceiver system to transmit data from the vessel's own navigation system – GPS, gyro compass and so on. Under regulations introduced by the IMO in the International Convention for the Safety of Life at Sea (SOLAS) AIS must be fitted aboard ships over 300 gross tons and all passenger ships regardless of size carrying out international voyages. In use AIS information is displayed on a VDU or electronic chart as an 'arrow-head' with annotations giving identification and navigational data.

The use of facsimile transmission and electronic mail (email) over various radio and satellite links has spread rapidly in the towage industry. It provides an ideal means of transmitting and receiving charts, weather maps, technical information,

The radio desk aboard the anchor-handling tug and ETV Anglian Sovereign houses the major items of equipment required to meet GMDSS (Area 3) regulations for worldwide use. A single sideband radio, VHF, Inmarsat, telex, fax, and cell phone are included, each with their necessary computers and printers. (Author)

drawings, contracts and other management information. The possibilities this presents to the towage and salvage operator are immense, with important documents being transmitted directly from owner's and agent's offices to tugs at sea conducting towage, salvage, or offshore operations.

The land-based cellular mobile telephone has also found an important place aboard the modern tug. Although its use is obviously restricted by phone network coverage, this type of telephone now appears in the wheelhouses of most tugs. Owners are finding such systems a convenient and relatively secure means of communicating with vessels in coastal waters. Business can be conducted in conditions of some privacy without broadcasting on international frequencies or resorting to encryption. More recent innovations such as 'Iridium' handheld satellite phones may well overcome the constraints inherent in the cellular systems.

LIGHTING AND SAFETY EQUIPMENT
Lights and Shapes

In general, the lights required by maritime law for navigational purposes are the same for tugs as for other shipping. There are, however, special conditions and requirements that affect tugs when they are towing. As in general shipping there are also day marks, or shapes, which are displayed for the same purpose during daylight hours.

Towing Lights and Shapes

To the uninitiated, the mast of a tug seems to carry an over-abundance of lights. The vertical array of lights fitted to the mast is a combination of towing and navigation lights. The towing lights are illuminated in a particular order to indicate to other shipping that the tug is towing and give some indication as to the nature of the tow. The regulations governing lights are revised from time to time but the following basic rules applied at the time of writing:

(a) Tugs below 50 metres in length need only one masthead steaming light. Larger vessels exceeding that length require two steaming lights, on separate masts, in the same way as a conventional ship.

(b) A tug with a tow of less than 200 metres in length, from the stern of the tug to the stern of the tow, must carry one additional white towing light at the forward mast 2 metres below the steaming light. A tug with a tow of over 200 metres in length must show two additional towing lights.

(c) A tug with a tow must show a yellow towing light aft, above its stern light.

(d) Three other lights are fitted at the mast of most modern tugs. These are two red lights, arranged vertically, separated by a white light. This is the international signal for 'vessels restricted in ability to manoeuvre' and is often used by a tug at sea with a tow. The lights must be visible from all round the vessel and on many tugs are mounted on brackets to separate them from the mast.

The mast of the tanker-handling tug Castle Point *displays the mandatory towing and navigation lights required for a modern tug of its type. Located on the wheel-house roof are the magnetic compass, two radars, a searchlight and an inflatable life-raft. The numerous antennae visible are required for MF and VHF radios, GPS, and domestic television services.* (Author)

Tugs of the tractor- or push/tow-type, which are capable of operating equally well stern first, may have two sets of towing and navigation lights fitted. The second set is positioned for use when the vessel is operating stern first.

During daylight hours a black diamond shape is hoisted to the mast of a tug with a tow exceeding 200 metres in length. The red-white-red light signal, 'vessels restricted in ability to manoeuvre', is replaced in daylight by two black ball shapes separated by a black diamond.

Portable lights are usually provided aboard tugs, to be installed temporarily on vessels in tow which have no lights of their own. The lights may be powered by gas from cylinders or electric batteries.

In some ports and inland waterways local by-laws require special signals to be displayed indicating when a tug is operating with a tow. These are usually flag signals or shapes which are hoisted on a small additional mast.

Searchlights

Powerful searchlights are an important part of the tug's equipment. Almost every type of tug will have one or more searchlights. They have many uses. During towing operations a searchlight is used to keep a visual check on the condition of the towline and the vessel in tow. It can also be useful to identify any likely hazards located close at hand by radar. Searchlights and floodlighting are used extensively during salvage and offshore operations to enable work to proceed around the clock.

Boats and Life-Saving Equipment

The type of boat carried aboard tugs has changed drastically in the past twenty years. Rigid, full-size lifeboats, once common on tugs of most types, are now rarely seen aboard anything but the largest vessels. Rigid boats carried on tugs engaged in ship-handling work were a particular nuisance. Such boats are difficult to stow without impairing the vision from the wheelhouse and are easily damaged when the tug is working close alongside a ship. Most owners throughout the world were quick to dispense with the rigid lifeboat once a suitable alternative evolved. The vast improvements made in inflatable life-rafts and durable rigid inflatable boats (RIBs) have been responsible for sealing the fate of the conventional boat. A modern RIB is most commonly carried as a rescue craft and can be used as a general-purpose tender when required. A simple, single arm davit, or the tug's hydraulic crane, is used to launch and recover the boat.

Life-Rafts and Other Aids

For life-saving purposes the inflatable life-raft, stowed on deck in a sealed container, has proved to be highly convenient for a number of reasons. The space required for stowage is insignificant and if necessary the number of rafts provided

A typical rescue boat and its launching davit being tested aboard a tanker-handling tug. The davit is being manually operated. An alternative electric winch is also fitted. The quick-release hook above the boat is clearly visible. (Author)

can be increased without difficulty. A single modern life-raft can easily accommodate the entire crew of all but the very largest of tugs. The life-raft container is usually stowed in a cradle incorporating a hydrostatic pressure sensing mechanism which will release it automatically should the tug sink. Among the other life-saving aids provided are traditional lifebuoys, distress flares, marker floats and position indicating devices such as EPIRBs and SARTs (mentioned above). A growing number of harbour craft now carry recovery devices, designed to enable personnel to be recovered from the water without the need to lower a boat. These take the form of slings, scoops or sophisticated ladder devices operated from a small davit or, again, a hydraulic crane,

Workboats

Boats are frequently needed for purposes other than life-saving. In earlier days the rigid lifeboat often doubled as a workboat. A workboat is often necessary to collect stores, transfer personnel, put towlines aboard other vessels, and many similar tasks. More often than not those duties are now undertaken by sturdy RIBs equipped as workboats and propelled by powerful outboard motors. Such boats are durable, light to handle, and with suitable engines can be quite fast. Larger versions of the RIB have a reinforced plastic lower hull and possibly an inboard engine. This type of boat is easy to stow, launch and recover. Very large seagoing and salvage tugs may still be equipped with rigid boats. These may take the form of lifeboats or purpose-built workboats with diesel engines sufficiently powerful to cope with difficult sea conditions and handle heavy equipment during salvage operations.

SALVAGE EQUIPMENT

Almost every tug carries some items that come under the heading of salvage equipment. Even the smallest barge tug will probably have some additional pumping equipment on board to enable it to pump out or refloat flooded barges. The amount of equipment carried will again depend on the type of tug and its employment. Salvage is a very complex subject on which much has been written; in the following paragraphs it is intended only to outline the basic equipment deployed for salvage work. With the number of dedicated salvage tugs falling, many salvage specialists store and maintain salvage equipment in a form that can be quickly mobilised and put aboard any suitable tug or anchor-handling supply vessel capable of attending a casualty. Many of the items mentioned here fall into that category and will be sufficiently portable to allow them to be transported by air to any part of the world.

Salvage Pumps

Additional pumping equipment is one of the most common facilities provided. In salvage tugs this usually takes the form of high-capacity pumps fitted to the tug's auxiliary machinery. The diesel-driven generators, air compressors, and other auxiliaries located in the engine-room may have a salvage pump fitted that can be engaged when required. Such pumps are piped to connections, easily accessible, on deck to which suction hoses can be fitted. The purpose-built pumps fitted for salvage work are capable of moving water at an extremely high rate.

Additional portable salvage pumps are carried aboard tugs operating regularly in salvage or may be supplied from specialists ashore. These are usually diesel-driven, self-contained units or submersible pumps driven by an electrical or air supply. Diesel pumps are stowed aboard the salvage tug and can be lifted onto the deck of a casualty if the necessity arises. Submersible pumps are sealed units, connected to a hose and designed to be lowered into the flooded areas of a casualty. A common type of submersible pump popular on tugs is one driven by high-pressure water. There are no electrical hazards involved and a suitable water supply is readily available on most vessels.

Anchors and Ground Tackle

Among the most common items found aboard a large seagoing or salvage tug are additional anchors. These are generally somewhat heavier than the vessel's own

The Chinese salvage tug De Da *is well equipped for long-distance towing and salvage. A powerful crane, fully protected lifeboats, an aft control cabin and towing rails are all visible. Note also the fire monitors on the forward gantry mast and additional lights on the short mast forward denoting a vessel of over 50 m in length.* (H. Hoffmann)

anchors and may well be of a special design. Additional anchors are used to assist with the refloating of vessels that are aground. They may be incorporated in ground tackle, very heavy multiple-pulley systems rigged to exert a much greater pull than would be possible by towing alone.

Line-Throwing Equipment

Most tugs, of any size, have on board some means of getting a light heaving line to vessels that for some reason cannot be approached too closely. If a ship is aground in shallow water, or if the weather is exceptionally bad, the tug will not be able to manoeuvre alongside in the normal way. The most common method of making a towing connection under these circumstances is to fire a light line over the vessel by rocket or line-throwing gun. Once contact is made in this way heavier lines and eventually a towline can be hauled aboard the casualty and made fast. Line-throwing equipment varies from simple expendable rockets, which give one attempt, to guns that can be reloaded with fresh projectiles and line. Reloadable line-throwing guns operated by compressed air are popular and have the advantage of increased safety where inflammable cargoes or vapours are present.

Pollution-Control Equipment

One of the first considerations for the salvage master is that of pollution control. Problems with leaking oil or other contaminants must be dealt with as a matter of priority and tugs of almost any size can be involved in deploying protective booms and carrying out supporting duties. Tugs employed at or near oil terminals may be equipped with booms or have provision to take pre-prepared boom-laying equipment on board. This subject is described in greater detail in Chapter 7.

Underwater Equipment

There is an obvious need aboard a salvage tug for some form of diving capability. In larger vessels this may be part of the tug's equipment, or alternatively provision may be made to accommodate specialist gear and personnel when required. The range of equipment carried can again vary enormously, from simple scuba-diving gear to full-scale deep-diving outfits with a decompression chamber provided on board.

Included under this heading is equipment for cutting and welding and the means of carrying out other repair work underwater. Special tools are available for use underwater, such as spanners, drills, and hammers driven by compressed air. Some provision may also be made for the storage and use of explosives. These are used in salvage work for cutting purposes, to disperse wreckage and blast away rock.

Highly specialised equipment such as small remotely operated vehicles (ROVs) carrying cameras are sometimes used to carry out underwater inspection work during and after salvage operations. This equipment will only be stowed permanently aboard the largest fully equipped salvage tugs but can be readily transported and used from any suitable vessel.

FIRE-FIGHTING EQUIPMENT

Fire-fighting equipment of some kind is installed on board virtually every tug. This capability usually extends beyond that needed to protect the vessel itself from fires on board. The equipment fitted ranges from the provision of a few hose connections and extinguishers to sophisticated installations capable of undertaking important fire-protection duties. Specialist fire-fighting tugs, their equipment and duties, are described in a later chapter. The following paragraphs deal with the more common and less specialised installations.

Fire Mains and Hoses

The term 'fire main' refers to a water supply, generally provided by a powerful pump in the engine-room, which can be used to fight fires on board or to assist another vessel. A fire pump can be driven by one of the auxiliary engines or in some tugs by the main engine. The fire main is a system of pipes routed to deliver a supply of water to hose connections within the vessel and on deck. Hoses are attached to these connections and may be fitted with suitable nozzles for fire-fighting. In most vessels the fire main is identified from the mass of other pipework by painting it red.

Indee, *the first prototype Z-Tech tug, has a typical installation of two powerful 'short barrel' fire monitors mounted forward of the wheelhouse. The monitors are remotely controlled and standard equipment on most tugs of this type and many other modern harbour tugs.* (P.S.A.)

Monitors

Because of the difficulty in accurately directing high-pressure jets of water during fire-fighting operations, some form of nozzle is often used which is fixed to the structure of the vessel. These are known as monitors. In its simplest form a monitor is a nozzle located on a mounting designed to enable the water jet be controlled with some accuracy. This is usually achieved by a system of hand-wheels and simple gear mechanisms. In the more sophisticated installations the monitor will be capable of delivering either water or a water/foam mixture. The output from a high-performance fire monitor can vary from approximately 1,500 to as much as 60,000 litres of water per minute. If fire-fighting foam is used, the chemical compound needed is introduced into the water supply, prior to the monitor, from storage tanks installed on board. When foam is in use the volume delivered by the monitor is considerably higher than with water alone.

CHAPTER 5

Small Tugs and Multi-Purpose Vessels

It is increasingly difficult to put tugs at the lower end of the scale into neat categories. Many small tugs, of less than 26 metres in length, now in service equal many larger and older vessels in terms of power and agility and are frequently used for full-scale ship-handling. Where this is the case much of the information contained in Chapter 6 will apply. This chapter is intended to embrace the most prolific and diverse, and in many respects the most interesting, sector of the towing industry. Tugs in this category are employed to carry out a whole host of different and sometimes unusual tasks. Included are tugs and work vessels employed in small commercial ports where they are true 'maids of all work', assisting small ships, working with barges and dredgers and involved in many routine port maintenance tasks.

A great many tugs in this category are employed by specialist towage contractors supporting dredging operations and marine civil engineering work in harbours and at riverside and coastal locations. Many are owned by very small companies or 'owner-operators' working under contract for individual jobs, or employed regularly to carry out a particular towage operation. Included in this 'small tug' category are the growing numbers of powerful purpose-built shallow-draft vessels capable of towing, pushing and many other services required by dredging and construction companies.

Some tasks involve long coastal or short sea voyages to fulfil contracts in other ports and/or other countries. To meet those requirements some of the most recent examples have increased in size and are equipped for full seagoing service.

Many small modern tugs and multi-purpose vessels are very suitable for mass or series production. This has resulted in a proliferation of proprietary 'standard' vessels being purchased to undertake many of the duties described in this chapter.

There are many small vessels, other than tugs, that regularly give assistance to other craft by towing or pushing but are excluded here because towing is very

Dutch Partner, *shown here off the coast of Norfolk with the back-hoe dredger* Manu-Pekka *in tow, is one of a new generation of shallow-draft tugs built by Gebr Kooiman in the Netherlands. The tug is 27.8 m in length, powered by two Caterpillar diesels generating a total of 2,780 bhp for a bollard pull of 30 tonnes.* Dutch Partner *is owned by Englesman Towage & Salvage of Makkum.* (Author)

much a supplementary duty. Workboats, passenger launches, construction vessels and even pilot cutters often have some provision for securing a towrope and when needed undertake small towing jobs but cannot be regarded as tugs. For the purposes of this chapter the starting point will be the small tug/workboat of some 20 gross tons and larger.

Traditional Barge Tugs

Barge tugs of traditional design are still widely used in port areas and on inland waterways where barge trades have survived. Europe has a large population of such craft operating in Holland, Belgium, France and Germany. Many of these have been adapted to push or tow their barges, as circumstances dictate. In Britain very few have remained in their traditional trade and a diminishing number are still to be found employed as small harbour tugs and contracting vessels. The term 'barge tug' in the USA and Canada can mean a small craft, similar to those used in Europe, or a very much larger vessel used on major waterways or in coastal operations. This chapter deals only with the towing tug – examples of those vessels dedicated to pushing are described in Chapter 9.

The smallest of the traditional barge tugs is the 'launch tug', known as a 'tosher' in some British ports. These are terms that describe a very small tug of a traditional design used mainly to handle single barges or other small craft. Originally intended for use in the barge and lighterage industries, several of these craft remain in service in Britain, Holland, Germany and elsewhere. Few tugs of this type were built after the mid-1960s but they have remained popular due to their sturdy construction, rounded hull form, and low profile. An average launch tug will have a length of some 12–15 metres and gross tonnage of about 20 tons. They are generally single-screw vessels powered by a diesel engine of 125–400 bhp housed in an engine-room taking up most of the space within the hull.

Knab *is a rugged pilot vessel and tug built for the Lerwick Port Authority to work in the sometimes arduous conditions around the Shetland islands. The 20.3 m twin-screw vessel was built in Denmark in 2006 and powered by Volvo main engines of 1,442 bhp (total) to achieve a 22-tonne bollard pull and free-running speed of 11.4 knots.* (Lerwick PA)

The launch tug was originally developed to handle barges singly or in small numbers and marshal such craft in readiness for larger tugs to undertake the longer journeys. To that end the hull is strongly built to withstand hard use and the low profile enables the craft to proceed under river and dock bridges without the need for them to be raised or opened. Some barge companies still employ these vessels for their original purpose but in many ports they are being replaced by more modern tug/workboats of similar size and power.

Like their smaller sisters, the larger traditional barge tugs are invariably strongly built to withstand heavy contact with their charges. A feature which often identifies them from a ship-handling tug of the same size, is the height of the bulwarks which

The launch tug Merano *is typical of many similar vessels built for use on the Thames and Medway in Britain and many major European ports. Owned by Medtow Marine Ltd, it is a vessel of 14.6 m built in 1949 and powered by a single Volvo engine of 380 bhp. A low profile is an important feature when working in the enclosed dock systems with many low bridges.* (Author)

are generally tailored to provide some protection yet low enough to avoid fouling tow ropes or sustain undue damage from contact with barges. In size, most British and European barge tugs will be below 100 gross tons and 24 metres in overall length. Many earlier vessels are fitted with a single conventional screw propeller. In the past twin-screw tugs were avoided by many owners because the propeller blades could be easily damaged by contact with barges. The main engine will be a diesel of 350–1,200 bhp. Their larger American and Canadian cousins are often much more powerful. The engine and gearbox will be controlled from the wheelhouse and most engine-rooms can be left unattended for long periods. Thrust-enhancing nozzles of the Kort type are used by some owners and may be of the fixed or steerable type. Some older barge tugs have been fitted with nozzles in later life to improve their performance – with a fixed nozzle being the most likely choice.

On European waterways the modern 'standard' tug is replacing some of the smaller traditional craft. Vessels of the tug/workboat type, with main engines of 750–1,200 bhp, excellent handling characteristics, and good accommodation for a small crew, can often be seen working with barges in Holland and Belgium in much the same way as their earlier counterparts.

The methods used to handle barges depend on the type and size of barge and the conditions on the waterway concerned. On some waterways the total length of the tug and its tow are governed by local by-laws. Barges towed astern may be

General VIII *is a single-screw barge tug built in 1966 for the Thames fleet of Cory Environmental Ltd. It is designed to tow refuse barges away from central London and retains many traditional features including a low air draft allowing it to pass beneath the river's many bridges. The tug is 25.7 metres in length and powered by a Lister Blackstone diesel of 1,196 bhp.* (Author)

Seaspan Tempest *is a modern twin-screw barge tug in daily use in Vancouver and the Fraser River in British Columbia towing bulk cargo barges. Built in 2003 with sister* Seaspan Venture, *this 19.5 m vessel is powered by two Cummins KTA38 engines with a total output of 1,700 bhp.* (Author)

arranged in 'strings', two or three long and two or more abreast. On the River Thames, for example, a string of barges of 250 tonnes each, three long and two abreast, was commonplace when the lighterage industry was thriving and transporting large amounts of cargo. Such tows still continue but the cargoes are mainly domestic rubbish for disposal, building materials and excavated spoil. The tendency now is to use fewer but larger barges. When operating on tidal waterways, journeys are timed to make the maximum use of any advantage that can be gained from the flow of the tides.

In continental Europe, the USA and Canada barges are generally very much larger and used mainly for bulk and containerised cargoes. Barges used for sensitive cargoes likely to be damaged by the ingress of water, such as paper, grain or fertilizer, incorporate hatches that can readily be opened, closed and sealed. Single barges are often towed with the tug secured alongside. The tug is positioned very near to the stern of the barge, often described as 'on the hip'. This arrangement enables the tug and barge to be controlled very much as one vessel and is particularly useful with light craft which some times tow badly astern. In many regions, pushing from astern remains the most popular means of handling barges over long distances on inland waterways. In Europe the majority of barge tugs are fitted with a suitable bow fender and two small hand winches with securing wires, to enable the tug to revert to pushing when required.

Standard Tugs and Tug/Workboats

Vessels of this type have become so prolific in recent years that they warrant a category of their own. Whole ranges of small tugs and tug/workboats have been designed and marketed with great success, largely by specialist builders in Holland. Such vessels are obtainable almost 'off the shelf' and sold in large numbers to small harbour authorities, dredging concerns, and civil engineers. The vessels on offer generally range in size from approximately 12 to 25 metres in length.

At the smaller end of this range, up to 19 metres in length, the vessels invariably fall in the category of tug/workboat. These are constructed in great numbers and are fitted out to the owners' requirements, and tend to be used for towing, and a host of other tasks where a robust, highly manoeuvrable vessel is required. In recent years vessels of this type have increased enormously in power. Most are twin-screw and commonly powered by a pair of diesel engines producing a total of anything from 300 bhp in a 12-metre vessel to 2,000 bhp in a tug of 19 metres. Fixed high-performance propulsion nozzles are normally fitted as standard and a vessel of this type, dependent on size, will produce a bollard pull of up to 30 tonnes. A large wheelhouse is provided and sufficient accommodation for a crew of two or three. A small 'flying bridge' with duplicated engine and steering controls is sometimes fitted to give improved all-round vision.

These vessels have sufficient power to carry out a very wide range of duties extremely economically. They are used in many smaller ports to assist ships, carry out survey work, act as pilot boats, and perform simple dredging and other

The Damen 'StanTug' 1907 Bruiser *is one of an improved twin-screw tug/workboat design of 19.33 m in length, fitted with two Caterpillar engines producing 2,000 bhp to give the vessel a bollard pull of 27.8 tonnes.* Bruiser *is employed by Clyde Marine Ltd of Greenock, Scotland, on ship-handling and general towage duties.* (Author)

maintenance work. The dredging industry was one of the first serious commercial users of these modern standard vessels. They have proved ideal tugs to handle the hopper barges used to take spoil away for dumping, assist with repositioning dredging plant, and transport personnel.

Where bigger and more powerful tugs are required there are alternative vessels on offer in standard ranges and again the power available in a relatively small tug has increased dramatically in recent years. In the small tug category a number of compact designs are employed, up to about 26 metres long and with engines of up to 3,500 bhp. In general these follow closely the designs used for larger ship-handling and coastal tugs but scaled down and equipped for a particular purpose. Many are employed as small ship-handling tugs or to carry out coastal tows or more specialised duties. Larger pieces of plant such as floating cranes, dredgers of all types and similar pieces of marine construction equipment all require towage assistance in some form.

Shallow-Draft Tugs

The current high level of activity in the marine construction industry and the proliferation of wind farm construction and oil exploration in coastal waters has created the need for a new breed of shallow-draft tug. Many of these vessels are between 19 and 30 metres in length and often designed to work in water of 2.5 metres or less. A useful bollard pull of 28–35 tonnes is common. To achieve the necessary bollard pull in a shallow-draft vessel of this type a twin- or triple-screw propulsion system is normally employed in order that the size of propellers and nozzles can be reduced. In many cases the propellers and nozzles are located in shallow tunnels on the underside of the hull.

Shallow-draft tugs of this type normally have a long clear afterdeck with a towing and anchor-handling winch, stern roller and line-handling equipment fitted in much the same configuration as a full-size offshore anchor-handling supply vessel. A powerful deck crane is also installed in virtually every case to assist in marine construction. Vessels of this type are increasingly built to standards that allow them to undertake coastal and short sea-towage operations, without restriction. The standard of accommodation is high, with air-conditioning and facilities to enable the vessel to operate in both hot and cold climates.

A standard design that has been progressively developed to encompass this particular market is the Shoalbuster, designed for series production by the specialist Dutch shipbuilder Damen Shipyards. Originally introduced as a small, shallow-draft vessel for the dredging and marine civil engineering market, this design has been developed almost beyond recognition. The latest versions of between 25 and 32 metres in length are intended for full seagoing operation and

Delivered in 2008 André-B *was built in the Netherlands for Dutch owners BMS Towing. The tug is one of the latest of a series of shallow-draft anchor-handlers designed to work on oil-related projects, wind farm construction and other projects where draft is an important factor. André-B measures 31 m in length and has two Mitsubishi main engines of 3,400 bhp (total). Twin nozzles and four rudders give a bollard pull of 48 tonnes and good manoeuvrability.* (BMS)

Giessenstroom *of Van Wijngaarten Marine Services is a vessel from the top end of the range of Damen Shoalbusters. This 30 m tug, with Caterpillar engines and a bollard pull of 40 tonnes, is a vessel that can carry out a wide range of duties on marine construction and major dredging sites in shallow waters yet is capable of undertaking long tows at sea. (Damen)*

embody most of the features described in earlier paragraphs. Although constructed as a 'standard' vessel, tugs in the Shoalbuster range are frequently 'customised' to fulfil the exact requirements of their owners.

Tractor Tugs

The only very small tractor tugs to enter the towage business have been those using the Voith Schneider propulsion system. An ability to manoeuvre with great precision in any direction has obvious advantages, particularly when handling awkward craft in very confined spaces. A substantial number of vessels of this type were built in Europe in the past, with the vast majority being used by port authorities and naval dockyards.

The British Ministry of Defence (Navy) built twenty small Voith Schneider tractors, using two designs, for vessels of 330 bhp and 650 bhp. Both types have propulsion systems using only one Voith propulsion unit. The smaller of these was built to a design derived from a commercial prototype dating back to 1964. In naval dockyards their primary function is to work with the many barges and other non-propelled craft used to service warships. Many of these former naval vessels have now passed into commercial hands.

In continental Europe, tugs of a similar size are in use but embodying twin propulsion units, considerably enhancing their agility and handling characteristics.

The small former British naval tractor tug Lilah *has a single Voith Schneider propulsion unit beneath the bow and large skeg aft and is powered by a single Lister Blackstone main engine of 330 bhp.* Lilah *is shown handling a floating marina pontoon for current owners the Milford Haven Port Authority, UK. (Author)*

Tugs of this type are particularly useful in docking and undocking small vessels at dry docks and slipways, but their main employment in commercial service is to work with barges and civil engineering plant in and around harbour areas.

Although many of these vessels remain in regular use, no small tractor tugs of this type have been built during the past two decades. The relatively high capital costs involved in fitting sophisticated propulsion units and the increasing popularity of more powerful, twin-screw designs has turned the tide against them.

The Multi-Purpose Work Vessel

A popular and relative newcomer to the towage industry is the multi-purpose work vessel. Often referred to generically as a 'multi-cat' this is a vessel that started life resembling a small pusher tug with long open foredeck. Within the past five years this is a vessel that has 'come of age'. Some of the most recent examples are formidable craft capable of towing, lifting, transporting and providing a wide range of services on marine construction sites.

The hull is normally a simple rectangular pontoon shape, with a wide beam, equipped with a conventional twin- or triple-screw propulsion system. Popular sizes range from 15–26 metres in length, powered by main engines with a total power of between 750 and 2,500 bhp. Fixed propulsion nozzles are usually fitted and bollard pulls of up to 35 tonnes are achieved in the most powerful vessels. Push knees are located at the bow and a small superstructure and wheelhouse at the stern or offset to the port side. A towing hook or bollard is installed aft and a powerful winch amidships. The winch is frequently a double-drum machine used for towing, lifting and anchor-handling. To facilitate lifting over the bow a roller is fitted at deck level between the push knees. The open foredeck is used as a working and cargo area and at least one powerful hydraulic deck crane is installed.

Because of their rectangular pontoon shape the vessels have a shallow draft and large reserve of buoyancy making them ideal for load-carrying and lifting. The result is a powerful multi-purpose craft capable of working with construction barges and carrying out a wide range of towing and other duties. Vessels of this type are employed mainly by companies specialising in work for the marine civil engineering industry and harbour authorities.

Shannon 1 is a 19 m 'MultiCat' work vessel delivered to Shannon Foynes Port in Ireland by Damen Shipyards in 2008. Clearly visible is the timber-clad work deck, hydraulic crane, anchor-handling winch, and demountable 'A' for plough dredging. The vessel is powered by two Caterpillar main engines producing 960 bhp to achieve a bollard pull of 13.2 tonnes. Note the hydraulic deck crane. (Damen)

USING SMALL TUGS AND MULTI-PURPOSE VESSELS

The duties of the harbour tug and barge-towing vessel are perhaps obvious, but there are many forms of employment for the small and medium-size tug that are more specialised and worthy of further description.

The Ports of Jersey authority in the Channel Islands employs the well-equipped multi-purpose tug Duke of Normandy *for a wide range of tasks including ship-handling, survey work, buoy maintenance and small salvage operations.* Duke of Normandy *is a Damen Shoalbuster of 26.2 m and 2,200 bhp with a 28-tonne bollard pull. In this photograph the tug is lifting a 9 tonne buoy onto its after deck.* (Author)

Port Services

In ports where one or perhaps two small tugs are the only harbour craft of any size and power, a key requirement will be versatility. Vessels of this type will have sufficient power to give effective towage assistance to ships, but may also be required to perform a wide range of other duties.

A task frequently placed upon the harbour tug is the maintenance of the buoys and channel markers of various kinds in use around the port. This work will vary from routine maintenance, requiring only the servicing of lights and equipment *in situ*, to towing a complete buoy into port. In order to carry out this type of operation some means of lifting is needed to deal with the heavy 'sinker' or anchor keeping the buoy in place. A lifting sheave (pulley) in the bow, or a stern roller, may be used in conjunction with a winch, or a suitable crane may be fitted. A larger harbour tug carrying out this work may even take the entire buoy onto its after deck.

With the advent of much larger and more powerful marine cranes, capable of being mounted on tugs and work vessels, buoy handling has become simpler and much safer. A modern tug or multi-purpose work vessel of the pontoon type, equipped with a powerful crane, is not only ideally suited for such work but is also capable of providing a wide range of useful services around the port. It is now common for repairs to quay walls and fendering, small salvage and wreck-clearance jobs to be undertaken by such vessels, which can often access parts of a port not easily reached by land-based lifting equipment.

Another duty frequently falling to the small harbour tug is transporting pilots and personnel to and from ships at anchor or in transit. Where this is a regular duty the tug may be required to conform to local regulations regarding the carriage of passengers. This generally involves the provision of additional safety equipment and an upper limit on the number of passengers allowed. Going alongside ships to put pilots aboard can be a hazardous business whilst they are under way, particularly in poor weather. Although the tug may be well fendered and equipped to do this work, additional handrails are often fitted for the safety of personnel transferring between vessels.

A small, manoeuvrable port tug may also be equipped to carry out regular surveys in the port and its approaches to monitor water depths, and detect accumulations of mud or other hazards on the seabed. Special transducers will be fitted beneath the vessel's hull and accurate echo-sounding equipment will be installed in the wheelhouse or accommodation. In order to produce precise results a DGPS or other accurate position-finding equipment may be required. The results of such surveys take the form of printed sounding records or charts.

The port tug may also be used to assist with dredging operations and/or raking as described later in this chapter.

Tugs for Military Use

The navies of the world are well versed in the use of tugs of all types. Small tugs are employed in large numbers at dockyards and around naval bases to handle the smaller types of warship, fuel and ammunition barges, and similar vessels. Many navies employ 'off the shelf' standard tugs with little modification. Others may develop their own designs in order to cope with special conditions and needs. They may have conventional screw propulsion or employ systems giving superior manoeuvrability. A feature to be found in many naval tugs used for handling submarines is fendering fitted below the waterline to avoid damage to the pressure hull whilst working close alongside during berthing/unberthing operations. Tugs working with aircraft carriers need adequate overhead clearance and sometimes folding masts, to enable them to work safely under the overhanging flight decks.

In recent years there has been increasing political pressure on many navies to cut the costs related to essential, but peripheral, services in naval establishments. This has resulted in some instances in the employment of commercial contractors to manage and operate the supporting tug fleets. Other navies have begun the process of handing over the entire towing and ship-handling operation to commercial operators using their own tugs.

Many armies around the world also operate tugs of various types. Most are very small vessels used to support temporary military bridging operations and are outside the scope of this book. But in the USA there is still a very real tug fleet in the hands of the Army watercraft units and the Corps of Engineers. Much of the equipment owned by the Army is for use in setting up temporary military ports in times of war or civil emergencies. A large proportion of this fleet is held 'mothballed' in a state of preservation until required. The majority of tugs employed are of relatively basic designs, intended to work with barges, floating cranes, and other harbour equipment. The US Army Corps of Engineers is quite a different matter, operating a wide variety of tugs and floating plant on a continuous basis, maintaining and improving inland waterways.

Atlas *is part of a large fleet of tugs owned and operated by Serco Denholm in naval bases around the UK under contract to the Royal Navy. The 25 m twin-screw 2,200 bhp tug has a 30-tonne bollard pull and is used to handle ships and dockyard plant. Note the rope overlay on the bow fender to prevent damage to warship paint.* (Author)

Line-Handling Tugs

Craft known as line-handling tugs or mooring vessels are widely used to assist with mooring large tankers at oil and LNG terminals. They are employed to handle the heavy mooring ropes during berthing operations, towing them away from the ship to the jetty or adjacent mooring dolphins. At terminals where the tankers are required to moor at buoys mooring vessels are required to make the ship fast to the mooring buoy while ship-handling tugs hold it in position. Where tankers load or unload at special mooring buoys, often some distance from shore, it may also be the task of the mooring vessels to tow floating hoses into position so that the necessary connections can be made. The same craft may form part of an anti-pollution organisation stationed at the tanker terminal and will be used to tow protective booms into place, either as a precautionary measure or if an oil spill occurs.

In order to carry out these duties satisfactorily many such vessels are based on established tug designs. They must have sufficient power to handle the heavy gear and the ability to manoeuvre easily and precisely throughout the operation. Mooring vessels designed for the work described are easily identifiable by an array of protective guards fitted to prevent mooring ropes becoming entangled with the mast, radar, wheelhouse and other parts of the superstructure. Many have an open stern and bulwarks of reduced height to enable protective booms and hoses to be brought on deck easily. The size of vessel varies enormously, depending on the location at which they are required to work and the other duties they may have to perform. A small mooring vessel of about 14–16 metres in length is common at many terminals and would be employed mainly to handle ropes and act as a tender to transport personnel and stores. Larger and more powerful vessels may be employed to carry out a wider range of duties, including giving towage assistance to small ships on adjacent jetties and providing fire-fighting and anti-pollution services in an emergency.

When handling mooring ropes at oil and gas terminals, it is common practice for the line-handling tug to manoeuvre close to the ship to accept one or two mooring ropes at a time. The rope ends are secured on the foredeck of the tug and as the ropes are paid out by the ship's winches they are towed to the jetty or mooring dolphin. By working over the bow and manoeuvring for much of the time stern first, the ropes are kept clear of the tug's propellers.

Similar procedures, using much smaller and less powerful boats, are common in ports throughout the world for handling mooring lines for container ships and other very large vessels.

The single-screw line-handling tug Bram *is in service with Buksér og Berging at the Mongstad oil terminal in Norway. Built in Norway in 1988 it is a vessel of 11.5 m in length, fitted with a Volvo main engine of 300 bhp. Note the protective guard-rails and sturdy, compact design.* (Author)

The shallow-draft multi-purpose tug Afon Cefni *from the Holyhead Towing Company fleet in the UK is shown working with a dredge pipe on the shoreline, typical of the tasks undertaken by this type of vessel.* Afon Cefni *is a 22.5 m tug with a draft of only 2 m, powered by two Cummins diesels of 1,300 bhp (total) for a bollard pull of 17 tonnes.* (Author)

Tugs and the Dredging Industry

The dredging industry has traditionally been a regular user of tugs to support its operations in ports and rivers around the world. Depending on the type of dredging operation in progress, tugs may be employed to carry out any of the following duties: towing non-propelled (dumb) hopper barges, moving and attending dredgers, surveying and raking. The tugs used are owned by port authorities, dredging companies or contractors specialising in providing tugs for this type of work. In the industry today conventional screw tugs or small purpose-built vessels of approximately 16–25 metres in length are often used. The latter are frequently built to 'standard' designs and employed because of their versatility. They are highly manoeuvrable, economical to operate, and usually have suitable accommodation to house modern surveying equipment. In many cases the same tug can also be quickly adapted to tow a rake or plough.

The towing methods used are not in any way unusual. Hopper barges vary in size considerably, as does the length of journey to the dumping ground. Barges with a carrying capacity of 1,000 tonnes or more are common and in some instances the tug is required to make long voyages towing loaded craft out to sea to be discharged. On other occasions spoil may be taken to a pumping plant where it will be pumped ashore for reclamation purposes. The tug may also be required to reposition the dredger, pumping plant, and floating pipelines. This often entails

Among the many small tugs engaged in dredging, using a towed plough, is the Dutch built Herman Sr, *seen here with its plough clearly visible.* Herman Sr *is a single-screw vessel of 15.85 m in length powered by a 575 bhp Caterpillar engine, operated in Britain by H&S Marine Ltd.* (Author)

re-laying the anchors used to keep the dredger in the correct position. Winches on board the dredger are used to control its position by hauling on the anchor cables. The tugs selected for a particular dredging operation are chosen with all these factors in mind.

Anchor-handling for a dredger is little different in principle to the operations carried out at sea for large oil rigs. The smaller anchors used with dredging craft may weigh a couple of tonnes or so and the tug may be required to recover and re-lay them when necessary. Using a modern tug, with an open stern and a stern roller, the anchor will be taken on deck or suspended just below the stern roller and secured using the tug's winch wire whilst being 'run out' to a new position.

Much of the work carried out by dredging companies is concerned with land reclamation and improving and maintaining coastal defences. Using modern suction dredgers, it is now common practice to pump ashore, or redistribute, vast quantities of sand and ballast. This is carried out using the powerful pumps installed aboard the dredgers and, often long, lengths of rigid steel or floating flexible hose. The pipes and hoses can be up to one metre in diameter and sometimes several hundreds of metres in length, enabling the dredger to remain safely afloat offshore. Assembling and laying these pipelines requires considerable skill and effort. Shallow draft tugs and multi-purpose work vessels, built with the dredging and marine construction industries in mind, are ideal for the purpose and designed to enable dredging pipes to be taken on board during assembly, dismantling and repair.

133

An operation that is carried out by dredging tugs throughout Europe and elsewhere is raking or ploughing. These terms refer to a very old process that has experienced something of a revival in recent years due to changes in modern dredging methods. To carry out the work a tug is used to tow a specially constructed steel rake along the sea or river bed to move unwanted mud or silt from around berths, moorings and in shipping channels. Often the tug works in conjunction with a self-propelled suction dredger and moves the spoil way from shallow areas and jetties to a point where the dredger can manoeuvre easily to pick it up for dumping at sea. This is a much cheaper method of keeping harbours cleared to the correct depth than employing more specialised dredgers. In order to carry out this work the tug requires a small winch and some form of A-frame on the after deck to raise and lower the rake, which is usually towed by means of two chains or wires secured amidships, one on either side of the tug.

Sophisticated electronic surveying equipment is increasingly employed by major dredging companies to enable accurate depth soundings to be carried out prior to, during, and after dredging operations. This work is important to ensure that the correct depths have been achieved and the required amount of spoil removed. This equipment is often installed in one of the supporting tugs and may comprise depth-sounding equipment, coupled to an electronic charting system, to enable an accurate picture of the sea or river bed to be displayed on visual display units and recorded in the form of a printed chart.

Tugs in Marine Civil Engineering

The marine civil engineering industry is involved in construction projects such as bridges, tunnels, new port installations, and increasingly the redevelopment of old dock systems throughout the world. Perhaps a less obvious area of the work is the continual improvement of sea defences and beaches, and the reclamation of new areas from the sea. As with the dredging industry, that is also heavily involved in some of this work, the use of tugs is almost unavoidable. Much of the work to be done, such as pile-driving, excavation and the installation of concrete and steel structures, can only be done using floating plant and equipment. Cranes, piling barges, work platforms and barges for the transportation of materials all require assistance from tugs. Small, powerful, twin-screw tugs, tug/workboats and multi-purpose work vessels have proved ideal for such tasks. Much of the work, particularly with respect to sea defences, requires craft with sufficient power to handle unwieldy barges or pieces of floating plant but with a draft shallow enough to work close inshore without constant risk of damage. The work of tugs and other vessels engaged on civil engineering projects is arduous and not unlike that carried out in the dredging industry, as previously described. Working close alongside other vessels and pieces of floating plant for long periods, sometimes in a moderate swell, demands tugs of sturdy construction with carefully designed fendering.

Also gaining in popularity, as previously mentioned, is the multi-purpose work vessel, widely known as the 'multi-cat'. The 'multi-cat' has proved to be a very useful vessel to the civil engineer due to its shallow draft, generous deck space, powerful deck crane and ability to tow. They are well suited to supporting pipe-laying, lifting, piling and diving operations. Most vessels of this type have a large portion of the hull divided into tanks for diesel fuel and fresh water, and are usually fitted with suitable transfer equipment to enable them to supply other vessels or plant.

Yogi *is a modern triple-screw Damen MultiCat of 26 m in length with a beam of 11.5 m, powered by three Caterpillar main engines generating a total of 2,435 bhp. With a bollard pull of 32 tonnes, a towing/anchor-handling winch and two powerful cranes,* Yogi *is employed on dredging, construction and wind farm projects.* (Author)

Among the growing list of projects that now fall in the marine civil engineering category are the construction of offshore wind farms and other alternative sources of energy such as tide and wave power. Many shallow-draft tugs and work vessels are finding employment in this sector. New wind farms are frequently situated in shallow coastal waters and the tugs and work vessels described in earlier paragraphs are ideal for supporting the specialised craft used to erect the wind turbine towers. Wind-farm projects also involve cable-laying and transporting personnel and equipment during final assembly and testing.

Fish Dock Tugs

In the early days of towage, the fishing industry made good use of tugs to assist sailing vessels into port. A small number of tugs are still employed by the industry throughout the world but in a quite different way. Once trawlers arrive in port after a lengthy voyage they are normally berthed to unload and the crews paid off. The vessel may then be required to move several times, to be repaired, refuelled, and prepared for the next trip. Without a crew, it is regarded as a 'dead ship' and generally moved around the harbour by a tug. The tugs engaged in this work are often small single-screw diesel vessels of about 300–500 bhp. Most of the towing is done with the tug fastened alongside its charge. This method requires no crew on the fishing vessel to steer or handle lines. A tug with a sturdy hull and good fendering is required. It must be a 'handy' vessel, sufficiently manoeuvrable to work in the frequently congested confines of a fish dock. In some parts of the world, where substantial fishing fleets are based, a larger tug may be employed to provide support for fishing vessels at sea. Such a vessel is used to tow home trawlers with machinery defects, transfer fuel and stores and provide similar services.

Among the smallest vessels employed by the Canadian timber trade are 'dozer tugs' such as the Tidal 5. *These 'one-man' vessels are powered by a single diesel engine coupled to a small fully steerable azimuthing propulsion unit, resulting in an extremely agile craft for sorting individual logs when making up sections and booms for towage.* (Author)

Tugs in the Timber Business

In Canada, North America, Scandinavia, and other areas where forestry is a thriving industry, timber is still transported by water in one form or another. Tugs are often involved in the process of getting tree trunks from riverside sites to sawmills using the rivers and coastal waterways. The timber industry in British Columbia and the American north-west in particular employs large numbers of

Harken No. 6 is photographed working with a typical log boom tow in Canada's Fraser River. The twin-screw tug is only 11 m in length, has main engines generating a total of 608 bhp, has very little freeboard and is highly manoeuvrable. Note the array of floodlights at the top of its very tall mast – essential when making up log booms at night. (Author)

small and medium-size tugs. Once logs are placed in the water they are made up into rafts, known as 'sections', about 20 metres square. The sections are then coupled together using chains to form a 'boom' capable of being towed long or short distances as required. Depending on the route and river conditions a complete boom can be anything up to 30 'sections' in length – with 10–15 sections being quite common on busy rivers where other traffic has to be considered. Very small tugs are used to marshal the logs and sections at either end of the journey and larger and more powerful vessels undertake the long-distance tows.

Alternatively, logs may be transported for longer coastal journeys on special barges equipped for rapid loading and unloading. Where timber is to be pulped for the manufacture of paper or used in other wood-based products it may be reduced to wood chips at a plant near the forestry site. The chips are then transported in huge, high-sided barges to the paper mills or factories.

The vessels engaged in this work, with log booms and barges, are of heavily reinforced steel construction and average between 9 m and 14 m in length. A high-proportion are twin-screw, with keel cooling to enable them to work in shallow water, and fitted with propulsion nozzles to give maximum bollard pull. Most tugs working in or around the timber industry have a series of forward-facing teeth fitted to the stem, beneath the bow, to give the tug some grip on the logs when pushing them into position. Towing winches are fitted on all but the very smallest vessels to assist with handling the towing gear for log booms and barges.

Preservation and Leisure Use

No chapter on small tugs would be complete without the mention of the many small tugs, and some not so small, that at the end of their working lives end up in the hands of private owners of groups of enthusiasts. An interest in tugs is almost a national sport in several countries. There are two main aspects to this interest in owning and caring for what are more commonly known simply as 'Tugboats' to many people. A strong desire to preserve something from our maritime history is overwhelming in many individuals and small groups and an elderly tug, often a vessel of great character, frequently benefits from that enthusiasm. To preserve, refurbish, and care for a vessel of any size is a significant undertaking and even a modest-sized tug can still be a major undertaking. Many elderly tugs around the world, still in good working order, owe their longevity to dedicated individuals and groups of enthusiasts.

Another aspect of tug ownership is the private individual who is looking for a vessel as a yacht for purely leisure purposes. In countries such as the Netherlands many dozens of small tugs are in private hands for just this purpose. Again the character inherent in so many tugs is the major appeal, along with a manageable size and reliable machinery. It is certainly not for the amount of accommodation – the largest space in tugs of almost any size is the engine-room.

In both cases the effect is the same: an increasing number of elderly tugs are being maintained in excellent condition and remain part of our maritime heritage.

The diesel tug Kent *is a former ship-handling and barge tug renovated and beautifully kept in running order by the South Eastern Tug Society at Chatham in the UK. Kent was built for J. P. Knight Ltd of Rochester in 1948, a single-screw tug of 26.8 m, powered by a direct reversing British Polar main engine rated at 880 bhp running at 275 rpm. (P. Barker)*

CHAPTER 6

Ship-Handling and Coastal Tugs

S hip-handling and coastal towage is regarded by many as the 'core business' of the towage industry. From a commercial and technical point of view this sector of the industry continues to change at an alarming rate. As previously mentioned, the first few years of the new millennium saw the introduction of three completely new types of tug – the 'Rotor Tug', 'SDM' and 'Z-Tech' – all of which are now in service in the ship-handling business. A great deal of money and effort continues to be expended by owners, naval architects, and propulsion manufacturers to refine the vessels and equipment even further and to meet current and future environmental standards.

There is no doubt that the ship-handling and coastal-towing sector will continue to develop. Ship-handling tugs will be needed in significant numbers for the foreseeable future. There are certain types of ship that will always require tug assistance and port areas that will remain accessible to ships only if towage can be provided. In many parts of the world individual fleet sizes continue to reduce but demand for new tug fleets is growing. During 2007–8 more tugs were on order, building or entering service than at any other time in the history of the industry. That growth is due to new and expanding ports in developing countries and a significant increase in the transportation of liquid natural gas by sea. This has resulted in new terminals being opened to distribute and receive LNG cargoes. A massive increase in the size of container ships has also had a significant effect on demands for improved tugs and tug services. The construction of terminals for oil, gas and bulk cargoes in locations with challenging weather and tidal conditions has also had a profound effect on tug design and research into this mode of operation continues.

Routine ship-handling services also include escort and emergency response duties in many ports. There are additional services involving the use of tugs to accompany very large ships, usually with volatile or otherwise hazardous cargoes, to and from locations well outside the seaward limits of the ports concerned.

A massive increase in the shipment of liquid natural gas by sea has created added demands on tug companies to provide service of a very high standard at the various importing and exporting terminals. Tugs from the Adsteam fleet (now Svitzer) assist the gas tanker Berge Arzew *on its first visit to a new UK terminal in the Medway.*

Purpose-built escort tugs and their equipment are described in Chapter 7 but the ship-handling aspects of their work are covered later in this chapter.

Tug owners in the ship-handling business exist to provide the services mentioned above but remain under constant pressure to do so at a reasonable cost, while facing increasing demands for power, performance and sophisticated equipment. Commercial pressures continue to have a profound effect on tug design and operation. Tug owners now have a wider choice of hull and propulsion technology available to them than ever before, the aim being to meet the demands of their clients effectively, safely, and economically. This chapter attempts to show how those choices are being exercised and give some idea of what ship-handling entails.

Coastal tugs involved in the towage of ships, barges and other floating plant have been included in the same category as ship-handling vessels because the two types are so often fully interchangeable. In many parts of the world there is a thriving coastal towage sector, where tugs and barges are the principal means of transport for a wide variety of cargoes. The tugs involved in those services are in many cases also used for ship-handling in their home ports.

THE TUG OWNERS

The ownership of ship-handling tugs is rarely a simple matter of local commercial interests. In the major ports of the western world individual tug fleets continue to

This picture shows the 24 m 'compact' stern-drive tug Adsteam Shotley *(now* Svitzer Shotley*) after assisting the container ship* Olivia Maersk. *The 5,600 bhp, 69-tonne bollard pull tug was subsequently taken over with the Adsteam fleet, joining the massive Svitzer organisation and part of the A. P. Møller (Maersk) group.* (Author)

get smaller and the influence of major multinational tug-owning groups is increasing. The effects of 'globalisation' in all aspects of tug operation, procurement and construction are having a profound effect on the industry. Multinational companies, based in Europe, Australasia, Scandinavia, the United States of America, and the Far East now control a significant share of the world's towage companies. There are now groups of companies operating fleets totalling in excess of 500 vessels worldwide and some of those groups continue to expand.

Individual tug fleets operated under the umbrella of these large groups are generally quite small, employing anything from 1–10 vessels in each of the various ports. In Britain, for example, the Svitzer group provides towage services covering virtually every major port. Svitzer is a member of the Danish A. P. Møller – Maersk group which operates a fleet of over 500 tugs in 35 countries worldwide. In recent years the company has acquired, among others, the Australian group Adsteam Marine and Dutch-based Wijsmuller group. Those acquisitions gave Svitzer a major share of the towage markets in western Europe, Australasia and the Pacific. This pattern is repeated with Moran, Foss and Crowley in the USA and Pacific, Grupo Boluda in Spain, France and South America, and Smit International in the Netherlands, Belgium, South America and many other locations worldwide.

By operating internationally in this way towage organisations are able to deal with ship owners on a global basis, often with some financial advantages for both parties. A useful by-product of group ownership is additional flexibility and improved vessel utilisation. The ability to transfer tugs of various types from one location to another within the group ensures that vessels are properly employed and that individual ports have the most suitable craft available, and this is now taking place on a global scale. There are also benefits to be gained from the purchasing power of a large group and the collective experience of employees working in different operational environments.

141

Within Europe there is stiff competition among tug operators serving the major ports, often resulting in volatile situations, originally reported in the press as 'Tug Wars'. This competition has resulted in Dutch tug companies operating fleets in German ports and various alliances being formed in Holland, Belgium, France and elsewhere.

Small independent operators in the ship-handling business continue to suffer mixed fortunes, particularly in the major ports of the world. Few ports have sufficient business to support more than one or two independent tug companies. Major established towage companies in some locations face fierce competition from smaller independent operators and foreign groups bidding for specific ship-handling contracts. This has resulted in substantial reductions in the rates charged for towage operations, a situation welcomed by the ship owner but increasing the pressure on tug owners to reduce costs. The only remedy available to many companies is to employ fewer vessels, and often more sophisticated tugs that can be operated by smaller crews.

A large proportion of the French harbour towage fleets, formerly owned by Bourbon, are now operated by the Spanish Boluda Group. The nine tugs pictured in Le Havre are operated by Boluda, in a highly competitive and increasingly global market. (Boluda)

Many specialist services, involving fire-fighting, tanker-handling and escorting for example, require huge capital investment in vessels and are beyond the means of many smaller independent operators. This is particularly the case at the growing number of LNG terminals where both the tugs employed and the operating procedures have to meet very high standards. Tug fleets are likely to be employed on long-term contracts of up to 20 years in some cases, to allow investment in 'state of the art' vessels. The services provided are likely to include escort duties, fire-fighting cover and other supporting services such as enforcing exclusion zones around LNG tankers while they are on the loading/unloading berths.

In the present commercial climate, most major port authorities prefer not to become involved with providing towage services using their own vessels. In very small ports, where towage assistance is necessary but where levels of traffic are low, services may be provided by the harbour authority, a small local operator, or by one of the larger groups. In the interests of economy it is sometimes worthwhile to employ a tug from a neighbouring port, entailing a short coastal passage, or manning it only when it is required.

Ship-handling at naval bases in most of the major countries has traditionally been undertaken by fleets of tugs owned and operated by the navy concerned. In the past this has resulted in large resident tug fleets maintained almost exclusively for the purpose. As the number of warships requiring tug assistance has declined, as part of the so-called peace dividend, tug fleets have also been reduced. In many cases towage work has been put into the hands of commercial operators in order to cut costs. The type of work done at naval establishments involves ship-handling of the kind described later and some coastal operation.

The Voith tractor Bustler *is one of a fleet of tugs taken over from the British Ministry of Defence now owned and operated by Serco Denholm, a contractor providing a wide range of marine services to all UK naval bases. Seen escorting an aircraft carrier,* Bustler *was built in 1981 and is a vessel of 38.8 m in length and 2,640 bhp.* (Author)

Coastal towage is an activity that in many areas goes hand in hand with the ship-handling business. Some tug owners whose principal business is operating ship-handling tugs derive useful additional revenue from coastal towing or offshore operations, which also helps to ensure that tugs are fully utilised. To this end, major fleets often include vessels suitably equipped for coastal and short sea voyages with ships, barges, or contracting plant in tow. Such vessels are equally capable of providing assistance to disabled ships in need of towage in coastal areas.

In many parts of the world, and the coastal regions of the USA and Canada in particular, coastal and short sea towing with cargo barges is an important business and the core activity for many companies. Large fleets of tugs are employed to service barges carrying bulk cargoes, vehicles and shipping containers, operated by specialist companies or subsidiaries of major towing concerns. Coastal towing is also an activity that attracts the small owner or one-man business. In remote areas, such as Alaska and many island groups in the Pacific, many small towns and outposts receive supplies of fuel and other essential goods almost exclusively by tug and barge services.

TUGS FOR SHIP-HANDLING

As mentioned in Chapter 1, a wide variety of tug types are used for ship-handling operations. The choice available to tug owners is greater than ever before, including conventional screw tugs, stern-drive vessels, the Z-Tech, Voith and azimuthing tractors, Rotor Tugs and SDMs.

Stern drive tug Smit Barbados *applies full power astern to stop and control the container ship* CSCL Xiamen *as it enters a lock in the UK port of Liverpool. The tug is powered by Caterpillar main engines of 4,930 bhp and has a bollard pull of 58 tonnes.* (Author)

The major factors governing the type of vessel used include the operational environment and the size of ships to be handled, as well as building, manning, and running costs. Limitations placed on hull size and construction may apply to all of the available types. The maximum size of many ship-handling vessels may be governed by the size of locks and dock entrances or the size and depth of the waterways. Where locks are concerned, it is often desirable for tugs to occupy the same lock as the ship being assisted or to be small enough to pass along its side. Those limitations will apply regardless of the tug type but there is a current downward trend in the size of harbour tugs. Many new designs being produced in large numbers fall in the 'compact' category and well below the norm of over 30 metres of 25 years ago.

A tug operating in exposed locations, or involved in coastal work, may require a hull with a raised forecastle to improve its sea-keeping qualities and help to keep the decks, where men have to work, free of water. A good free-running speed is a common requirement for ship-handling tugs to enable them to move quickly between tasks and possibly escort ships in the seaward approaches to a port. Figures of 12–14 knots are common, regardless of propulsion system.

Conventional Screw Tugs

The number of conventional screw tugs, employing open-screw propellers, Kort nozzles and other thrust-augmenting devices, is rapidly declining in the major ship-handling fleets of the world. This time-honoured type is quickly being replaced by vessels employing tractor or stern-drive propulsion systems. In major British and European ship-handling fleets the remaining tugs with conventional screw propulsion fall into two distinct categories, the older traditional single- and twin-screw tugs and smaller modern twin-screw vessels.

The former are rapidly disappearing. Those remaining in service vary in size from 25–40 metres in length and 150 gross tons upwards, ranging in power from 1,000–3,500 bhp. At the larger end of the scale they have bollard pulls of up to 50 tonnes and are used for work with large ships, or engaged in a high proportion of seagoing operations. The real advantage of the deep-draft Kort-nozzle tug is its ability to produce a high bollard pull at moderate power settings. By modern standards, its handling characteristics may be limited but quite adequate for the work that it does. Relatively large tugs of this type, employed as part of a ship-handling fleet, are often equipped with suitable deck and navigational equipment to enable them to operate efficiently at sea. Towing winches, carrying towlines suitable for both harbour towage and sea work on separate drums, are fitted to enable them to change roles with a minimum of additional preparation.

Smaller, modern, twin-screw tugs of 19–26 metres in length remain popular in smaller ports for ship-handling and some coastal work. Many of the most recent designs are well-equipped vessels with bollard pulls of between 20 and 45 tonnes capable of providing a good level of assistance for medium-sized ships.

An important feature of any tug intended to work with ships is its ability to reposition itself quickly during the towing operation, in order to apply power in

The twin-screw tug Smit Japan, *built in 1986, is from the fleet of Smit International Harbour Towage in Rotterdam. Seen here assisting a large tanker, it is a vessel of 28.60 m in length with two Stork Werkspoor main engines producing 2,400 bhp and driving twin screws revolving in Kort nozzles.* (Author)

Vera Bisso, *owned by the Bisso Towboat Company of New Orleans, is a modern twin-screw tug designed for ship-handling and other duties. The 32 m long tug has two EMD diesel engines giving a total of 3,900 bhp driving propellers rotating within Kort nozzles. Note the clear after deck and towing winches fore and aft.* (Bisso)

the required direction. In this respect the conventional screw tug is somewhat limited and can in fact be endangered by the vessel in tow. One of the most common hazards is the risk of being capsized by the towline if the ship makes an unexpected movement when the tug has the towline over its beam whilst repositioning. This phenomenon, known as 'girting', 'girding' or in North America 'tripping', has been responsible for the loss of many tugs. Among the safety features used in modern conventional tugs to minimise the risk are righting arms on tow hooks and the use of gog ropes. These have been described in preceding chapters. The ability of a modern tractor or stern-drive vessel to reposition easily and safely is probably its most important advantage when compared with the conventional screw tug.

The USA was initially slower than many other countries to move away from tug designs employing the conventional screw propeller. Only in the last ten years has the popularity of tractor and stern-drive vessels begun to accelerate dramatically among owners in the ship-handling sector. Twin-screw tugs with conventional screw propulsion systems are still built in the USA in large numbers, particularly for owners engaged in ship-handling and coastal towing. The majority of modern conventional tugs employed to handle ships are twin-screw vessels, often with fixed nozzles of the Kort type. An additional refinement may be the installation of flanking rudders, fitted ahead of the propellers. The power ratings quoted for some of the most recent vessels are as high as 6,000 bhp. Although comparable in size to their European counterparts, the American tug is often of heavier construction. The ship-handling methods used in the USA demand much more contact with the ship and thus pose an increased risk of damage. Towing bollards are still in use in many fleets, fitted on the foredeck and aft, with towing winches installed aft on the more powerful and versatile vessels. In the last few decades the towing gear on some American tugs has been installed further forward than was common in the past, closely resembling European practice. This is usually the case in vessels intended to work extensively with a towrope over the stern, rather than close alongside the tow.

The conventional screw tugs used for ship-handling in many American and Canadian ports are very much multi-purpose vessels, employed in fleets engaged in both ship-handling and barge-towing. Such vessels are fitted with all of the equipment necessary for their alternative roles and particular attention is paid to fuel capacity and consumption. Many of the barges are very large and the journeys on rivers and coasts very long. Barges are pushed or towed depending on the circumstances. The process of pushing barges is dealt with in Chapter 9.

Tractor Tugs

The tractor tug has become a very popular means of assisting ships, particularly in ports where there are enclosed docks or riverside berths requiring intricate manoeuvres in difficult tidal conditions. The first tractors, introduced with the Voith Schneider propulsion system, brought a new dimension to the work. Their ability to apply thrust in any direction and handle equally well when going astern offered many new possibilities. Operating with the towline secured close to the stern virtually eliminates the possibility of the tug being capsized by its tow, improving safety considerably. Use of the tractor concept has spread to ports throughout the world. Voith Schneider tractor tugs of over 5,000 bhp, with bollard

Fratelli Neri is one of a new class of 'compact' azimuthing tractor tugs built for Fratelli Neri spa of Livorno, Italy, in 2007. Only 23.8 m long and 12 m in beam, the tug has two Caterpillar diesels of 5,706 bhp powering two Schottel propulsion units. The tug has a bollard pull of 65 tonnes and is very well equipped for such a small vessel. (RAL)

Wolf *is a Voith tractor tug, forming part of the tug fleet operated in Bremerhaven and Hamburg by German tug owners Bugsier Reederie and typical of many similar vessels operating in Europe.* Wolf *was built in 1993, is 31.57 m in length and powered by two MAK main engines of 3,944 bhp (total) driving two Voith propulsion units.* (B. Dahlmann)

pulls in excess of 50 tonnes are now common. Such vessels are also used at sea, particularly when awkward positioning operations are carried out with barges or floating structures. A continuing emphasis on escort services for very large ships has resulted in the development of large, powerful, and highly sophisticated Voith tractor tugs for use at oil and gas terminals. These vessels are designed to make maximum use of their large underwater skeg in the indirect towing mode. The use of Voith tractor tugs in escort towing is described in Chapter 7.

Tractor tugs incorporating azimuthing propulsion units have been chosen by some operators for ship-handling and occasionally coastal towing but have fallen from favour thanks to the continuing development of stern-drive designs. This type of tractor combines the higher bollard pulls possible with the azimuthing unit with the inherent advantages of the tractor concept. A factor governing the use of tractors of either type may well be their draft. Although the overall draft may be no more than a deep conventional screw tug, the position of the propulsion units protruding from the hull bottom plating makes them particularly vulnerable. In spite of nozzle or guard plates, the propellers of both types can be subject to damage if the tug is grounded. An objection raised by some owners is the additional complexity and cost of supporting this type of vessel during dry-docking or hauling out onto a slipway.

The SDM Endeavor *is shown assisting a bulk carrier with other vessels from Marine Towing of Tampa. Built in 1999, the vessel is powered by two Wärtsilä main engines producing a total of 4,000 bhp and a bollard pull of 50 tons that can be applied in almost any direction. (Author)*

The new alternative tractor designs, the Ship Docking Module and the Rotor Tug, offer additional advantages when ship-handling, if compared with the original azimuthing tractor concept. Although the two designs differ dramatically, both have the ability to apply a very large proportion of their bollard pull to the towline whilst moving sideways. In some ship-handling operations this can offer a distinct advantage. In the case of the SDM, it is highly praised for its manoeuvrability and ability to deal with large ships, but its sizeable beam and almost elliptical planform makes it an unwieldy vessel for use in locks and enclosed dock systems. The vessel is first and foremost an excellent ship-handler but lacks the versatility of many other designs. The Rotor Tug has proved to be not only an efficient and very powerful tractor tug for ship-handling but extremely useful in a number of other roles, such as coastal towing, and work with barges and rigs in the offshore oil industry.

Stern-Drive Tugs and the Z-Tech

A high proportion of new tugs entering service with ship-handling fleets are of the azimuthing stern-drive type. As we have seen, the basic design was first conceived in the Far East but the concept has spread rapidly in the last 15 years or so to fleets in most parts of the world. Britain and Europe were slower to adopt the concept as were operators in North America and Canada, a situation that has rapidly been reversed.

A powerful propulsion system, sophisticated hull design, an efficient towing winch, a sophisticated central control station, and accommodation for a small crew make up the basic specification for many new tugs. The stern-drive ship-handling vessel is always, by its nature, a twin-screw tug. Close-quarters towing whilst ship-handling is invariably carried out by towing astern using a towing winch located on the fore-deck. Operating in this way the tug is remarkably agile and can reposition, or move in to push with its fendered bow, very quickly. In this mode of operation, the risk of girting is virtually nil. The bollard pull and free-running speed when going ahead or astern are almost identical in the majority of

The stern-drive Svitzer Milford *is one of a series ten similar ('M' class) tugs built in 2004 by Svitzer for use in various UK and European ports.* Svitzer Milford *is 30 m long and fitted with two MAK diesel main engines of 4,890 bhp (total) coupled to Rolls-Royce propulsion units with controllable-pitch propellers giving a bollard pull of 60 tonnes.* (Author)

vessels. Coastal work or operations requiring a much longer towline are carried out from a second winch or tow hook at the stern, in much the same way as with a conventional screw tug.

The introduction of the Z-Tech and advanced azimuthing stern-drive tugs with deep box keels has added a new dimension to ship-handling. Both concepts enable the vessels to be used very effectively in the indirect towing mode of operation whilst working with large ships. The Z-Tech is capable of taking matters one stage further, offering true omni-directional operation. When it is necessary for the tug to tow at sea it simply travels in the opposite direction using the same winch and benefiting from a 'bow-shaped' stern that is configured for the purpose.

Vicky M. McAllister, *built for McAllister Towing & Transportation in 2001, has a configuration now common among US-designed stern-drive tugs. This example is 29.26 m long, with two EMD main engines generating 5,000 bhp (total) coupled to Schottel propulsion units and giving a bollard pull of 58 tonnes.* (Eastern SB)

SHIP-HANDLING OPERATIONS

Handling ships with the use of tugs is a huge subject on which many volumes have been written, by highly qualified ships' pilots and ships' captains. The paragraphs that follow are intended to give but a very brief overview, showing

Bocas Del Toro (2007) is one of a large series of Z-Tech tugs purchased for use in the Panama Canal. Designated the Z-Tech 6000 type, they measure 27.4 m long and 11.65 m beam and have Wärtsilä main engines producing 4,890 bhp to drive Lips propulsion units. These highly agile tugs have a bollard pull of 60 tonnes and a free-running speed of 12.5 knots. (RAL)

how the various types of modern tug are used and some of the more common ship-handling situations.

Tugs are employed to assist ships that, due to their size or design, are not capable of manoeuvring safely under their own power in the confines of the ports they may have to visit at either end of a voyage. Likewise a port may have wharves or other facilities that cannot be accessed by ships of a certain size or type without the assistance of tugs. The circumstances can vary from the use of a single relatively unsophisticated harbour tug assisting a medium-sized ship to its berth in a small port to a complicated operation involving several powerful tugs working with a modern tanker or bulk carrier of several hundred thousand tonnes.

The Need for Tugs

The need for tug assistance is determined by a multitude factors. The size of the ship in relation to the area it is to enter, the need to negotiate locks, pass through bridges, or perform other complex manoeuvres to berth or unberth are all common reasons for employing some form of tug assistance. Difficult tidal conditions or high winds can impose severe limits on the handling of a ship in a confined waterway and many small or medium-sized ships require assistance only when weather conditions are very poor. For example, large modern car and passenger ferries are well-equipped ships designed to handle well in all but the very worst weather conditions, but such vessels have very large superstructures that make them extremely susceptible to the effects of the wind in very bad conditions. A high wind, directly on its beam, may prevent such a ship berthing or leaving safely without the assistance of a tug.

Larger ships have additional problems, related to their sheer bulk and the enormous amount of kinetic energy inherent in their mass. A large ship, moving only very slowly, has sufficient stored energy to do a vast amount of damage should it collide with another object or even make contact with a jetty too heavily.

151

It is the duty of the attendant tugs to assist such ships, slow them down, move them onto their berth and stop any forward or sideways movement at exactly the right moment to prevent damage. The ship may need to be turned ('swung' in towage terms) in order to present the correct side to the berth for loading or discharge, and positioned precisely fore and aft to enable cranes or other handling equipment to be used effectively. Dock systems are often entered through locks and once inside can be congested, with narrow passages between the various basins. Tugs may be required to carry out these operations in a variety of weather conditions, which alone can pose serious problems for large unwieldy vessels.

Many jetties and terminals built solely for the shipment of various ores, coal, oil or gas are situated in remote and exposed locations. Tugs giving assistance at facilities of this kind may be faced with difficult tidal conditions and/or a heavy swell. Such harsh conditions present particular difficulties with regard to towing gear and fendering, and require exceptional skill on the part of the tugmasters and pilots.

Whether or not a ship requires the assistance of tugs is often an automatic decision. Many ports have by-laws or regulations laying down strict rules governing pilotage and towage. These rules generally place limits on the size and type of ship that can navigate in the area without tugs. Rules and procedures laid

A typical tanker berthing operation is depicted in this picture of tugs from the Spanish owned Boluda group working at the Charco Azul oil terminal on the Pacific coast of Panama. Four tugs are holding the 154,348 gt tanker Crude Progress *in position whilst the mooring lines are secured.* (Boluda)

down by the ship's owners, insurance underwriters, wharf or terminal operators can also demand the assistance of tugs for certain vessels and circumstances. These rules frequently give precise instructions on the number, type and power of the tugs to be used. When a very large ship enters port, decisions regarding its movements, pilotage, and towage are usually made well in advance, leaving little to chance. In many such cases a formal 'passage plan' is agreed in advance and communicated by fax or email.

Computer Simulation

It is now common practice to use computer simulation to determine the way that ship-handling operations are to be conducted, to train tug crews and pilots and to evaluate new tug designs. Computer simulation is particularly valuable when a major new towage situation arises: for example where new berths are being commissioned for very large ships, a different type of ship is to use a facility, or new vessels are joining the tug fleet. Computer programmes used for the work simulate local geography, tide and wind conditions, a ship's handling characteristics and the operational characteristics of each of the tugs employed. During a simulated ship-handling operation the positions of the tugs and their towing connections can be determined, and the heading of each tug and the power it exerts can be changed at will – in exactly the same way as in an actual towage operation – the main difference being that the ship on the computer screen cannot be damaged or run aground causing expensive damage. From the information derived, decisions can be made regarding the number, position, and power of all the assisting tugs and the optimum methods of carrying out a particular manoeuvre. As tugs have become more sophisticated and more powerful, computer simulation has become an essential tool in determining precisely how they will be used.

Computer-based simulators are also being used to train tugmasters, pilots, and vessel traffic controllers, in order to achieve safe and efficient ship-handling services. In some of the more sophisticated simulators the entire layout of a ship's bridge is reproduced, allowing ships' masters and pilots to practice a wide variety of manoeuvres. This includes the use of tugs for docking and undocking and the tugmasters are included, having their own realistic simulated bridge, controls and communications. The simulator has available the operating profiles of various full-size tugs, which are used and directed in exactly the same way as in real life. The effects of the tugs pulling or pushing are then apparent on the behaviour of the ship. Simulation work of this kind is generally undertaken by specialist maritime institutions or training establishments with strong links with the towage industry.

The Role of the Pilot

The role of the pilot during ship-handling operations using tugs is an important one. Pilotage arrangements differ from country to country, but in all cases the pilot

The simulator at the Lairdside Maritime Centre at Birkenhead on Merseyside, UK, is used to train tugmasters and pilots, and to evaluate methods of handling various ships and the tugs required. The system in use has identical controls to a Voith tractor with displays of radar images, electronic charts and data from the tug's propulsion system. A set of controls, for an azimuthing stern-drive tug are visible in the background. (Lairdside)

is an individual with specific local knowledge of the port, its tides, and the effects of weather on the movement of ships. In most ports the use of a pilot is mandatory for ships above a certain size. Throughout Britain and Europe pilots are supplied either by the port authority or by a pilotage organisation and join ships entering or leaving the area to advise the ship's master on the safe navigation of his vessel. Similar systems operate in many other parts of the world. In the USA the pilot may well be a senior tugmaster, from one of the tugs assisting the ship, put on board to take charge of the operation. It is necessary for a pilot, using tugs in a modern port, to have a sound knowledge of the capability of the various tugs in use and appreciate the advantages and disadvantages of the various propulsion systems. During a ship-handling operation the pilot is in charge of the tugs and communicates his orders directly to the tugmasters by VHF radio. The use of whistle signals between tug and ship has been superseded by radio in most ports, except in emergencies.

BASIC SHIP-HANDLING MANOEUVRES

To the experienced tugmaster every towage operation is unique: different weather and tidal conditions, different ships each with their own characteristics, and perhaps different pilots. All of the foregoing factors play an important part in towage operations in almost any port in the world.

The next few paragraphs are not intended as definitive examples but simply to illustrate some of the very basic manoeuvres that tugs are regularly expected to perform whilst ship-handling. They also give some indication of how these operations vary with the type of tug. The descriptions do not take into account the possible effects of wind and tide, which can transform the simplest operation into a virtual nightmare. It is also worth considering that these operations are carried out daily by tug crews, working not only in fine daylight conditions but also at night and throughout the winter months. The work has to continue in the dark, with the tug rolling and with decks and ropes covered with ice or snow. Even in the best-equipped modern tug, personnel are still required to work on deck to handle the towline and make that essential connection between ship and tug.

Picking Up the Tow

One of the most interesting operations to watch, and one requiring a great deal of skill from both tugmaster and crew, is 'picking up a tow' whilst the ship is under way. When a ship enters port, or approaches a berth, the pilot will often try to maintain sufficient speed to enable it to steer effectively until the tugs have their towlines connected. The tugs may have to approach the vessel and connect towlines with the ship moving at 5–6 knots or even faster. This can be a hazardous operation, particularly for the tug selected to take charge of the ship's bow – the

This photograph shows the stern-drive tug Svitzer Victory *manoeuvring 'bow to bow' ahead of a large container ship in order to connect its towline while both are under way. A 'heaving line' has been thrown from the ship and secured to the towline which is being hauled aboard by the ship's crew to be secured on the ship's bitts.* (Author)

'head tug'. The flow of water around the hull of a large moving ship produces a phenomenon known as 'interaction'. A situation can arise in which the tug passes into a low-pressure area adjacent to the ship's bow, causing loss of control. A mistake can result in a collision or in the tug being run down by the ship.

In order for a towline to be passed the tug will manoeuvre within a very few metres of the ship's bow. A conventional screw tug is the most vulnerable during this operation. Tractors or stern-drive tugs are able to control the thrust from their propulsion units to combat any risk of collision whilst in the interaction zone. Some stern-drive vessels are able to manoeuvre astern at speed and may use this (bow to bow) method to position the bow of the tug in readiness to connect a towline from the forward winch.

Once the tug is in position, a heaving line is thrown down from the ship to the waiting tug crew. A heaving line is a very light rope, weighted at one end so that it may be easily thrown. The heaving line is tied to the end of a light 'messenger' rope, which is used to haul the towline aboard the ship. In some ports a rope from the ship may be used, but with the special nature of modern towropes and the use of towing winches it is now more common for the tug's ropes to be used. With the towline secured, the tug can move into a towing position.

For tugs at the stern or alongside the ship, picking up the tow is slightly easier. A stern tug may be affected by wash from the ship's propeller. A conventional screw tug or stern-drive vessel will approach from astern and put its bow in a position very close to the ship's stern prior to receiving a heaving line. Tractor tugs in the same situation usually approach in the same manner but travelling stern first. Once the towing connection is made a tractor or stern-drive tug will simply drop back into a towing position paying out the towline to a convenient length. A conventional screw tug will make a towing connection on its winch or hook aft and move out to one side, continuing to go ahead parallel to the ship until the speed of the ship is reduced sufficiently to enable it to safely turn through 180 degrees and take up a towing position.

Conventional screw tugs working in American ports will move in alongside the ship and each make a connection, in the positions indicated by the pilot, with short towropes from the bow of each tug. Tugs that are to remain alongside for the whole operation may also be secured with a rope aft.

Slowing the Ship Down

Prior to positioning the ship for berthing it will be slowed down and stopped in the correct position. Using European methods, the stern tug will be positioned to tow astern and slow the ship, leaving the head tug to control the ship's direction. Under these circumstances the tug or tractor is towed along, stern first by the ship, applying power when necessary and acting rather like a rudder. A stern-drive tug will operate in much the same manner but be connected from its bow and apply power by going astern. Alternatively, the pilot will rely on the ship's own power to stop the ship and use the tugs to assist in steering.

Compact tug Svitzer Warden *uses its 69-tonne bollard pull to slow the container ship* Hyundai Tokyo *and assist with steering.* Svitzer Warden *is a 24 m vessel built by Damen to the ASD 2411 design and operated by a crew of three.* (Author)

American tugs apply power astern, selectively, at the pilot's instruction to keep the ship on course. If required, a selected tug can reposition easily and move ahead or tow astern.

When a tug is operating in the escort role the process of slowing a ship down can have entirely different implications due to the probable size of the ship, its speed and the momentum involved. Escort duties are described in Chapter 7.

To 'Swing' a Ship

Swinging a ship is a basic manoeuvre used to turn the vessel through 180 degrees, into a tide prior to berthing, or to ensure that the correct side of the ship is in contact with the quay for loading or unloading purposes. A partial 'swing', may be used to turn a ship into a lock or dock entrance. If the ship is to be turned to starboard, using European practice, the head tug will move round to tow at 90 degrees to the ship's starboard side. A stern tug will position itself similarly port and the ship will be turned bodily under the direction of the pilot. If other tugs are involved with berthing the ship they may be called in to push on bow or stern to assist or control the swing. In some cases more than one head tug will be used. If tractor tugs are used, repositioning to tow to port or starboard is a simple matter and can be achieved safely while keeping control of the towline. Again, the stern-drive tug will perform in much the same way – towing astern or pushing on the ship's bow or stern.

In order to take advantage of the modern ship-handling tug's ability to operate in a push–pull mode, the towing point aboard the ship will be selected accordingly. During a relatively straightforward berthing operation the head tug may make fast on the ship's port or starboard bow (depending on which side will go onto the quay) and stern tug will make fast on the stern quarter, on the same side. This enables the tugs to push or pull to maximum advantage as required and also control forward or astern motion.

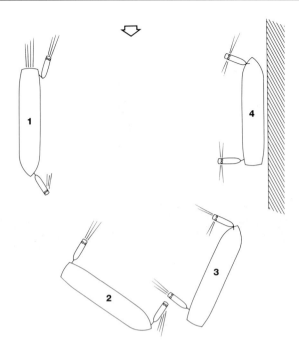

A swinging and berthing operation with modern stern-drive tugs is normally undertaken with each tug connected by a towline from its bow. The arrow indicates the direction of the tide, the direction of thrust from each of the tug's propulsion units is also shown.

The position of the tugs, and the amount of power needed, during this type of 'swinging' manoeuvre is very dependent of the 'natural pivot point' of the individual ship. Every ship has such a pivot point and its position will move fore and aft along the vessel, depending on whether the ship is moving ahead or astern. The pivot point will be estimated by the pilot and tugmaster using their experience, at any given time during the 'swinging' operation. Knowing approximately the location of the pivot point, about which the ship will turn easily, enables the tugs to be positioned where they can apply maximum 'leverage'.

If the ship is to be turned into a lock or entrance, the head tug is responsible for aligning the ship's bow with the opening. The stern tug then has the task of holding the stern in line, working to counteract any crosswind or tidal flow. Additional tugs may be deployed along the ship's side to push or guide the vessel, reducing the contact with the lock walls.

In American practice, tugs undertaking a 'swinging' operation will tow astern to port or starboard as appropriate or push on the ship's bow and stern. If tugs are positioned on either side of the ship, secured bow and stern, one will put its engines ahead and the other astern – creating a powerful turning moment. Moving the ship into an entrance is done in much the same way, pushing or backing away on the short towlines.

Berthing a Ship Alongside

Any swinging manoeuvre carried out with a ship prior to its arrival at a wharf or jetty is usually designed to end with the vessel positioned conveniently near the

Modern cruise ships rarely require the assistance of tugs unless they are berthing under very difficult circumstances or in very high winds. In this photograph Queen Elizabeth II *is being 'swung' in the confines of the River Maas on its farewell visit to Rotterdam. The azimuthing tractor tug* Thamesbank *of Smit tows the bow to port while two other tugs (out of sight) tow the stern to starboard. (H. Hoffmann)*

berth. Often this results in the ship positioned parallel to the berth but some distance away. In European practice head and stern tugs will tow towards the berth, moving the ship sideways. By co-ordinating the work of the tugs at each end the pilot can also ensure that the ship is correctly positioned longitudinally. Additional tugs may be employed to push on the vessel's side. Once the ship is close enough for mooring ropes to be passed, one or other of the tugs may be released, leaving the other to hold the ship in position against any tide or wind.

Conventional screw tug Shannon *is made secure beneath the bow of a tanker ready to push or tow astern when required. A line from its towing winch is used to help control its stern. Note the control position above the winch. (Author)*

The stern-drive tug SD Gironde *and azimuthing tractor* ZP Montelena *work together on the stern of a large ship.* SD Gironde *tows astern from its winch on the foredeck and* ZP Montelena *tows ahead from its winch on the after deck. When required either or both tugs can easily shorten their towlines and move in to push.* (H. Hoffmann)

The free tug may then be used to push on the ship's side to relieve the pressure on mooring lines until all the ropes are secure.

The use of tractors or stern-drive tugs in the operation simplifies matters considerably, since they can apply power in a push–pull fashion. A tractor will tow the ship into position in much the same way, but once the first mooring lines are passed it can adjust the length of its towline and move in quickly to push with its stern, without the need to disconnect. Stern-drive tugs, working from a bow winch, operate in the same manner.

Tugs Hopetoun *and* Cramond *from the BP fleet at Hound Point, Scotland, hold the giant tanker* Berge Sigval *(306,430 dwt) on the the berth while mooring lines are secured. The tanker was berthed after being swung, ready to depart once its cargo was discharged.* (Author)

160

American tugs carrying out the same operation remain connected by the bow and move round to push at 90 degrees to the ship. If some adjustment is required to the longitudinal position one or more tugs will move parallel to the ship and apply power in the necessary direction.

Although the practice of tugs pushing on a ship's side is an inherent part of ship-handling operations, it is undertaken with some caution. A powerful tug is capable of causing serious damage to the side plating of some ships. In a heavy swell it may be particularly difficult to keep the tug properly positioned on the ship's side. Some modern ships have marks painted along their sides indicating the correct 'pressure points' where assisting tugs may push without causing damage.

Assisting a Ship Away from a Berth

For relatively large ships, the procedure for leaving a berth is very much the reverse of that used for berthing. Depending on the size of the ship, the weather, and the need for any subsequent manoeuvres, a little less assistance may be needed. Ships are often berthed 'head down', heading downstream or towards the port entrance, having been 'swung' on arrival – simplifying matters when they depart. The head and stern tugs are connected as before and positioned initially to tow the ship sideways off the berth. Tractor or stern-drive tugs may push on the bow and stern while the mooring lines are being released, and move away to tow off when ordered by the pilot. Any additional tugs may be used to push on the ship's side and back off in the same manner. Once the ship has been moved far enough off the berth, the head tug will impart some forward motion, towing the ship in the direction it is to head. Generally, the head tug will remain connected until any other tugs have been released and the pilot is sure that the ship's steering and propulsion systems are working correctly. If the ship is to have a 'tethered' escort to the seaward limits of the port, the escort tug will remain secured to the ship's stern throughout.

In high winds even ships which do not normally need assistance from tugs may have difficulty leaving a berth without help. A ship can be held firmly against the

The Rotor Tug Innovation *assists a large car carrier from the locks at Bremerhaven. Using its unique triple-unit propulsion system, this 6,300 bhp vessel can exert its full bollard pull of up to 70 tonnes in almost any direction to control the ship's bow.* (Author)

161

quay by a stiff breeze. The assistance of just one tug may be all that is required to tow the vessel's bow or stern away from the berth and perhaps impart some forward movement. Equally, a ship may be 'blown off' the quay by adverse wind conditions. Under these circumstances tugs are used to control the ship while the moorings are released and until it is safely under way.

Indirect Towing

Considerable effort has been applied to ensure that a modern tug can apply 'indirect towing' methods as a means of exerting dynamic forces on the towline considerably greater than its static bollard pull. The masters of early steam and motor tugs, with very low bollard-pull performance, often used the weight and bulk of their vessels to exert additional force to stop or turn a ship. This was done, with careful use of a gob rope, by turning the tug at an angle to the towline and using its power to control its position – producing an effect rather like a massive rudder or sea anchor. The term 'indirect towing' is relatively new but the principles involved can be traced back to those early days of the towage industry.

Indirect towing is now often used to improve the performance of escort tugs working with very large ships, particularly ships under way, requiring assistance to stop or be steered. Many will argue that the Voith Schneider tractor tug is inherently suited to the task due to its very large underwater skeg. When acting as a stern tug, with a ship under way, the tractor is turned obliquely to the towline to produce an 'otterboard' or 'paravane effect'. The tug can be positioned to produce a steering force or braking effect of at least twice the vessel's normal bollard pull using this method. A tractor tug used extensively in this manner will be provided with an additional towing fairlead further aft than that normally used for ship-handling. The fairlead is positioned above the trailing edge of the underwater skeg to reduce steering forces when the tractor is being towed stern first.

Leader is one of a series of six tractor tugs introduced by Crowley Maritime in the USA in 1998. The vessels are 32 m Voith tractor tugs of 4,800 bhp, optimised to operate in the direct-towing mode. Note the normal towing staple aft and towing winches at each end. (Crowley)

The escort tug Boris *of Buksér og Berging is shown carrying out indirect towing trials with a large tanker under way. The tug is using its Voith propulsion units to maintain position out on the starboard quarter. In this manner the tug can exert towline forces of twice its static bollard pull.* (Buksér og Berging)

Indirect-towing methods are now used most effectively by stern-drive tugs, the Z-Tech and Rotor Tug operating in the escort role. The effectiveness of such vessels in this role has been achieved by adopting an underwater hull form that increases lateral resistance when operating at an oblique angle to the towline. Stern-drive tugs and the Z-Tech operating in this way normally tow from their forward winch and use their propulsion units to maintain position.

Stern drive tugs are capable of applying indirect towing methods to increase the line pull available to stop or steer a ship in much the same way as a tractor, by using the dynamic properties of a deep escort skeg or long box keel. Sertosa Treintaycuatro *is a 37 m terminal tug delivered in 2008 by Astilleros Armon for Remolques Ibaizabal of Spain. The tug has a static bollard pull, towing ahead, of 122 tonnes.* (Armon)

Retrieving the Towline

The final action, once a towing operation is completed, is to retrieve the towline safely without fouling the propellers of the ship or the tug itself. Even when a ship is stationary there is need for caution. A conventional screw tug, operating with a towline aft, normally moves steadily away from the ship allowing the towline to stream astern. Norman pins may be erected at the after rail to ensure that the rope does not pass over the side and become drawn into a propeller. Tugs fitted with towing winches can retrieve their ropes quickly and efficiently. Others may use some form of rope-recovery technique, using a messenger rope and a capstan or some other means of getting the rope inboard with as little manual effort as possible. Caution is also required with tractors and stern-drive tugs, though these have the advantage of the propellers being located further away from the towing gear. The master is also able to manoeuvre easily to reduce the danger of fouling the propulsion units.

COASTAL TOWING

Coastal towing is a generic term often used to cover a wide range of operations, away from the confines of the port. In Europe, voyages between neighbouring countries are often shorter than many coastal trips elsewhere but encounter similar conditions to true deep-sea towing. Coastal towing around the land masses of North and South America, Africa, Russia, and Southern Asia is quite a different matter and can involve vast distances. In the context of this chapter coastal towing covers the tasks likely to be undertaken by ship-handling tugs or vessels of similar size and type.

There are regulations governing the towage of ships and other floating objects on coastal and intercontinental voyages and these continue to become more stringent. Such regulations are laid down by the various national transport authorities, classification societies, insurers and coastguard agencies. Within the various rules and guidelines are requirements governing the size and power of tugs, suitable manning scales, the type of towing gear used, minimum standards for safety equipment and often recommendations governing the conduct of voyages. Many tugs employed primarily for ship-handling are also designed to meet the conditions laid down, in terms of manning and accommodation, power, bollard pull, and equipment. Vessels operated by companies specialising in coastal towage have to conform as a matter of course and possibly meet higher standards for worldwide operation.

The Tug and its Equipment

Obviously, the size and power of the tug used for a particular towing operation is related to the nature of the vessel to be towed. As we have already seen, vessels in the smaller tug categories also make coastal voyages under certain circumstances,

The twin-screw tug Island Scout, *built for Island Tug & Barge of Vancouver in 2006, is a coastal tug of 23.92 m powered by Cummins main engines of 1,600 bhp (total), giving a bollard pull of 25 tonnes and speed of 11 knots.* Island Scout *is used for pushing and towing fuel and other barges to towns on the coast of British Columbia and Alaska.* (Author)

and in order to do so must meet certain standards and recommendations. Tugs regularly involved in this type of work will range in power from 1,200–6,000 bhp and in size from 150–500 gross tons. Many vessels operating regularly on the coastal routes of the American continent may well be even larger and more powerful. The majority of tugs employed for coastal work will be single- or twin-screw conventional tugs with good seakeeping characteristics but a growing number of powerful stern-drive and tractor tugs are being used for coastal and short sea towing.

A tug equipped for regular coastal work will be fitted with a suitable towing winch to enable the length of the towline to be adjusted with a minimum of effort. Such winches are usually of the drum type and are likely to carry at least one steel wire towline of 600–1,000 metres in length. Much longer towlines are needed for towing at sea than for harbour or ship-handling work. It is now rare for a tug without a towing winch to be used for towing operations of this type. If no winch is fitted the crew will require a powerful capstan or some other aid to handle the towline, particularly at either end of the voyage.

The range of a tug employed in coastal towing may be a serious issue for some operators. Tugs from ship-handling fleets working around the coasts of Europe are likely to have sufficiently large fuel tanks to carry out the majority of short sea operations. Vessels in countries such as the USA where long distances are involved will have special provision made when the vessel is built to ensure that sufficient range is available without the constant need to refuel. Fuel consumption is heavily dependent on the type of tow and the weather conditions.

A full outfit of radar, communications, and electronic position-finding equipment is a requirement for coastal vessels under most national regulations. Sufficient capacity is needed to stow domestic stores, food, fresh water, spare ropes, and other equipment to make the vessel relatively self-supporting for the duration of the voyages undertaken.

The Towing Operation

In essence, a coastal or short sea towage operation is tackled in very much the same way as a full-scale oceangoing voyage. The basic principles are similar and many of the same considerations apply. The type of vessel to be towed may also be similar. A common task for the coastal tug is the small and medium-sized ship that requires assistance due to machinery damage or which cannot travel under its own power for some other reason. Similarly, unmanned vessels are frequently towed between ports for repair or to scrap-yards for breaking. In recent years, the delivery of partially completed vessels of all types has provided regular employment for coastal tugs, particularly in Europe. The hulls of such vessels are regularly towed from shipyards in Russia, Poland and Romania to shipyards in north-west Europe for completion. Barges of all types, dredgers, construction rigs, and cranes are all vessels regularly towed between ports and marine construction sites. Barges used to transport construction materials, such as stone, steel piles and concrete structures, are often in constant use – towed by various contractors in different areas as the work dictates. In some areas cargo barges, carrying bulk products, oil, containers, vehicles and even rail wagons, are commonplace.

Some of the vessels requiring towage behave very badly under tow and can present difficulties for the tugmaster and crew. With many vessels the need to be towed was not a serious consideration in the original design. Awkward tows behave in various ways: some yaw from side to side, others sheer off to one side and may even overtake the tug under certain conditions. The most dangerous and challenging for the tugmaster is one that behaves in a totally unpredictable

The coastal tug Rivtow Princess *is shown in the Fraser River with a 'tandem tow' of two woodchip barges. A 26.64 m tug of 1,740 bhp, the vessel is owned by Smit Marine Canada Inc of Vancouver and operates along the coast of British Columbia in support of the timber trade.* (Author)

Elbe is a powerful Voith tractor tug owned by Unterweser Reederei AG and used for ship-handling duties at Bremerhaven and operations in the North Sea. Built in 2006, the 37 m vessel has Voith propulsion units powered by MAK main engines of 7,180 bhp, giving it a bollard pull of 75 tonnes and top speed of 14 knots. In this picture Elbe *is towing a construction barge.* (H. Hoffmann)

manner. Ships are generally among the easier subjects for towing at sea, but even some of these can prove difficult.

Before leaving port a survey is carried out by a marine surveyor on behalf of the insurers, the classification society, or the relevant government agency. The tug's specification and documentation will be checked, as well as the towing gear and the condition of the vessel to be towed. Some temporary preparation may be required in readiness for towing. On a small ship, windows and openings may be boarded up, deck equipment lashed down and the rudder firmly secured in the amidships position. The propeller shaft may be disconnected to enable the propeller to rotate freely without causing drag, or firmly secured to prevent rotation and possible damage to machinery.

The towing gear will be rigged aboard the tow in a manner designed to reduce the possibility of the connection breaking due to wear or chafing. The towline is particularly vulnerable to damage where it passes through fairleads and is secured around bitts. Short lengths of chain may be used to make the towing connection at this point. A length of large-diameter nylon rope or other manmade-fibre rope is often coupled into the towline as a spring to absorb some of the shock loads that occur during towing. An additional emergency towline may also be rigged and stowed on the towed vessel where it can be quickly retrieved should the main towline break. In an unmanned tow, provision is also made for the necessary lights to be rigged and working before the vessels leave harbour.

A tug leaving harbour with a tow may need the assistance of another tug to help control the tow until open water is reached. Alternatively, if the towed vessel is small but awkward the tug may be secured alongside, to give the tugmaster better control. The towline will be rigged in readiness and the vessel streamed astern when there is sufficient 'sea room'. Once at sea the length of the towline will be adjusted. The length required will be determined mainly by the size of the tow and the weather conditions. The effects of towline length and other factors concerning towing at sea are explained in a later chapter on deep-sea tugs and towing. In a tug with a towing winch this is a minor matter, but for vessels without this facility lengthening a towline and later shortening it to enter harbour can be a major task. The process involves the use of the capstan and gripping devices known as 'stoppers'. This is a time-consuming operation, requiring a high level of seamanship, in which the towline is paid out or hauled in in short stages.

While the tug is at sea with a tow a constant watch is kept on the condition of the towing gear. Any points on the towline where it might become chafed and damaged, through contact with tow beams or other parts of the vessel, are protected. Where a towing winch is used the towline can be moved in or out by just a few metres to ensure that wear does not take place in the same place. At night the towline, and if possible the vessel in tow, will be inspected using a searchlight. The crew will work to a seagoing watch system of four hours on duty and four off, but in coastal waters the tugmaster is unlikely to leave the wheelhouse for any length of time. Radar will be used to monitor the position of any other traffic in the vicinity of the tug or tow and radio contact will be maintained with coastguards or other shore stations. In some areas regular contact with coastguard and vessel traffic systems (VTS) is mandatory.

Western Titan *from the fleet of Seattle-based Western Towboat is moored alongside a container barge of Alaska Marine Lines in Juneau, Alaska. The 33 m twin-screw tug was built at the owner's own yard in 1997 and fitted with Caterpillar engines of 4,500 bhp (total) Along with other tugs in the fleet,* Western Titan *operates a regular barge service to ports in Alaska, often carrying out the entire operation unaided – including berthing.* (Author)

CHAPTER 7

Escort, Anti-Pollution, Fire-Fighting and Ice-Breaking

Among the specialist duties carried out by tugs, in addition to their normal towage role, are escorting, fire-fighting, pollution control and ice-breaking. Although at first these functions appear diverse, they do in fact fit in well with the vessels' main role and to some extent help satisfy the tug owners' quest for improved vessel utilisation. The towage industry is becoming ever more involved in the protection of life and the environment from marine pollution and the hazards of fire at marine terminals. An increasingly important part of that protection is the provision of escort services to very large tankers and other ships carrying hazardous cargoes. Resulting from this involvement has been a period of almost continuous development of purpose-built tugs designed to deal with all aspects of escort, fire-protection and pollution-control work.

Winter ice is a less emotive but continuing problem for northern ports. For many decades an ice-breaking service has been provided by local tug fleets to keep shipping lanes open as long as possible in winter. Throughout the Arctic ice-strengthened tugs are essential to keep ports and oil and gas terminals working during the winter months. Equally important is the continuing exploration for offshore oil and gas. Those activities also require the use of ice-strengthened tugs and support vessels to ensure that maximum use can be made of what seasonal access is available in these remote regions.

ESCORT SERVICES

A number of serious oil tanker accidents in the 1990s, resulting in oil pollution of catastrophic proportions, caused enormous public and political pressure to improve the safety of marine transport and tanker operations in particular. Once a very large tanker goes aground, and sustains serious bottom damage, the result can be a massive uncontrollable escape of oil into the marine environment. The current philosophy, much publicised by the shipping and salvage industries, is to promote every possible means to 'keep the oil in the ship'. It recognises that large tankers are at their most vulnerable in coastal waters and the approaches to ports and harbours, and that every precaution must be taken to prevent groundings and similar accidents that could lead to a release of oil. One of the ways that oil companies and tanker operators have reacted to this pressure is to implement the greater use of escorting tugs for large ships in coastal waters – the intention being to have a tug immediately to hand should a fully loaded tanker suffer a loss of power, defective steering, or other serious failure. The extent of this service varies considerably with geography and the client's perception of the potential risk. Escort services have become common at oil terminals around the world and, with the massive increase in the use of large LNG tankers, demand continues to rise. Although the consequences of a serious incident involving an LNG tanker in a grounding or collision might be quite different, the escort services provided are virtually identical.

The Voith tractor tug Phenix *is a sophisticated escort and tanker-handling vessel operated by Solent Towage (a subsidiary of Østensjø Rederi of Norway) at the Fawley oil terminal near Southampton, UK. A vessel of 37 m in length, the tug is powered by two Bergen main engines developing a total of 6,850 bhp to drive a pair of Voith propulsion units. A highly developed hull form and skeg enables the tug to tow in the indirect mode safely and effectively.* Phenix *has a static bollard pull of 67 tonnes and can exert braking and steering forces of 150 tons at 10 knots. (Author)*

Escort tugs need a good turn of speed in order to make a towing connection with moving ships at sea. The Norwegian tug Boxer *of Buksér og Berging is a Voith escort tug designed to operate 'skeg first' and put into service in 1999. A vessel of 38.85 metres in length, with two Deutz main engines producing 6,800 bhp, it has a bollard pull of 65 tons and a top speed of 15 knots.* (Author)

The majority of true escort duties currently require the tug to be made fast by its towline to the stern of the ship and remain connected for the duration of the operation. This is known as an 'active' or 'tethered' escort. If the tug escorts a ship without making a towing connection it is regarded as a 'passive' escort but its success in an emergency is dependent on the tug making that connection before the incident becomes serious.

A typical requirement, in many locations, is for oil, gas and often chemical tankers of over 60,000 tons dead weight to be escorted in and out of ports and rivers adjacent to the oil or gas terminals at which they load or discharge. This frequently means providing an escort between the ship's berth and the seaward limits of the port, often covering distances of 5–25 miles, and sometimes further. If a propulsion or steering failure occurs aboard the tanker it is the task of the tug to stop or steer the ship effectively and control it until further assistance becomes available, or a safe anchorage is achieved. To stop or steer the offending ship sounds simple enough in normal ship-handling terms but the size and speed of the ship become critical factors in this scenario. A fully loaded tanker of perhaps 250,000 tons approaching its destination may well be travelling at over 10 knots when it is met by the escort some miles from shore. In the approach channels the ship's master and pilot may be reluctant to reduce speed until absolutely necessary in order to retain a reasonable degree of steerage. Therefore the escort tug requires not only the power to render real assistance but a good margin of speed.

171

For the tug operator escorting raises a number of serious issues, mainly concerned with ensuring that such services can be provided effectively and economically. The ability of a single tug to perform the necessary duties is a key issue, particularly where long distances are involved. Many oil terminals are in remote locations with dedicated tug fleets on station to provide ship-handling assistance and often fire-fighting protection. The additional demand for a tug to escort ships long distances to and from jetties can impose a serious burden on many such fleets. There are also serious legal implications for the tug operator regarding liability should an incident occur whilst an escort tug is in attendance – fortunately a matter still to be tested at the time of writing. Although there have been known instances where the escort tug has prevented a serious grounding, it is almost impossible to quantify the value of such a service.

The Escort Tug

The important issue of 'what type of tug can be fully effective' in the escort role has been one of the most contentious aspects of the whole subject. In the past, most new demands placed on ship-handling tugs have been met with more powerful vessels or advanced propulsion technology to improve manoeuvrability

Svitzer Waterston *is a stern drive escort and tanker-handling tug built for Svitzer in 2008 to be employed at a major gas terminal in Britain. Built to a new Robert Allan RAstar design the 33.6m vessel is powered by two General Electric 7FDM-16 main engines of 7,880 bhp (total) driving Schottel azimuthing propulsion units. This arrangement gives the tug a bollard pull of 107 tonnes and maximum speed of 13.7 knots.* (Astilleros Freire)

and safety, but with escort tugs there are other factors to take into account. Bollard pull is important but may not necessarily be the deciding factor when working with a large ship at high speeds. Bollard-pull figures between 65 and 95 tonnes are often quoted but the towline forces exerted by a modern escort tug operating in the indirect-towing mode are frequently double that figure. The bollard-pull figure is one that can be met by an increasing number of modern ship-handling tugs but the environment in which the escort vessel may have to operate and the distances involved may render them unsuitable. An escort tug may be required to cover a route that involves long distances at sea, in areas with predominantly poor weather for much of the year. A substantial forecastle is a prime requirement in many purpose-built vessels. Free-running speed is also an important factor – the typical maximum speed of a ship-handling tug of 12 or 13 knots is regarded as marginal in many instances.

The towage industry remains divided as to the type of propulsion technology ideally suited to escort duties. A large stern-drive tug of some 35–45 metres in length, with a high forecastle, and a bollard pull of between 60 and 95 tonnes has been the choice of many operators. Such vessels are of course equipped to tow over the bow and will have a hull form designed to be effective in the indirect-towing mode. Other operators have put their faith in large, powerful, Voith Schneider tractor tugs optimised to perform well when operating stern first. A tractor for use in escort work is likely to have a stern giving more freeboard than usual and a towing fairlead positioned very close to the stern. On the north-west coast of America at Puget Sound, Voith tractors of very large proportions are employed to escort tankers over long distances in an ecologically sensitive area. The tugs concerned are 47 metres in length, with a massive draft of over 6 metres, and powered by main engines of almost 8,000 bhp. Tractor tugs of this type, and

Nanuq is one of a pair of Crowley Marine Services escort tugs stationed in Alaska in 1990, to help protect Prince William Sound and Valdez. With sister Tanerliq *it remains the largest and most powerful Voith tractor in the world, having a length of 47.24 metres, and a pair of Caterpillar main engines of 10,192 bhp (total), giving a static bollard pull of over 95 tons. Both tugs can work in ice and are fitted for fire-fighting.* (Crowley)

A view from the wheelhouse of the escort tug Boxer *shows the tug in position on the stern of the* Irving Galloway, *a tanker of 300,000 dwt leaving the oil terminal at Mongstad in Norway. The towline is maintained at a predetermined length by the tug's towing winch.* Boxer *is travelling in a comfortable position just to port of the tanker's propeller wash. In an emergency the high performance HMPE towline must be capable of withstanding loads well in excess of 150 tonnes.* (Author)

many smaller highly developed vessels built for use in Norway and elsewhere, have a proven ability to exert towline pulls far exceeding their bollard pull when towing in the indirect mode, due to the very large surface area of the underwater skeg and other hydrodynamic factors.

Among the most important features in a 'state of the art' escort tug are the towing winch and towlines. The winch is invariably one that has a sophisticated control system that can be preset to maintain a certain length of towline and monitor and control the load imposed on the towline under differing circumstances. In the majority of cases the towline used will be manufactured from manmade HMPE fibres, which are extremely light, buoyant, and have similar strength characteristics to steel.

In most fleets the ability of an escort tug to stop or steer a tanker of a particular size is tested periodically for certification and training purposes. This can only be achieved by carrying out a realistic trial using a suitable ship, representative of tankers regularly using the port. A trial of this kind enables tugmasters, pilots, and ships' captains to gain experience, and the tug's performance to be evaluated. Most purpose-built escort tugs are fitted with instrumentation in the wheelhouse that can be used to monitor the tug's position in relation to the ship, towline forces and length. It is not uncommon for such trials to start with the tanker travelling at up to 10 knots, and for the tug to be used to make specific course changes without assistance from the ship's rudder. In other trials the tug may be required to stop the ship, again without the use of the ship's engines or rudder. During trials of this kind, escort tugs of the Voith tractor type, with a static bollard pull of 65 tonnes have recorded towline forces of over 150 tonnes when working with a tanker at 10 knots in the indirect-towing mode.

An escort tug is sometimes referred to as an 'intervention vessel' or an 'emergency response vessel'. These terms may refer to vessels that are employed largely to provide safety orientated services such as escorting, fire-fighting and pollution-control work and may have little involvement in the actual berthing of ships. More commonly the escort tug is equipped to carry out those functions in addition to its normal ship-handling duties. To that end a 'state of the art' escort tug will be fitted for fire-fighting to a high standard and often carry the necessary equipment to deploy protective booms and carry out oil retrieval. All of these subjects are dealt with later in this chapter.

ESCORT OPERATIONS

The duties of the escort tug with regard to incoming ships start at a rendezvous point at sea, often at the seaward limit of the port concerned. In most cases on meeting the tanker a towing connection will be established, with the tug's towline

Stern drive tug Adsteam Victory *(now* Svitzer Victory*) is one of many similar tugs regularly carrying out escort duties, in this case with the LNG tanker* Berge Arzew. *The 33 m tug was built in Australia in 2000 and fitted with two Daihatsu main engines of 4,850 bhp (total) driving Niigata Z-Peller propulsion units, to achieve a bollard pull of 64 tons and a maximum speed of 13 knots.* (Author)

being made fast at a central point on the stern of the ship. This is regarded as an 'active' escort, where the tug can respond immediately to assist the ship to steer or stop if required. An alternative arrangement would be to have the tug accompany the ship at close quarters without making a connection until much later in the operation. This involves a time delay should the ship require help in an emergency.

Approaching the ship to connect a tow presents no great problem for either the stern-drive or purpose-built Voith tractor tug in spite of the ship's speed, which may well be in excess of 10 knots. A stern-drive tug or Z-Tech will be positioned with its bow close to the stern of the ship and pass the towline from the forward winch in the normal way, an operation that can be carried out relatively safely at sea. The tractor tug will turn stern (skeg) first and make a connection from the winch in the same manner, passing the towline through the appropriate towing fairlead.

Once a towing connection is made the tug will maintain a position astern of the ship, usually keeping the towline slack. In this way the ship is not inhibited in any way by towing the tug and wear on the towline is considerably reduced. If the ship suffers a serious malfunction, the prime task of the escort tug is to assist the vessel to achieve a safe anchorage or maintain a course within the designated shipping channels. It is generally considered most likely that the tug will be required to slow and steer the ship rather than attempt to bring it immediately to a halt. In either case considerable skill and effort is needed to provide the necessary assistance to a very large ship of up to 500,000 tons deadweight.

The stern-drive tug in this situation may initially apply full power astern, with the azimuthing propulsion units directing thrust forward, to slow the ship. Alternatively, when assisting a ship at very high speed, a method known as the transverse arrest mode may be used. In this mode the propulsion units are turned outboard to their normal neutral position but with full power applied, a method claimed to produce massive drag and very high towline forces. A tractor tug will likewise apply full power astern, but both types of tug will quickly resort to indirect-towing methods in order to apply sufficient force to the towline to slow or steer the ship successfully.

In most locations the same large ships are also escorted on the outward bound journey from the berth to sea. The extent of escort services in other areas often depends on whether the ships are fully loaded or in a light condition, with fully loaded vessels being accompanied by a tug at all times. Escorting a tanker to sea is almost the same procedure in reverse, but one requiring special care when the towline is released from the ship. Retrieving the towline at speeds of 7–10 knots at sea may require the tug to change course immediately in order to ensure that the loose end of the towline is kept well away from the tug's propulsion units.

FIRE-FIGHTING

The enormous traffic in ships carrying oil, petrochemicals, and hazardous liquefied gases has resulted in comprehensive fire-protection measures being put into place in ports and at specialist loading and unloading terminals. Those

Tugs from Semco Towage & Salvage fight a serious fire aboard the bulk carrier Nina *in Singapore. The tugs are using their monitors and hoses to cool the decks, hatches and hull structure.* (ISU)

measures usually include the provision of specially equipped fire-fighting vessels and that duty is frequently undertaken by the local tug fleet. Where tugs are already on station to provide ship-handling services, often on a 24-hour basis, it makes good economic sense to install comprehensive fire-fighting equipment

Purpose-built fire tug and harbour service vessel RPA 12 *is operated by the Rotterdam Port Authority, specifically for dealing with fires on ships and harbour installations and other emergencies. Built in 1999, and based on a twin-screw design,* RPA 12 *is equipped with monitors and hoses, including one remotely operated monitor mounted on a hydraulically controlled arm. Towing bollards are fitted for use only in an emergency.* (Author)

aboard some or all of the vessels involved. The cost of providing continuous fire-fighting protection is generally met by special contracts placed with the tug owners by the oil terminal operators or port authorities. Additional finance may also come from local or central government sources.

A number of port authorities in the USA and Europe employ special fire-fighting vessels to carry out patrol and fire-fighting duties in the areas under their jurisdiction. Many of these vessels use an easily recognisable tug design and may be equipped with towing gear. This is only used in a dire emergency and the vessels have no regular towage commitments.

An important factor in the operation of fire tugs is the provision of specialist fire-fighting expertise. The approach varies. Tug crews often receive special training in fire-fighting in order to achieve their vocational qualifications. A common method of providing additional expertise is to take on board trained fire fighters when a full-scale emergency occurs. This procedure is used extensively in Britain, where local fire brigade personnel regularly go aboard fire-fighting tugs to become familiar with the equipment and to train with the tug crews.

The Fire Tug

Fortunately, fire-fighting is very much a secondary duty – the vast majority of fire tugs have never been called upon to combat a serious fire. Therefore when vessels are built and equipped, towage requirements remain paramount.

There are a number of basic features the tug must possess to be suitable for use as a fire-fighting vessel, the most important being adequate power to operate the fire pumps and at the same time retain a high degree of manoeuvrability. High-performance fire pumps installed in modern ship-handling tugs are usually driven by the main engines, often with one pump coupled to each main engine. Using this method, the engine or propulsion controls are designed to ensure that sufficient power remains available to manoeuvre the tug whilst the pumps are in operation. Where pumps are driven by the main engines, particularly in stern-drive tugs and tractors, 'step-up' gearboxes are often installed to enable the pumps to rotate faster than the speed of the engine. This arrangement improves fire-fighting capability and gives more precise control of the propulsion system.

Alternatively, pumps driven by separate auxiliary diesel engines may be installed. Ideally these are located in the engine-room, for protection and stability reasons, but they are occasionally located in the superstructure or on deck. The power needed and size of the fire pumps varies with the number of monitors fitted and their capacity but figures in excess of 600 bhp are not uncommon.

Manoeuvrability is an important consideration. In the event of a fire – aboard a ship or at a shore installation – the tug must be accurately positioned to enable the fire fighters to do their work. A less obvious need is the ability to manoeuvre precisely and at the same time counteract the thrust generated by the monitors. Very powerful monitors produce considerable thrust, and can make controlling the vessel's position extremely difficult. For this reason highly manoeuvrable

The tanker-handling tug Aeger *demonstrates the power of its two remotely controlled high-level fire monitors. Now operated as the Danish* Asterix, *the 32 m stern-drive tug is a vessel of 5,445 bhp, built in 2003, and fitted with a fire-fighting system capable of delivering a total of 2,700 cu/metre of water per hour.* (Author)

tractor tugs and stern-drive vessels make ideal fire tugs. During a fire-fighting operation there may be circumstances when the jets of water or foam from the monitors can only be directed satisfactorily by manoeuvring the entire vessel. If the monitors have no remote controls, once they have been adjusted it may be too hot for the crew to remain on deck to control them. Under these conditions it is essential that the tug handles well with the fire monitors in operation.

Fire-fighting Equipment

Fire-fighting monitors have already been mentioned a number of times, including a brief description in Chapter 4. In the modern fire tug at least two high capacity monitors will be installed, of a type capable of delivering either water or foam. The figures used to describe the output of monitors vary widely and include litres per minute, gallons per minute, cubic metres per hour, and sometimes tons per hour. Cubic metres per hour will be used here to give some indication of output. The output capacities required vary with the type of tug and the work that it does. Stringent standards are laid down by oil and gas terminal operators and reflect the requirements imposed by the various international classification societies for fire-fighting vessels. A common notation applied to oil and gas terminal tugs is known as FiFi 1 – which lays down certain parameters for pumping capacity, performance of the monitors and levels of protection for the tug itself. A typical modern oil or gas terminal tug will have a total pumping capacity of 2,400–2,800 cubic metres per hour to supply two remotely controlled monitors capable of delivering water or foam. A FiFi 1 system, with a capacity within that range, would normally have two pumps installed, one driven by each main engine. The pumping system described will also supply the tug's 'self protection' water-spray equipment.

The salvage tug Abeille Liberté, *operated by Les Abeille as an ETV on behalf of the French Navy, has a fire-fighting capability meeting the requirements for FiFi 2. The total output from the triple high-level fire monitors is 7,200 cu/metre of water per hour. A vessel of 80 m in length,* Abeille Liberté *has a twin-screw propulsion system powered by four MAK main engines to achieve a bollard pull of 200 tonnes and a maximum speed of 19 knots. (Author)*

Oil-rig supply vessels and some larger tugs working extensively in offshore oil fields are often equipped with fire monitors capable of delivering far in excess of those figures and have classification society notations of FiFi 2 or FiFi 3.

A modern high-capacity monitor is capable of throwing water to a height of over 150 metres when elevated at something like 45 degrees. In vessels where the monitors are mounted fairly low on the tug the height and distance achieved can be of great importance. Each monitor has a means of controlling the elevation and direction of the nozzle and in many designs the shape of the nozzle can also be adjusted. The monitors may be controlled manually, although it is now common for the entire outfit to be remotely controlled either from the wheelhouse or from a special control cabin. The remote controls are operated by hydraulic or electrical systems, or by turbine-driven mechanisms using water pressure from the fire-fighting system. The latter have the advantage of being unaffected by heat or moisture.

It is the manner in which the monitors are mounted, often high above the vessel's superstructure, that gives a fire tug its distinctive appearance. Many earlier tugs working with tankers have at least one monitor mounted very high above the waterline, in order to be able to play water or foam over the ship's decks. With a very large tanker in ballast the main deck may be over 18 metres above the waterline. It is not unusual, therefore, to have one monitor fitted at the tug's masthead approximately 21 metres above the waterline. There are a number of problems associated with having a relatively heavy fire monitor so high above the tug's deck. Apart from any influence on stability, the effects of vibration and forces imposed on the mast are considerable. The alternatives were to build substantial platforms or use a form of mounting which can be raised and lowered. Both concepts have been used extensively in the past but are rarely found in new vessels due to much improved monitor design giving a more effective water jet.

Variable height monitor mountings take two basic forms. The simplest and least obtrusive is the telescopic mast. A telescopic mechanism is usually incorporated inside a normal mast or a similar structure in order to house the tubular extending sections. Such masts can accommodate only one monitor and this may be of limited capacity. The second option is a hydraulically operated platform, similar to those used on land-based fire-fighting vehicles or for overhead maintenance. When not in use the platform folds down into a convenient stowage position. Platforms of this type are capable of carrying more weight than the telescopic type and can be manned if required.

The use of fire-fighting foam is a common means of combating oil fires. Foam is used to blanket a fire by helping to exclude oxygen. It comprises a mixture of water, air, and foam compound. The formulation of the compound varies, as does the proportion of water and compound, giving some control over the density of the resulting foam. The foam compound is automatically injected into the water supply, in carefully metered proportions, before it enters the monitor. Most monitors are capable of delivering approximately three or four times more foam than water. The foam compound is carried in specially designated tanks within the hull of the tug. As we have seen, the monitors are normally designed to handle water or foam and in many fire-fighting operations only water will be used. Often when a tug is called to a shipboard fire its job will be to cool down the hull plating of other parts of the vessel's structure. Known as boundary cooling, vast quantities of seawater are used, in operations that may take many hours. Hose connections fitted at deck level are used to enable additional hand-operated hoses to supplement the monitors if required and to enable fire fighters to take hoses aboard the casualty.

Measures are also needed to protect the tug itself from the hazards of working in close proximity to fire. Reports of tugs working at major incidents mention scorched paintwork, cracked windows, and conditions too hot for crews to work

The Voith tractor tug Tystie *shows off its fire-fighting and self-protection spray system. Small nozzles around the bulwarks and super-structure produce a drenching spray to keep the wheelhouse and upper works of the tug cool during major fire-fighting operations.* Tystie *is a 38.37 m tanker-handling and escort tug of 5,760 bhp and 56-tonne bollard pull operated by Shetland Towage Ltd. (Author)*

on deck. On some earlier tugs steel plates are provided that can be erected to protect bridge windows. In most modern vessels a dousing, or self-protection spray system is installed. This consists of an arrangement of spray nozzles that continually envelop the vessel in a protective curtain of water. In order to prevent salt deposits building up on warm wheelhouse windows, the more sophisticated wetting systems use a separate fresh water supply for this part of the superstructure. The nozzles used to spray cooling water over the superstructure and wheelhouse are often conveniently, and unobtrusively, located in the handrails at boat deck level.

POLLUTION-CONTROL DUTIES

As a direct result of public and political pressure, pollution-control measures in areas where major oil installations are located continue to become more stringent. Such measures generally comprise a comprehensive planned approach to preventing occurrences of significant oil pollution and ensuring that the means are in place to deal with any spill of oil should those measures fail. Considerable effort and resources are put into strict operating procedures and the provision of equipment to deal with any emergencies that arise. The resident tug fleet and any purpose-built escort vessels inevitably become part of these 'emergency response' arrangements. Their availability and the ease with which they can be adapted to carry the necessary equipment has made them obvious candidates. Pollution-control duties involving tugs can be split broadly into three categories: oil dispersal, containment, and retrieval. The extent of an oil spillage can vary from a small accidental discharge from a tanker in port, to a major incident involving thousands of tons of cargo released from a damaged vessel at sea. The type of oil discharged can also effect the treatment necessary. Light diesel fuel, that may evaporate relatively quickly, presents quite a different problem from a spill of heavy, tar-like crude oil. Huge advances in the development of equipment and pollution-control procedures have taken place in the last decade.

Ajax of Østensjø Rederi, Norway, is seen deploying its on-board oil skimmer. Note the skimmer hose, hydraulic crane and reel of inflatable protective boom. The skimmer and boom are housed in a 'garage' within the superstructure. Built in 2000, Ajax is a Voith escort tug of 41.60 metres, with Caterpillar main engines producing a total of 10,340 bhp, for a bollard pull of 92 tons. (Author)

Oil Dispersal

For many years the principal means of dealing with large- and small-scale oil pollution has been to treat the offending slicks with a chemical dispersant. Dispersal operations are carried out by tugs in a wide variety of circumstances, both at sea and in harbour. More recently, it has been recognised that this method may in itself be environmentally unsound in some circumstances. Therefore chemical dispersant is only used under strict control and guidance from local and/or national maritime authorities. Although dispersal is less popular than in the past, many tugs continue to be equipped to carry out the work.

In general the equipment carried on board a tug is intended to apply chemical dispersants and when necessary break up the slicks after the chemicals have done their work. Most fire-fighting tugs and many ordinary ship-handling vessels are capable of carrying several tons of chemical dispersant, in specially designated tanks. The spraying equipment used is sometimes permanently fitted and stowed in a convenient location on board or removable and taken ashore when not required. The more complex arrangements consist of long tubular spraying arms rigged to extend outwards, one from each side of the tug. Nozzles spaced along the arms discharge a spray of chemicals downwards onto the surface of the water. This enables the vessel to cover a wide path at each pass, as the tug manoeuvres to cover the oil. For much smaller operations, such as small spillages in harbour, hand-operated spraying equipment may be used by crew members working from the tug's deck.

The approach to breaking up oil slicks continues to change and several different methods are in use. A common method, still used in some circumstances, is to tow specially designed 'breaker boards' through the oil. The boards are simple structures intended to cause a mixing action, agitating the surface of the oil and water. This method is particularly suitable for anti-pollution work at sea where very large areas have to be covered. Some operators rely on the action of the tug's propellers to do the work. A further alternative method is to use the tug's fire monitors to direct high-pressure water jets at the surface.

Booms and Oil Retrieval

Pollution-control measures currently in use at many ports and oil terminals place great emphasis on the containment and retrieval of any oil spillage. In some parts of the world the use of a boom, a flexible floating barrier, is mandatory at oil terminals, while tankers are being loaded or discharged. Once a tanker is berthed a boom is put in position around the vessel before any transfer of oil can commence. This is a safeguard against damaged hoses or other failures in the loading or discharging equipment that may cause a spillage. Booms may also be used when an incident resulting in a release of oil occurs in sheltered waters, floating booms being used to contain the oil and prevent slicks being spread by the action of wind or tide. The boom is positioned around the damaged ship or oil slick as a barrier to contain the oil, and perhaps enable it to be retrieved. The use of booms at sea, even in relatively calm conditions, is quite a different matter due to the difficult task of keeping the light-weight booms in position against wind and tide.

Booms generally consist of a series of flexible floats assembled to form a long continuous barrier. A flexible rubber or canvas 'skirt' is an integral part of the boom and is arranged to extend a metre or so below the floats to help prevent the passage of oil. There are various designs in use including inflatable, fully portable types, which are stored on reels when not in use. Such booms are now becoming normal equipment for many tanker terminal tugs and escort vessels. A length of boom can be accommodated on a reel stowed on the superstructure or at the forward end of the after towing deck, and deployed through an opening in the

A workboat tows the protective boom from its storage reel aboard the escort tug Ajax. Designed for rapid deployment and retrieval, the boom inflates automatically on being pulled away from the tug and deflates while it is being wound in. The boom can encircle spilt oil or a leaking vessel, so that the oil can be retrieved using a skimmer. (Author)

Don Inda is one of a pair of highly sophisticated emergency response vessels built by Astilleros Zamakona for the Spanish Maritime Safety Authority SASEMAR. This aerial view shows the vessel deploying a side sweep oil-skimming system. Oil retrieved is pumped into dedicated internal tanks. Note also the boom reels, cranes and rescue equipment. The 80 m twin-screw tug is powered by four Bergen main engines generating a total of 21,740 bhp to give the vessel a massive bollard pull of 220 tonnes and a maximum speed of 17.6 knots. (Zamakona)

stern. As the boom is deployed the outer end is handled by a workboat or another tug. Booms that are in regular use at oil terminal berths are usually attended by purpose-built pollution-control craft, small tugs or workboats that tow booms into position and ensure that they are properly maintained.

Once an actual oil spill is contained by a boom, it can be dealt with in one of two ways. The oil can be treated with a chemical dispersant or steps may be taken to retrieve it. The latter procedure can be accomplished in very calm conditions by simply pumping the oil and surface water into tanks. The resulting water/oil solution is allowed to settle and taken ashore for treatment. This very basic method of removing oil from the surface of the water has been superseded by far more sophisticated means. Among devices designed to remove only the oil, with a minimum of water content, are rotating mops that soak up oil and various skimming devices. A skimmer of some kind is again becoming standard equipment on tugs involved in pollution-control duties. The skimmer is housed aboard the tug and lowered by a deck crane into the oil contained by the boom. Hoses connect the skimming device to pumps aboard the tug where the water/oil solution is stored in specially allocated settling tanks.

An alternative retrieval method is to have a short length of boom rigged from one or both sides of the tug, with its outer end attached to a long lightweight spar. The boom is rigged so that a bight is formed when the tug moves slowly forward. Any oil on the surface is collected at the after end of the bight. A skimmer is lowered into the bight to retrieve the oil as previously described.

Active anti-pollution measures such as spraying with dispersant, breaking up slicks by agitation, or retrieval require precise knowledge of the position, size and movement of oil slicks. In many modern vessels electronic charting and positioning equipment is installed for just this purpose. The positions of slicks are represented graphically on the VDU screen along with the real-time position of the tug. The direction the oil is likely to drift can be predicted and search patterns depicted on the screen.

ICE-STRENGTHENED TUGS AND ICE-BREAKING

The use of tugs for ice-breaking is a duty far removed from those previously described but in many parts of the world operating in ice is an essential part of tug work. There are many harbours and coastal waters which for some weeks or months each year can only be kept open to shipping with the use of some form of ice-breaker. In many cases the expense of a purpose-built vessel dedicated to this seasonal work is not justified. The use of a suitably designed tug, to be employed principally as a ship-handling vessel, is a different matter. In North America, Scandinavia, and Russia there are many such tugs. Some are employed to keep harbours, their approaches, and coastal shipping lanes open as small ice-breakers in their own right, often dealing with ice over 30 cm thick. Others are strengthened and equipped simply to enable them to continue about their normal business of assisting ships, unimpeded by ice.

A third and more recent category of ice-breaking tug is the large deep-sea vessel used for specialist towing duties by the oil industry. Offshore oil exploration has moved north into ice-infested areas such as those off Alaska and northern Russia. Much of the equipment used in these northern oil fields is transported by barge and towed by purpose-built ice-strengthened tugs. The same principles apply broadly to all such vessels.

The main constructional difference between an ice-breaking tug and any other lies in the strength and shape of the hull. The need for additional strength is obvious; the hull must resist not only the forces imposed by its forward motion through ice but any crushing which may take place. Additional strength is introduced by using thicker steel plating and increasing the number of supporting internal frames. The bow of the tug normally has a long, shallow, angled portion just below the waterline. In order to appreciate the purpose of this strange shape the principle of ice-breaking must be understood. The tug breaks ice not by battering it with brute force but by riding up over it and using its weight to do the work. The long sloping shape aids this process and acts as a form of cutting edge. There may also be a more rounded shape in the body of the hull to minimise the

Svitzer Sakhalin *is one of four heavy-duty ice class escort tugs built for use at the Prigorodnoye oil and gas export terminal on the coast of Sakhalin Island, Russia. The 34 m stern-drive tugs are winterised and powered by two Bergen main engines driving twin Rolls-Royce propulsion units. All four have a bollard pull of 73 tonnes and a free-running speed of 13.5 knots. (M. Piche)*

risk of the tug becoming 'squeezed' or crushed. A more rounded shape will simply be forced upwards if crushing occurs.

Other considerations concern the propulsion system. Nozzles are often avoided due to the risk of ice becoming jammed between the propeller blades and nozzle structure. Small protruding fins are often located ahead of the propeller and aft of the rudder to deflect ice away from those vital components. A number of stern-drive tugs and tractors with azimuthing propulsion units are successfully employed in fleets in Scandinavia, North America and Europe. The propulsion equipment of these vessels appears to be unaffected by ice, presumably due to the deep immersion of their propellers and the provision of protective fins.

Modern tugs built to operate in northern regions incorporate a number of features often described as 'winterisation'. Heating systems are sometimes incorporated in decks, bulwarks and other exposed areas and fittings to prevent the build-up of ice. Winches and towlines will also have some protection to ensure they are in working order when needed. The cooling systems for the main and auxiliary engines may also be modified. Cooling systems which can be operated without circulating seawater from outside the hull are often used to avoid problems resulting from frozen or blocked water intakes.

CHAPTER 8

Oceangoing Tugs and Offshore Support Vessels

Tugs in this category include the largest and most impressive vessels employed by the towage industry. Among them are the massive seagoing vessels involved in long-distance towing and salvage work, and anchor-handling tugs and anchor-handling tug supply vessels involved in supporting the offshore oil industry.

The broad sector of the towage industry in which most of these vessels operate is split into three specific areas of work, salvage, long-distance towing, and operations centred on the offshore oil industry. All three continue to experience economic and operational changes to a greater or lesser degree. Demand for tugs built specifically to carry out salvage work has, for economic reasons, suffered a substantial decline. In the European salvage and long-distance towing market there have been very few replacement vessels built in the past decade and many existing tugs are becoming elderly and in some respects outmoded. There has, however, been a marked increase in the construction of large, powerful tugs intended for long-range towing operations, with ships and other large floating objects.

An oceangoing tug of any type represents a massive investment for its owners in terms of capital and operating costs. Over the past decade operators in the long-range towage market have been forced to reconsider the best way forward. A small minority decided to concentrate on the towage of large, high-value vessels and floating plant, built and used by the offshore oil and gas industry. The standards of service required are high but in the present climate of long-term high oil and gas prices the rewards are equally worthwhile. Among the objects being towed, often over distances of more than 10,000 miles, are massive floating oil and gas storage and production vessels and oil exploration and production rugs. The result is a whole new generation of tugs, including significant vessels from the Netherlands, Singapore, China and elsewhere in the Far East. Vessels in this category often carry some salvage equipment but salvage is very much a secondary role.

The list of owners of oceangoing tugs, operating in the long-range towage and salvage sector still contains many well-known names, such as Crowley, Foss, International Transport Contractors (ITC), Moran, POSH Semco, Svitzer, Tsavliris and Fairmount. In the early years following the dissolution of the USSR a great many oceangoing tugs and oil-rig supply vessels were released onto the commercial market in order to earn badly needed foreign currency. Some of those vessels continue to provide stiff competition, due mainly to their low manning costs. Several Russian vessels joined established western fleets, on charter, or as part of joint operating arrangements but the majority are now back in the hands of their original owners or newly formed companies.

Included in the oceangoing sector are some of the less well-known tug and cargo-barge operations. Many of these services operate over long distances towing cargoes of containers, petroleum products, vehicles and various bulk goods. In addition to similar coastal operations US operators regularly cross the Pacific to the Hawaiian Islands and from the east coast of the USA to Africa and elsewhere.

Some navies, and many coastguard organisations, around the world operate deep-sea tugs for rescue and support purposes but rarely become involved in commercial towing. In peacetime oceangoing naval tugs are most likely to be engaged in training and perhaps the occasional tow with warships or dockyard equipment. Coastguards are, however, becoming increasingly proactive in the protection of the marine environment in coastal and sea areas under their

Nan Hai Jiu 101 *was the most modern deep-sea salvage tug to enter service with the China Rescue and Salvage Bureau when it was completed in 2007. Measuring 109.7 m in length and 4,091 gt, the tug was built to fulfil a wide range of towage, salvage and rescue duties. Two Wärtsilä main engines produce a total of 19,000 bhp to drive twin controllable-pitch propellers rotating in fixed Kort nozzles, giving a bollard pull of 200 tonnes and free-running speed of 22 knots.* (P. Sinke)

Blizzard *is one of three sister ships operated by International Transport Contractors (ITC) for deep-sea towing, anchor-handling and offshore supply services. Built for Maersk in 1987, it is a twin-screw vessel of 69.7 m in length fitted with two MAK main engines of 12,000 bhp (total). The vessel has a bollard pull of 140 tons and a maximum speed of 16 knots. (ITC)*

jurisdiction. Coastguard authorities frequently station tugs in vulnerable areas to offer an emergency towing service to ships breaking down, in danger of going aground or causing any form of marine pollution. The tugs involved are either purpose-built or commercial tugs, chartered for the purpose, and equipped to carry out emergency-response duties.

The market for large powerful vessels designed primarily to support the offshore oil industry continues to develop in step with the heavy demand for oil and gas. This development is, however, linked firmly to the amount of activity experienced in the offshore oil fields at any given time, and as a consequence is subject to wide short-term variations in demand. There are continuing demands for increasingly powerful anchor-handling tugs and anchor-handling supply vessels to work in deeper water and in many of the more inhospitable areas of the world. The result is a market where some of the older, well-equipped, versatile, but no longer 'state of the art', offshore anchor-handlers are proving viable in other deep-sea towage roles.

The majority of vessels working in support of the offshore oil industry are owned by specialist companies dedicated to providing services to that sector but rarely the oil industry itself. Among the vessels owned and/or operated by those companies are anchor-handling tugs – powerful vessels capable of towing oil rigs, barges and other offshore equipment, and dealing with their anchors, but with no significant cargo carrying capacity; and the anchor-handling tug supply vessel which is equipped to tow and handle anchors, and can additionally carry substantial cargoes, to and from the oil fields, on deck and in specially installed tanks.

OCEANGOING TUGS

'Oceangoing' or 'deep-sea' are both terms used to describe tugs intended primarily to operate at sea and undertake long-range towing operations. They vary in size from a vessel little larger than a harbour tug, of 35 metres in length and perhaps 350 gross tons, to massive vessels of over 100 metres long and over 5,000 gross tons. Anchor-handling tugs, employed largely by the offshore oil industry, also belong in this category but are equipped in a particular way for the work that they do. The special equipment required and the process of anchor-handling is dealt with later in this chapter. As previously mentioned, the anchor-handling oil-rig supply vessel is widely used to carry out work that was previously the primary role of the more traditional oceangoing tug. There are, however, significant numbers of the latter still in use and it is with those that the next few paragraphs are mainly concerned.

The ability to operate at sea in almost all weather and sea conditions is a vitally important feature of any oceangoing tug and is to some degree dependent on the size of the vessel. A large tug is, in every respect, a small ship, capable of withstanding the very worst weather conditions and with sufficient range to undertake long voyages, with another vessel or object in tow. In almost every case the hull design incorporates a high forecastle to afford maximum protection in heavy seas and some form of protection along its sides to guard against heavy knocks when working alongside other vessels. This usually takes the form of external steel rubbing-bands, with perhaps some diagonal reinforcement. Bow fenders are considered of limited use in many very large tugs and can be a distinct disadvantage in heavy seas.

Oceangoing salvage tug De Da *is employed on worldwide long-range towage services by China Ocean Engineering Services. The tug was built in 1979 to a traditional design, for a vessel of 98 m in length and 3,566 gt. Two Pielstick main engines produce 20,800 bhp to give the tug a bollard pull of 200 tons and free-running speed of 20 knots.* (H. Hoffmann)

Rotterdam, *formerly* Smitwijs Rotterdam, *of Svitzer is one of a series of oceangoing tugs of similar design originally built in 1975 for Smit International. The twin-screw vessel is 74.75 m long and 2,708 gt, with the wheelhouse located amidships. Two Stork-Werkspoor main engines rated at 13,500 bhp (total) drive two controllable-pitch propellers to give the tug a bollard pull of 151 tonnes and maximum speed of 14 knots.* (H. Hoffmann)

The superstructure in earlier designs tends to follow the traditional tug configuration, with the wheelhouse and bridge very close to the bow. This may necessitate a secondary control position further aft (often known among tug crews as a 'dog house') to give the tugmaster a better view astern when manoeuvring or picking up a tow. A control position of this kind may comprise a completely separate wheelhouse equipped with engine, steering, and winch controls. Another form of additional control position is the 'crow's nest', a very small wheelhouse located high above the normal superstructure. A number of older oceangoing tugs are equipped in this way to afford improved all-round vision when the tug is towing, searching for a casualty, or working its way through ice.

Later generations of oceangoing tug have a single wheelhouse located almost amidships, in a position giving a good field of view in all directions. Duplicate controls are provided at windows facing aft with a clear view of the towing deck. This configuration also affords greater protection to the wheelhouse in heavy seas. In the very latest designs of long-range tug, however, it has been found necessary to locate the superstructure forward to enable a long after deck to be incorporated, in much the same style as a very large anchor-handling tug supply vessel. The reason is commercial. Tugs of this latest generation have also been given the ability to assist with anchoring and mooring the oil-related equipment they tow on completion of voyages to offshore locations.

The propulsion system installed in the vast majority of large oceangoing tugs will be of the conventional screw type, incorporating some form of propulsion nozzle. Twin-screw vessels with fixed nozzles and controllable-pitch propellers are the most common, with each propeller driven by one or two main engines. Power output will of course depend to some degree on the size of vessel and can vary from around 3,000 bhp to a massive 25,000 bhp. The latter is the rating given to a pair of Russian-built tugs currently operating on the commercial towage and salvage market. Bollard-pull performance will also vary between approximately 45 tons and the 248 tonnes produced by those very large vessels. Free-running speed is more important in oceangoing tugs than most other types. The need to reach a casualty or the next task quickly is of the essence and may determine the success or failure of an operation. Speeds of over 18 knots can be achieved by some of the larger vessels. If present trends continue, those performance figures may well be surpassed very quickly by new vessels entering service. In the most recent examples of the modern long-range oceangoing tug good fuel consumption and endurance are also of prime importance. The majority of these vessels consume cheaper heavy-grade fuel oil and have very large bunker (tank) capacities to enable very long distances to be covered, whilst towing, without the need to refuel.

The handling characteristics of oceangoing tugs have to meet rather different requirements to the smaller vessels mentioned previously. An ability to handle well at sea, with perhaps an ungainly vessel in tow, is more important than extreme agility. Manoeuvrability remains important, however, particularly in tugs conducting salvage operations and working in the offshore oil industry. The installation of powerful transverse bow and stern thrusters is universal in large modern vessels. Integrated and dynamic control systems are also used extensively to simplify the handling of larger tugs whilst working in close proximity to other craft and offshore installations. Integrated control systems are discussed in Chapter 2 above.

Fairmount Expedition *is one of a series of five tugs built for Dutch-based Fairmount Marine BV. Completed in 2007 and 75 m long and 3,239 gt, the tug is powered by four Wärtsilä Vasa diesels generating a total of 16,000 bhp, and giving a bollard pull of 200 tonnes. The tugs are designed to operate economically over long distances.* (Fairmount)

A comprehensive outfit of towing gear is installed. The sheer size of the winches and towlines of a very large tug is impressive. The main steel wire towlines on large oceangoing tugs are 18–23 cm in circumference with a length sometimes exceeding 1,200 metres. Sufficient spare gear is carried to enable towing connections to be made using pendants of wire rope, chain cable, and possibly large-diameter nylon rope springs. Smaller 'tugger' winches and deck cranes are fitted to handle towlines and bridles and to assist in setting up towing gear or ground tackle. Hydraulically operated line-handling equipment, comprising tow pins and forks, developed originally for anchor-handling tugs, is now universal in large oceangoing tugs.

The towing winches in many of the larger vessels are located within the superstructure and several vessels built in the 1960s still have winches of the friction type. Because many winches cannot be seen from the wheelhouse, closed circuit television is frequently installed to monitor the movement of the towline passing round the various winch drums, thus avoiding serious problems from fouled or jammed ropes.

A stern view of the tug Salviceroy *shows the long after deck, high forecastle, compact superstructure and wheelhouse of a modern oceangoing tug. Built for POSH Semco Pte of Singapore in 2007, the 68 m twin-screw vessel is fitted with two Wärtsilä main engines generating 12,000 bhp.* Salviceroy *has a bollard pull of 157 tonnes and fuel consumption and bunkers to undertake long towage operations without refuelling. Note the enclosed winch housing and reels for spare towing gear.* (POSH Semco)

SALVAGE

The subject of salvage is an extremely wide one, on which many books have been written. The material that follows is intended only to give an indication of the work that salvage tugs must be prepared and equipped to carry out. Very few tugs

The British and French authorities regularly conduct exercises in the English Channel and the Western Approaches to hone the efficiency of their joint services. British Coastguard ETV Anglian Princess *and the French ETV* Abeille Liberté *work together to take the naval replenishment ship* Orangeleaf *in tow during an exercise.* Anglian Princess *is a 67.4 m anchor-handling tug of 16,400 bhp and 200-tonne bollard pull, built in 2002 and operated under contract by Klyne Tugs (Lowestoft) Ltd. (Author)*

are now employed solely in the traditional salvage role. Up to thirty years ago, it was common for many fully equipped tugs to be stationed in strategic locations around the world. Long periods were spent waiting to intercept a radio message indicating that a ship was in difficulties and required assistance. The rising cost of tugs and manpower has rendered this type of operation prohibitive for most operators. Vessels engaged in this kind of salvage work are now often subsidised, either by the owners themselves or by funds from government sources.

The fact remains that ships still suffer machinery breakdowns, weather damage or fires, and they still run aground. In most cases a well-equipped tug is required to give assistance and if necessary carry out a full-scale salvage operation. A ship would be very fortunate indeed to have such a commercial tug awaiting its calls on salvage station nearby; it is far more likely that a tug will be diverted from work elsewhere or dispatched from its home port, the exception being a government, or locally funded, tug on station or on patrol in the area.

Various serious accidents at sea and in coastal waters in recent years, where marine pollution has become a prominent issue, have persuaded an increasing number of governments to fund the provision of salvage vessels in a 'stand-by role' at sensitive locations. As previously mentioned those vessels are generally operated by coastguard authorities or other government agencies as 'emergency towing vessels' (ETVs) or 'emergency response vessels' (ERVs). The areas attracting most attention are those where shipping lanes are exceptionally busy, where a high proportion of hazardous cargoes are being carried, or where the coastline is particularly inhospitable and the weather unpredictable. In some cases, salvage tugs or other suitable vessels are contracted to provide cover all year round and in others for the winter months only when weather conditions are poor. The duty of an ETV is to attend the casualty as quickly as possible and render whatever assistance is necessary, the priority being to prevent the ship foundering and/or becoming a pollution hazard. Frequently, this involves standing by a disabled and drifting vessel while the crew make repairs but offering the security of a tow should the weather deteriorate or the situation worsen. When not involved with a specific incident an ETV may be used to patrol sensitive traffic zones, carrying out training or other duties for the employing coastguard agency. Many of the vessels employed are purpose-built and equipped not only for towage, salvage and fire-fighting but also for pollution control and recovery. Among the countries known to be operating purpose-built ETVS are Britain, France, Germany, Iceland, India, the Netherlands, Norway, Spain, Sweden, South Africa, and Turkey.

KV Harstad, built in 2005 to a Rolls-Royce Marine design, is an ETV of the Norwegian Kystvakt (Coastguard) owned by Remoy Shipping and operated under government contract. The 83 m vessel can undertake towing, salvage, fire-fighting and a wide range of other duties. It has a bollard pull of 110 tonnes and a maximum speed of 18.5 knots. (Rolls-Royce)

There remains a romantic notion that successful salvage operations produce rich rewards for owners and crews alike. This is still occasionally the case, but salvage specialists will argue that the massive costs of spectacular and the costs of difficult operations may not be fully covered by the resulting remuneration. This has resulted in a marked decline in the interest shown in salvage by some major operators. For many years the industry has relied heavily on 'Lloyds Standard Form of Salvage Agreement – No Cure No Pay', often known as 'Lloyds Open Form' (LOF), to ensure a fair and just settlement of salvage claims. This agreement, once made between tug and ship owners, enables salvage operations to take place immediately without the need for complicated financial negotiations before work can start. When the operation is completed a salvage award is eventually decided by an arbitration committee at Lloyds of London. If the salvage attempt fails, no payment is made. 'Lloyds Open Form' is still widely used in emergency situations where a ship is in danger and very little time is available to make other arrangements, and recent changes have been made to the agreement to encourage salvors to respond in sensitive cases were environmental damage may occur. Known as the 'Special Compensation P&I Clause' (SCOPIC), this element of the LOF agreement can be invoked where there is danger of a significant risk of pollution and where the likelihood of salvaging the ship is in doubt. This enables some payment to be made to the salvor in recognition of its services in preventing pollution regardless of the final outcome.

Incidents such as the sinking of the bulk carrier New Flame *off the coast of Gibraltar in 2007 can have serious consequences in terms of marine pollution. One of the first tugs on the scene was the Russian* Fotiy Krylov, *one of the largest and most powerful salvage tugs in the world, operated at the time by Tsavliris of Greece (now returned to its Russian owners). The first priority was to remove the heavy fuel oil from the ship.* Fotiy Krylov *is a 99 m vessel of 24,480 bhp with a bollard pull of 248 tonnes and maximum speed of 19.5 knots. (Tsavliris)*

In these days of improved communications other arrangements or agreements may be possible. The use of facsimile and secure radio transmission enables negotiations to take place and a contract to be made privately in a very short time. This may result in a tug being contracted on an hourly or daily basis or using some other criteria.

A major concern of the present-day salvor is the question of financial liability should a major pollution incident result from a salvage operation or occur whilst the casualty is in its charge. Stringent regulations and constraints are imposed on the movement of damaged ships into coastal waters by some local authorities and marine agencies and many place huge responsibilities on the salvage company. The

Tsavliris Hellas is a dedicated salvage tug from the fleet of the Tsavliris Towage & Salvage group in Greece. Built in 1977 as the French Abeille Normandy, *the twin-screw vessel measures 66.7 m and 1,487gt. Two main engines generate a total of 10,000 bhp, to achieve a bollard pull of 120 tonnes and a maximum speed of 15 knots.* (Tsavliris)

financial risk to the salvor and insurers is considerable and may deter some operators from becoming involved in the more difficult salvage operations.

There are a number of well-established specialist salvage companies who are not tug owners or operators. Those companies operate worldwide and respond to casualties using modern methods of communication and frequently make use of a network of specialist brokers. When a salvage operation is undertaken, any necessary tugs or other floating plant are hired from the nearest convenient operator. Salvage companies working in this way generally maintain a large inventory of specialist equipment and staff that can be flown anywhere in the world at very short notice. By operating in this way the companies are not burdened by the massive overheads incurred in keeping expensive salvage tugs at sea, in locations that may be days' of even weeks' travelling away from impending casualties. Several salvage companies have formed agreements, or alliances, with operators of oceangoing tugs of a known standard and will use their vessels if they are conveniently close to a casualty.

The term salvage tug is applied loosely to any vessel capable of carrying out the work in hand but it is generally accepted to be one equipped to a certain standard. A successful salvage tug must be self-sufficient to a large extent and will be large enough, and have adequate power, to assist casualties in a variety of different circumstances, often in remote parts of the world. The ship requiring a tow may be up to half a million tons. Tankers or bulk cargo carriers of huge proportions have required assistance from time to time due to propulsion or steering system failures and damage caused by heavy weather. Although the first tug to reach a very large casualty may not be sufficiently powerful to deal with it unaided it may be used to prevent the ship from drifting into danger or render other assistance

In the chapter on ship-handling, the process of picking up a tow was described as one requiring a great deal of skill. When an oceangoing tug is required to carry out the same procedure the hazards are multiplied. If the tug is called to a damaged ship in heavy seas, getting the tug in close enough to pass a towline in the usual manner, by heaving line, may be impossible. In high winds a ship without power may be drifting considerably and there are a number of alternative methods of making a connection. A line may be fired over the vessel using a rocket gun or floated downwind towards the vessel using a small buoy or float, and sometimes a helicopter can be employed to help.

Connecting a towline to a casualty can be an extremely difficult and hazardous operation in bad weather. The Dutch anchor-handler Boulder *is shown making a towing connection to the cargo ship* B Prus *disabled in heavy weather. The crew on the after deck are preparing to pass a messenger line whilst the tug manoeuvres close under the bow.* (ITC)

In order to simplify the business of taking ships in tow quickly in an emergency international maritime organisations are advocating the installation of emergency towing equipment in all vessels above a certain size, particularly tankers. The equipment called for is normally located at the stern of the ship and can take several forms. In general it comprises a steel wire towline or manmade-fibre rope, stowed on a reel or in a special sealed container. The inner end of the wire is securely fastened to a towing point on the ship and the outer to a long messenger line and a small coloured buoy. In the case of an emergency, the buoy and messenger line are thrown overboard by the crew to float away from the ship – for retrieval by the tug. The tug then hauls in the messenger line to pull the towline from its stowage.

There may also be difficulties when the casualty is aground in relatively shallow water. If a tug cannot approach due to its own deep draft a boat may be used, but in poor weather, line guns, floats, or other methods may have to be tried. To assist a ship aground the tug may require additional anchors and sufficient towing gear

Not all salvage operation require the services of very large and powerful tugs. When ships run aground on sandbanks in the busy River Schelde large numbers of ship-handling tugs are often employed to refloat them. In the case of the container ship Pelican 1 a fleet of local tugs, barges and a floating crane were used to remove some of the ship's cargo and gently refloat the badly damaged ship. (Multraship)

to make up 'ground tackles'. This is a method of increasing the tug's pulling capacity by using anchors and a multiple pulley system. The casualty may be damaged and require temporary repairs to its hull. For this work diving, welding, and cutting equipment will be needed and a supply of materials. Once repaired, the ship may have to be pumped out using pumps from the tug and perhaps portable units transported from shore. In more complex operations compressed air may be used to gain buoyancy and drive water from internal compartments. The need to discharge all or part of a ship's cargo before it can be refloated is a common occurrence. Electrical power may be needed to enable the ship's own cranes to be used. If the ship's engine-room is flooded or out of action for other reasons, power will be supplied either by the tug's generators or by transferring portable units. Where a large and badly damaged ship, such as a tanker, is aground it may be necessary to cut the vessel into two or more parts and refloat each section separately. This can be done with the careful use of small explosive charges or special cutting equipment. These common salvage tasks may have to be carried out in remote parts of the world where little or no outside assistance is available.

Fire aboard ship is one of the most serious hazards a mariner can experience and presents particular problems for the salvor. The fire may be fought using monitors and equipment installed aboard the tug similar to that described in

Chapter 7. But fires are not necessarily extinguished by simply dousing them with foam or water. Engine-room fires, caused by broken fuel pipes and similar failures are perhaps the most common occurrence. These are necessarily fought on board the ship and in this scenario the tug is likely to be tasked with cooling down the exterior of the hull and superstructure to prevent the fire spreading and to minimise structural damage. This is known as 'boundary cooling'. Cargo vessels with complicated stowage arrangements, or carrying containers, may have deep-seated fires needing other methods to extinguish them, such as injecting carbon dioxide gas. Bulk cargoes of grain, coal, and other combustible materials suffer problems with spontaneous combustion and are particularly difficult to extinguish. Flooding the ship with water to extinguish a fire may be the only solution but considerable thought has to be given to its stability. It may be necessary to beach the vessel on a suitable shore or take other precautions to prevent it capsizing due to the weight of water used in fire-fighting.

When the heavy lift ship Zhen Hua 10, *loaded with container cranes, was blown ashore on a tourist beach on the Netherlands coast it was refloated by the anchor-handling tug* Janus *and several powerful harbour tugs from Rotterdam.* Janus *was completed in 2007 for Harms Transport & Heavy Lift Gmbh of Germany and is a 65 m twin-screw anchor-handling tug of 19,000 bhp, with four engines and 219-tonne bollard pull.* (H. Hoffmann)

Collision is a common cause of shipping casualties, particularly in heavily congested coastal waters. The damage inflicted in a collision between two ships can vary dramatically from minor indentations to a vessel being virtually cut in two. Flooding due to damage below the waterline may be contained by pumping until a safe haven can reached or, alternatively, some form of temporary repair may be necessary. Once damage to the hull has been temporarily repaired it may be necessary to tow the vessel to port. In order to avoid causing further damage, towage operations are carefully planned. It is not unusual for a damaged ship to be towed stern first or at a particularly slow speed to reduce the pressure on bulkheads and other parts of a weakened hull structure.

LONG-DISTANCE TOWING

Long-distance towing covers a wide variety of operations ranging from the towage of conventional ships, to the safe transportation of all manner of floating objects from barges and dredgers to massive oil rigs and other oil and gas production equipment.

Towing ships over long distances is a well established task that has changed little in concept since tugs first went to sea. The size of ships likely to be towed has grown dramatically but it must be accepted that any ship currently in service may require towage at sea at some stage. Many oceangoing tugs now in service can deal efficiently with ships of any size. Ships are towed long distances for a number of reasons. Even the most modern vessel can be disabled by a machinery failure and require towage to a suitable shipyard for repair. Ship repairing and reconstruction is an extremely competitive business and ships are towed many thousands of miles to have work carried out. In the same way, new ships may have their hulls built in

Fairmount Glacier *is shown leaving Invergordon in Scotland with the semi-submersible oil exploration rig* Frontier Driller *in tow bound for Pascagoula in the Gulf of Mexico. The tug is an identical sister to* Fairmount Expedition *illustrated earlier. This is exactly the type of long-range towage operation this current generation of tugs was designed to undertake.* (Fairmount)

one location and be fitted out many thousands of miles away for sound economic reasons. Old and redundant ships, sold for breaking up, are towed to parts of the world offering the best prices for scrap steel. The cost of towage is part of the economic equation and competition for such work is fierce. A large tug, properly equipped, has been known to tow two, three, or even four ships at a time to shipbreakers in the Far East from Europe, the USA, and South America.

Towage operations concerned with other kinds of floating object can be considerably more complex. As the towage industry has developed, the subjects for transport by towing have become larger and stranger. Large pieces of floating plant, dredgers, cranes, oil drilling rigs, oil and gas production and storage vessels and similar items are frequently towed long distances. The products of heavy engineering are often too large and unwieldy to be shipped in any other way. Many of these objects are slow, difficult tows requiring great care, and particularly vulnerable in very bad weather conditions. In the last decade or so, however, 'dry towing' has eliminated some of those difficulties.

A typical 'dry tow' is pictured entering the New Waterway in Holland. The flat-top pontoon barge Sainty No 7 *is arriving from China in tow of the deep-sea tug* Salvage Champion. Sainty No 7 *is loaded with a dozen new, partially completed motor barges destined for the European waterways.* (H. Hoffmann)

Dry Towing

'Dry towing' refers to transporting such objects by loading them onto a very large barge. In order to allow large pieces of floating equipment to be loaded, some barges are designed to be submerged temporarily. The buoyancy of the barge is controlled by pumping and ballasting systems located beneath the single flat deck. Once the barge is submerged, the object to be transported is towed into position

Complex 'modules' destined to become part of giant offshore oil or gas production rigs are built ashore, taken to sea and assembled onsite. Barge OC 4126 from the fleet of Otto Candies Marine Transport & Towing is leaving port to be towed out to a site in the Gulf of Mexico with a 'module' welded to its deck. (Otto Candies)

over the deck, the barge is then raised and the object secured – usually by welding it temporarily to the deck. The welds, cradles, brackets and other items required to fasten the cargo securely to the barge are generally known as 'sea fastenings'. By this means complete oil rigs and similar pieces of equipment can be loaded and towed more safely and often much faster than would be possible if they were afloat. Dredging companies make good use of this method of transport. A whole dredging outfit, dredgers, dump barges, floating pipelines, and small dredging tugs are often loaded on to one barge. Once secured, the entire outfit can be towed to a new location, on the other side of the world if necessary.

Transporting large or awkward 'non-floating' items by barge is now commonplace. Flat-topped pontoon barges are normally used, some of which are extremely large, to carry items such as dockside cranes, sections for new bridges, huge oil refinery components, and fabricated sections of new ships. Offshore oil and gas production facilities, under construction many miles from shore, frequently have much of their upper-works and machinery built in modular form at engineering yards ashore. Individual modules, some weighing many hundreds of tonnes, are transported by barge to the construction site and lifted into place.

Bulk commodities such as stone, coal, ore, petroleum products, timber, and paper are also transported, in large quantities, long distances by tug and barge. Modern shipping containers, vehicles and railway wagons all form part of the regular tug and barge operations in some part of the world. In locations such as Alaska towed barges with all of the commodities mentioned play an important part in the area's infrastructure. The barges used in this work can vary in size up to a carrying capacity of 20,000 deadweight tonnes or larger.

The economics of any towage operation are governed not only by the cost of hiring suitable tugs but also by the expense of insuring both tug and tow. The premium for a major towage operation is based on many factors. Surveyors from specialist companies are often used to assess the risks, taking into account the type of tug, the nature of the vessel to be towed, the distance, route, and likely weather conditions. Recommendations may be made and conditions laid down regarding towing methods, the route, and the way the tow is to be conducted. The relatively lower insurance risks and costs involved have been partially responsible for the success of 'dry towing'. Unfortunately for the tug owner, the 'dry towing' method faces stiff competition from operators using self-propelled heavy-lift vessels offering similar services.

Towing Operations

The principles involved in towing over long distances are much the same as those previously described for coastal towing, only the scale of the operation differs. Preparations for a tow are made in exactly the same manner. The vessel to be towed is surveyed and any necessary steps taken to ensure that it remains seaworthy for the duration of the voyage. Ships, oil rigs, and similar vessels may have a small 'running crew' on board to care for the towing connections, pumps and lighting, and generally monitor the condition of the vessel. Provision is made for this small crew to be housed as comfortably as possible, in what may be somewhat austere conditions. Once the tow is at sea their only contact with the tug will be by radio. The vast majority of barge tows are unmanned, however.

A critical factor is always the towing connection. Considerable attention must be paid to the towline and its connections. Many large barges and some ships have special fittings permanently welded to their decks to enable towing connections to be made swiftly and efficiently. The most common are known as 'Smit brackets' and were developed by the Dutch towing specialists Smit International several decades ago, as part of a study to develop quick and efficient methods of taking large vessels in tow. The Smit bracket allows the eye end of a towline or bridle to be secured quickly by a large sliding pin. A bridle is usually made up from lengths of chain cable, or steel wire, coupled to the towline to form a 'Y'. Two legs of the bridle are then secured aboard the vessel to be towed. The bridles used on very large barges that are in constant use are extremely heavy and designed to resist the continual wear and chafing that takes place during towing.

When taking a ship in tow, over long distances, a chain bridle or the ship's own anchor cable are commonly used to make the towing connection. The anchor is removed from the cable and the towline connected in its place. A few metres of cable are then paid out, making a durable and effective connection. Alternatively, the anchor can be disconnected but left in place in the hawse pipe and the cable paid out through a suitable fairlead in the ship's bow.

Prior to leaving port an emergency towline will be rigged aboard the vessel to be towed. This takes the form of a length of steel wire towline, or high performance manmade-fibre rope, secured at one end to bitts on board the vessel, arranged along its sides or rails and held in place by rope lashings. To the free end of this emergency towline is coupled a length of light line and a small brightly coloured buoy. Once the tug and tow are under way the buoy and its line are thrown overboard to trail astern of the convoy. If the main towline should break during bad weather, the tug can rapidly locate the buoy and, using the light line, haul the end of the emergency towline on board and make it secure. As the tug takes up a towing position the remainder of the emergency towline breaks free from its lashings and extends to its full length.

The flat topped pontoon barge AMT Traveller (9,779 tonnes cargo capacity) is typical of many used to transport a wide range of unwieldy items. Clearly visible is the chain bridle, secured to 'Smit brackets' aboard the barge (left). The bridle is part of the barge's equipment and may be hauled aboard by a small winch in the bow.
(Author)

In many tows a length of large diameter manmade-fibre rope will used to connect the main towline to the bridle or cable. This acts as a 'spring' to help cushion the towline against shock loading. On board the tug some provision may also be necessary to ensure that the towline is protected against chafing. In the more modern vessels the tug's stern is designed to minimise contact with the towing gear. Where this is not the case, the towline will be protected by sleeves manufactured from rubber or composite plastics, or the contact points will be heavily greased.

Delivering ship's hulls or partially completed vessels by towing them long distances at sea is a very common practice. In this picture the hull of a new 'feeder' container ship is arriving in the Netherlands from Romania to be fitted out and completed. In charge of the tow is the Hellas, *from Greek operator Gigilinis Salvage & Towage, a twin-screw tug of 50.5 m and 5,200 bhp with a 75-tonne bollard pull.* (H. Hoffmann)

Once an oceangoing tug and its tow are at sea the main towline will be adjusted to a length suitable for the conditions. The towline will be paid out by the winch to several hundred metres in length, depending on the conditions. An important feature of the towline in deep-sea operations is its inherent sag or catenary. The length and weight of the towline act as a spring or damper, lessening the effects of snatching and shock loadings caused by the action of the waves and the relative motion of both vessels. A steel towline several hundred metres in length will sag considerably and remain deeply submerged. When the tug enters busy coastal sea-lanes the towline will be shortened to give the tugmaster better control and ensure that the towline does not foul the seabed. Alternatively, in poor weather, the towline may be lengthened further to reduce the strain on the towing connections.

When more than one vessel is to be towed, if at all possible a separate towline will be used for each. For example, if two ships are towed, a towline will be rigged for each from separate drums on the towing winch. This enables the respective towline lengths to be adjusted so that the vessels will not collide with each other

Sister tugs Sea Victory *and* Sea Venture *work together to tow a partially fitted-out oil exploration rig. The tugs are from the fleet of US operator Crowley Marine. Both are twin-screw vessels of 45.73 m, powered by EMD diesels of 7,200 bhp (total) for a bollard pull of 108 (short) tons.* (Crowley)

or foul the towlines. There are occasions when it is necessary to tow in tandem, with one vessel connected to another. This presents difficulties for tugmasters in that they have little control of the towline between the two vessels. Its length cannot be adjusted when entering harbour or for different weather conditions.

There are also occasions when more than one tug will be required to handle a particular tow. If two tugs are to be engaged to tow a large vessel over long distances, separate towlines will be connected directly to the vessel. The length of the towlines will be carefully adjusted and the position of each tug monitored carefully during the voyage to minimise the risk of collision and ensure that the towing loads are equally distributed. Very large tows, the positioning of permanent oil production platforms for example, may involve a whole fleet of tugs. The platforms are usually constructed at sheltered coastal sites, towed to their final location offshore and lowered into position by flooding parts of the structure. The tugs used for such an operation are selected by size, bollard pull, and handling characteristics. Each tug is connected to a particular position on the structure and the entire operation is controlled by a 'tow master' from a vantage point on board. The 'tow master' co-ordinates the movement of all the individual tugs to achieve the correct course and speed.

A less common towing method, used occasionally as a temporary expedient, is towing in tandem, where a towing connection is made from the winch or tow hook of one tug to the bow of the other. This method is sometimes used when additional power is required to assist a tug in difficulties or when refloating a ship aground.

Towing very large, high-value vessels used in the offshore industry for the production and storage of oil is an important source of revenue for the long-distance sector of the towage industry. The new deep-sea tugs Salveritas *and* Salviceroy *are pictured towing the Bohai FPSO from Shanghai to Singapore.* (POSH Semco)

Provided that the first tug has a towline of suitable strength it is a simple means of adding more power without the need to make another towing connection aboard the vessel in tow. A temporary tandem towing connection is sometimes made when a second tug makes a rendezvous with a tug and tow to transfer fuel or fresh water. In this situation hoses and other equipment can be hauled along the towline.

ANCHOR-HANDLING TUGS AND ANCHOR-HANDLING TUG SUPPLY VESSELS

Work in the offshore oil and gas industry is a highly specialised activity that becomes more complex as supplies of oil and gas become more difficult to locate and extract. This section is intended to give only a broad outline of the work involved and the vessels employed. Anchor-handling tugs and anchor-handling tug supply vessels perform duties that are arduous and often dangerous. In order to satisfy the current demands of the offshore oil industry such vessels must be able to participate in towing, positioning, and anchoring the current range of drilling rigs, pipe-laying barges, and similar pieces of floating plant, and keep them supplied with consumable stores. The offshore oil industry continues to explore in more remote locations and is now operating in deeper waters and in increasingly hostile climates – both hot and cold. To undertake this work the size of rigs and plant in general has also increased. Consequently, the vessels required to assist in these operations have, of necessity, become larger and more powerful.

209

Any major offshore rig or similar piece of plant will be supported by a number of vessels. If the rig or barge is of the 'jack-up' type it will be towed into position and the supporting legs jacked down to raise it above the surface of the water. A rig of this type operates in relatively shallow waters, and will then only require the services of a supply ship and a standby vessel. The oil-rig supply vessel will attend regularly to deliver supplies and remove unwanted waste and equipment. A standby vessel is a mandatory requirement in most locations and is constantly on station to ensure that other shipping remains a safe distance from the rig and to assist in emergency situations, such as the evacuation of a rig in the event of a serious fire. Occasionally a suitably equipped tug or supply vessel will be used to perform the duties of a standby vessel. The current practice in most areas is to have specially designed vessels, well equipped to spend long periods on station and deal with emergency situations.

Maersk Supplier *is an anchor-handling tug supply vessel built for the Maersk Company in 1999, a vessel of 82 m in length, capable of carrying out a wide range of anchor-handling, towing and cargo transport duties. A powerful vessel with a bollard pull of 212 tonnes, it is powered by four MAK main engines driving twin screws with a total of 18,000 bhp.* (Maersk)

Rigs and construction vessels of the semi-submersible type remain afloat and need to be anchored when they arrive in the selected location. Most semi-submersible rigs used by the offshore oil industry are moored using a system of eight or ten anchors deployed in a star-shaped pattern. Each of these anchors must be taken out in turn to an exact position and lowered to the seabed. Rig anchors weigh in the order of 12–45 tons, or larger in some special cases. When the rig moves each of the anchors have to be 'broken out' of the seabed, raised, and carried back to the rig. The anchor-handling tasks will be carried out by a team of anchor-handling tugs or anchor-handling tug supply vessels. Where the rig is operating in extremely deep water the size and weight of each anchor, and the length of wire and/or chain to which it is attached, becomes a significant factor in the choice of anchor-handler. In extreme cases the anchor-handling vessel may require a very high bollard pull, and winch capacity of over 400 tons in order to retrieve a single anchor. Where long lengths of chain cable form part of the rig's anchor system, the anchor-handler may be required to take on board the anchor and chain. In the more modern anchor-handling vessels the chain will be taken on board and stowed in special chain lockers provided below decks, adjacent to the winches.

While the semi-submersible rig is in position it requires much the same standby and supply services as the jack-up mentioned earlier. Anchor-handling tugs without a substantial cargo capacity will remain with a rig only if further moves are to be made in a short space of time. In the case of a pipe-laying barge, the tugs remain in use constantly, relaying anchors every few hours as the barge moves forward.

The Norwegian anchor-handling tug supply vessel Sea Lynx *of Deep-Sea Supply Shipping AS is towing the 'jack-up' rig* Ensco 102, *escorted by the tug supply vessel* Far Sovereign. Sea Lynx *was built in 1999, measures 73.9 m and 2,556 gt, with Wärtsilä main engines of 15,000 bhp.* (H. Hoffmann)

The Anchor-Handling Tug

The modern anchor-handling tug is a powerful, well-equipped deep-sea tug incorporating a high forecastle, a wheelhouse located close to the bow and always an open stern. Its prime purpose is to tow and deal with the anchors of rigs, barges and construction plant. Such vessels will have the ability to carry some cargo on the after deck but no specialist bulk cargo tanks below deck as found in the anchor-handling tug supply vessel.

The anchor-handling tug will almost certainly be a twin-screw vessel with propulsion nozzles, controllable-pitch propellers, bow and stern thrusters and an integrated control system. Those are common features in a vessel that spends much of its working life at sea and is frequently required to operate in close proximity to other craft. The size and power of a modern anchor-handling tug varies enormously but vessels of approximately 1,000 tonnes gross and perhaps 10,000 bhp can be considered common and economical in terms of manning. As anchor-handling conditions become more challenging larger tugs are entering service to meet that challenge. Among the most recent examples are tugs of 19,000 bhp with a bollard pull of 220 tonnes, and larger vessels are planned.

To enable the heavy and unwieldy anchors to be handled effectively the tug must have a completely clear afterdeck and a winch designed for the purpose. During the anchor-handling process the tug is often required to take the anchors on board by hauling them over its stern, along with their associated chain and other fittings. For this purpose a large, heavily constructed, horizontal roller is installed in the stern, usually at deck level. To prevent damage to the deck a thick wooden cladding, which can be easily replaced, is applied to the working area. Substantial guard-rails are usually fitted at either side of the working area to afford some protection to the crew and prevent fouling should an anchor break loose in heavy weather.

The modern anchor-handling tug Magnus *was completed in 2006 for the rapidly growing fleet of Harms Transport & Heavy Lift Gmbh of Germany.* Magnus *is a 58.5 m twin-screw vessel powered by two MAN diesels of 19,000 bhp achieving a bollard pull of 200 tonnes. This stern view clearly shows the winches, line-handling pins and stern roller.* (Harms)

The winch in an anchor-handling tug has at least two drums, with one designed specially for working with anchors and capable of producing a static pull much higher than that required for towing. The steel wire rope fitted to that drum is likely to be shorter than a towing wire but must be of sufficient strength to withstand the strain of breaking an anchor from the seabed and bringing it on board. In order to simplify the work of securing the anchors and their chain cables, and reduce the workload of personnel on the exposed after deck, special handling equipment has been developed. This equipment varies but generally consists of some form of jaw or gripping device. Line-handling gear of this type is located near the stern of the vessel, ahead of the stern roller, and retracts flush with the deck when not in use. 'Sharks jaw', 'Karmfork' and 'Triplex' are all well-known types of line- and chain-handling equipment. Most comprise a hydraulically operated jaw or other device that rises vertically from the deck to grip the chain or wire of a rig anchor securely once it has been hauled on board, over the stern roller. These devices are normally used in conjunction with at least two hydraulically operated stop pins. A common arrangement is to have two gripping devices, each served by a pair of stop pins.

The work of handling heavy anchors, chain, buoys, and other equipment on the after-deck is aided by the use of at least two small 'tugger' winches. Wires from the tugger winches are used in conjunction with various fairleads around the after end of the vessel to move heavy items around. A versatile hydraulic deck crane with a useful working capacity of 10–20 tons is invaluable aboard the anchor handler and found on virtually every vessel.

Anchor-Handling Tug Supply Vessels

Oil-rig supply vessels in use in offshore oil fields around the world can be broadly divided into three main categories: the pure supply ship – not fitted with any equipment for anchor-handling or towing; the much more powerful vessel fully equipped to tow, lay and recover anchors; and highly specialised vessels based on similar designs but equipped to provide a wide range of other services in the oil industry, such as diving support, maintenance and offshore construction.

It is the fully equipped anchor-handling tug supply ship with which this section is concerned. The size and power of oil-rig supply vessels is determined very much by the location in which they are intended to operate. When this type of vessel gained prominence in the very early 1960s most had evolved from the relatively small ships in use in the oil fields of the Gulf of Mexico. As offshore oil exploration spread to the Arabian Gulf, the Far East and North Sea, conditions became more demanding with a corresponding need for larger and more powerful supporting vessels. As those earlier anchor-handling tug supply vessels have become outmoded they have frequently found alternative employment as inshore salvage vessels or tugs, in employment where the inherent additional deck space is particularly advantageous.

The modern anchor-handling tug supply vessel embodies the towing and anchor-handling equipment previously described in the section on anchor-handling tugs but size and cargo capacity are the main differences. A typical example of an anchor-handling tug supply vessel working in the northern regions of the North Sea would be a ship of some 2,300 gross tonnes, 74 metres in length,

Olympic Octopus, *owned by Olympic Shipping AS of Norway, is a 78.5 m anchor-handling tug supply vessel designed by Rolls-Royce Marine and built in 2006 to incorporate some of the latest developments in remote line-handling on the after deck. The cranes visible above the bulwarks are used to manipulate anchor-handling gear remotely to minimise the need for personnel on deck.* Olympic Octopus *is a vessel of 1,600 bhp and 180-tonne bollard pull.* (Rolls-Royce)

with a long clear after deck capable of carrying 1,200 tonnes of cargo. The cargo carried varies considerably but will include foodstuffs and other stores in standard containers, engineering equipment and often drill pipe, casing and other long cylindrical items in large quantities. In addition, dedicated cargo tanks and handling equipment will be available below decks for cargoes of bulk liquids and cement. The liquid cargoes commonly carried by supply vessels are drinking water, drilling water, liquid mud, brine and fuel oil. Drilling water, mud and brine are special compounds used in the process of drilling for oil and may need special treatment while on board such as regular agitation.

The propulsion system of an anchor-handling tug supply vessel of the type described will certainly be twin screw, with controllable-pitch propellers rotating within fixed nozzles. Two or four main engines are common, with two driving each propeller shaft through twin-input/single-output gearboxes in the latter case. In the example of a North Sea vessel mentioned previously the total power available will average some 16,000 bhp giving the vessel a bollard pull of some 160 tonnes. Transverse thrusters are likely to be fitted fore and aft and possibly an additional, retractable azimuthing thruster in the bow. The propulsion and steering control systems in most modern supply vessels include a single-lever joystick control, working in conjunction with the main engines, propeller controls, and thrusters. As previously mentioned, systems of this kind are computer-controlled and also make use of inputs from the vessel's auto-pilot and gyro compass. This enables the ship to be moved bodily in any direction by the movement of a single lever and the heading to be changed or maintained by simply setting a compass bearing. Many of the propulsion controls and a joystick are provided at an after control station in the wheelhouse with an exceptional view of the after deck. The master of an anchor-handling rig supply vessel spends a great deal of time operating from this position.

When the vessel is employed in the 'supply ship' mode of operation, it is literally regarded as a very large and versatile maritime truck. Supplies of all kinds are taken on board in a convenient port and taken to the rig being supported, a journey that might vary in distance between a few dozen or a few hundred miles. At either end of the delivery voyage the vessel will be required to manoeuvre accurately and quickly. In port it may be necessary to move between various berths in order to load different bulk and containerised cargoes. When the vessel arrives at the rig it will be required to take up an allotted position beneath the appropriate crane and unloading area. In most cases this involves moving into position stern first and remaining in position whilst unloading takes place. Frequently, no actual mooring is possible and the supply ship must be capable of accurately maintaining the correct position and heading for long periods, sometimes in very difficult

Far Sapphire, *built for Farstad Shipping in 2007, is an advanced anchor-handling tug supply vessel of 92.7 m in length powered by four Bergen main engines generating a total of 21,760 bhp and coupled to twin screws. The vessel has a bollard pull of 240 tonnes (270 tonnes when the azimuthing thrusters are used) and a speed of 17 knots.* (Farstad)

215

The towing and anchor-handling winch (above) aboard Far Sapphire has three drums with line pulls of 350–675 tonnes. Note the size in relation to the man standing beneath the drums.

Karm forks (left) come in all sizes. Aboard Far Sapphire they can withstand a safe working load of 275 tonnes.

Far Sapphire is fitted with a unique 'anchor recovery frame' (left) to raise the height of the anchor-handling 'work' wire to aid the recovery of very large anchors over the stern roller. When not in use the ARF folds flush with the deck. (Farstad)

weather conditions. In this respect the single-lever control, or a dynamic positioning system, simplify matters considerably for the ship's master. The vessel is manoeuvred forward, astern and to either side quite easily while the auto-pilot maintains a pre-set heading. If necessary, cargo is moved around the deck by means of wires from the tugger winches. Bulk cargo is transferred through hoses, using the powerful pumping equipment installed in the vessel.

When towing, the anchor-handling tug supply vessel operates in exactly the same manner as any large open-stern tug. The after deck is of course cleared to ensure that there are no obstructions to foul or interfere with the towline. In most cases hydraulically operated line-handling equipment and stop pins are used to control the position of the towline and prevent it moving out to either side and endangering the vessel. Alternatively a gog eye will be fitted to the deck aft and the wire from a tugger winch used as a gog rope, with a large running shackle in place over the towline.

Many large and powerful anchor-handling tug supply vessels are equipped with high-capacity fire-fighting systems and monitors capable of fighting fires on exploration rigs and production platforms. In order to be suitable for this work monitors must be capable of projecting jets of water high enough to reach the upper levels of massive platforms, often over a hundred metres high. Supply vessels equipped in this way may well be engaged in a stand-by role that also involves rescue duties should a major incident occur on a rig or platform. Among the additional items of equipment needed for the task are small fast rescue craft, scrambling nets and other aids to retrieving personnel from the water. Some very large vessels are also equipped with a lightweight heli-deck to enable helicopters to land and take off to transfer personnel and stores.

Anchor-Handling Operations

The methods used to moor oil and gas exploration rigs vary considerably and are dependent on the type and size of rig, depth of water, the type of sea bottom, and prevailing tidal and wind conditions. The paragraphs that follow describe the sequence of events for a typical anchor-handling operation.

When the oil rig or barge arrives in the desired location, attendant tugs or anchor-handling tug supply vessels keep it in position until the anchors are laid and known to be holding satisfactorily. Each anchor is connected to a steel wire rope or chain cable deployed by winches aboard the rig. The entire operation is controlled by the supervisor in charge of the rig using VHF radio communication with all the vessels involved.

There are two main methods of laying and retrieving the large anchors used by rigs and large work barges. An early well-established method involves the use of a steel wire pennant permanently attached to the head of the anchor. The free end of the pennant passes through a large steel buoy and when the anchor is laid, the buoy and pennant remain attached with the end of the pennant supported on the surface by the buoy, ready to aid retrieval.

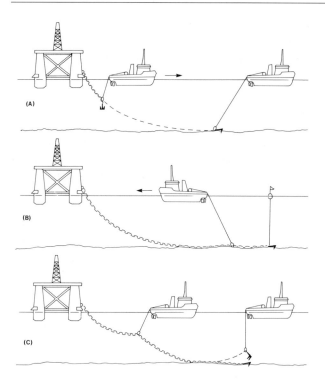

Anchor-handling.

(A) The tug hauls the pennant and 'chaser' under its stern and takes the anchor out to the required position, lowers it to the seabed and tows it out to tension the chain.

(B) Either, a buoy is secured to a permanently attached pennant, or the 'chaser' is towed back to the rig.

(C) To retrieve the anchor the 'chaser' is towed from the rig along the anchor chain to engage the anchor, or the buoyed pennant is retrieved, to haul the anchor from the seabed to be returned to the rig.

A more modern system, developed for use in much deeper water, does not use a buoy. The pennant is attached to a 'chaser' – a shaped steel collar that is free to move along the anchor cable and locate on the shank of the anchor. The pennant is used to carry the anchor out to its position but is 'chased' (towed) back to the rig for retention until required for the retrieval operation at a later date.

To lay an anchor, the tug must first take on board the free end of the pennant. The tug manoeuvres close to the anchor stowage position on the rig and the pennant end is passed down to its after deck by crane. The pennant is coupled to the anchor-handling winch wire and hauled in until the anchor is secured, hanging beneath the tug's stern roller. If a buoy is used it is taken on deck or also secured at the stern. The tug then moves away from the rig to a predetermined position as the anchor cable is paid out. Once in position, the anchor is lowered to the seabed and towed along to tension the chain cable. The pennant is then secured to its buoy or, when a chaser is used, returned to the rig. The operation is repeated until all anchors are in position. If the seabed is such that anchors do not hold the rig properly, two anchors may be connected to each anchor cable. This may entail the tug taking the anchors on board, along with their connecting chain, to transport them to the position where they will be laid.

To lift the anchors, in readiness for a 'rig move', much the same process will be repeated in reverse. A chaser pennant is collected from the rig and towed along the anchor cable until it is positioned on the anchor. With a buoy system the pennant is connected to the winch wire and the buoy secured or taken on board. With the pennant connected the tug hauls on the anchor to 'break it out' from the seabed. It is then raised and taken back to the rig as the cable is reeled in.

The operation is not always straightforward. If a pennant breaks or for some reason the anchor cannot be retrieved in the normal way the vessel will have to retrieve the anchor wire by 'grappling' for it using a specially designed grappling hook or a device known as a 'J' hook or 'shepherd's crook'. This is a tedious process, involving towing the grapple across the seabed until the wire is 'caught' and hauled aboard. The anchor-handler may also be required to service the rig's anchors and replace pennants or anchor cables. Many vessels equipped for anchor-handling are provided with additional, large power-operated storage drums to enable these items to be taken on board.

Anchor-handling operations must continue day and night in all weathers until the work is completed. It may take a couple of anchor-handling tugs or anchor-handling supply vessels anything from twelve hours to several days to lay a pattern of eight anchors in poor conditions. The crew on the after deck may be working for long hours with heavy gear, sometimes waist deep in water with the vessel rolling and pitching in an alarming manner.

In the very latest anchor-handling tug supply vessels a great deal has been done to improve the protection available to the crew working on the after deck and where possible mechanise the process to obviate much of the manual handling necessary in earlier vessels.

In this photograph the anchor-handling tug supply vessel Boulder *is manoeuvring close to the pipe-laying barge* Castoro Sei *to pick up an anchor pennant and buoy prior to laying the anchor in a new position.* (ITC)

CHAPTER 9

Pusher Tugs and Pushing

A less obvious form of towage, used widely throughout the world, is pushing. Large numbers of tugs spend most of their working lives pushing barges of all shapes and sizes, either on inland waterways or at sea. In some countries the movement of cargo by pusher tug and barges on inland waterways is an important feature of the national transport infrastructure. The tugs employed in this unlikely form of towage fall into two quite distinct breeds. There are the true 'pushers' – known in American parlance as 'towboats' – designed to operate almost exclusively on inland waterways. They are invariably rectangular in plan-form and unlike any other type of tug. There are also tugs of a conventional type that spend much of their working lives pushing. Of these, many operate inland but others form part of seagoing transport systems working with very specialised barges or as part of fully integrated tug/barge systems.

Elsewhere in this book the emphasis has been on towing astern, which raises the valid question – why is pushing so widely used? There are two main reasons: improved handling and economy. Once a pusher tug is connected astern of its barge or train of barges the whole tow behaves in much the same way as a single vessel, achieving not only improvements in handling but also in propulsive efficiency and fuel consumption. The aim of all tug and barge combinations is to maximise the use of the most expensive components of the transport system – the power unit and the crew. One tug can service many barges, delivering cargoes, returning empty craft, or deploying them to other locations to load return cargoes. The tug does not have to remain idle during loading or unloading operations and, if properly organised, can remain in operation more or less continuously. A useful by-product of the barge is that it can provide a convenient means of short-term storage, particularly for bulk cargoes. Once loaded, suitably weather-proofed barges can, if necessary, remain at convenient moorings until required, offering a high degree of security.

Manning costs related to tug and barge operations can also offer very large savings. When compared with self-propelled vessels with similar cargo capacity the manning scales that legally apply to a pusher tug are frequently much lower than those required for a conventional ship of a similar size. This is particularly noticeable in the case of tugs working with very large barge trains, or with tugs pushing a single seagoing barge with a cargo capacity of many thousands of tons.

The inland waterways of the USA and Europe form an important part of the transport infrastructure. Veerhaven X, *the most recent addition to the Dutch fleet of Thyssen Krupp Veerhaven BV, is seen pushing loaded iron ore barges from Rotterdam to the Ruhr in Germany.* Veerhaven X *is a triple-screw pusher of 40 m in length, 15 m beam and 1.74 m draft, built in 2007. Three MAK main engines generate a total of 5,544 bhp to drive fixed-pitch propellers rotating in high-performance nozzles. Extensive accommodation is provided and considerable effort has gone into reducing noise and vibration.* (Kooiman)

For pushing to be effective on inland waterways, the barges must be firmly secured to the bow of the tug and each other. The barges built for use with pusher tugs have square ends and are easily secured together as a single unit. The manner in which barges are prepared for pushing varies considerably with the waterway and geographical location. In areas where the waterways are mainly narrow rivers or canals, barges are pushed singly or in tows of two or three barges in line ahead. The need to use the largest barges practicable, and handle several with a single tug, has made conventional towing uneconomic on many waterways.

Large American towboats handle vast tows of up to thirty barges on the wide rivers of the southern states of the USA. Push-towing on inland waterways is common throughout Europe, North and South America, Africa, and some parts of Asia. Many of these areas have wide but sometimes shallow waterways running for many hundreds of miles, acting as major thoroughfares for cargoes moving inland from coastal ports. On the major waterways in north-west Europe large pusher tugs ply the routes between the major coastal ports and industrial centres inland with barges carrying shipping containers, vehicles and bulk cargoes of coal, ore and many other commodities. In Britain the inland waterways are generally very narrow and less suited to push-towing with vessels of any size, resulting in a very small population of true and rather specialised pushers. To undertake push-towing operations under these differing conditions a wide variety of vessels of different sizes and designs are used, but all operate in a similar manner.

Pushing operations at sea are complicated by weather conditions that can dramatically affect the performance and safety of the tug and its barge. The tug used in this type of operation is normally of the conventional screw type, suitably modified or purpose-built for the work. Single barges are used, shaped at the stern to accommodate the bow of the tug. In recent years there has been significant development in the field of 'articulated tug and barge' (ATB) units where the tug fits into a deep notch and is secured by one of a variety of sophisticated coupling devices. Fully integrated, tug/barge systems are also in use and closely resemble a ship when assembled, with the tug fitting closely onto the stern of the vessel to form a rigid unit.

THE INLAND WATERWAYS PUSHER TUG

The true pusher tug comes in a variety of shapes and sizes, but virtually all are based on a hull that is rectangular in shape. Above the waterline the bow is square and incorporates two or more heavily fendered vertical 'push knees'. This is the tug's interface with its tow. The knees are often several metres high to enable good contact to be made with the barges being pushed, regardless of whether they are fully loaded and deep in the water or empty with a great deal of freeboard. Steps are constructed in the rear face of the knees or a special ladder provided to enable crew-members to gain access to the deck of the barges, whatever their height.

The methods used to secure the barges to each other and to the tug vary greatly with the geographical location and with the individual operator. Steel wire ropes are generally used to make the various towing connections but an important feature of the operation is the means used to tension the securing wires. Throughout Europe and in many other locations small deck winches are fitted at strategic locations on the pusher tugs and aboard the barges. The winches are generally hand-operated, via large distinctive handwheels, and designed to produce the required tension in wires connecting the barges to each other and the tug with little manual effort. Similar winches may also be installed on multi-purpose work vessels and small conventional screw tugs to facilitate pushing operations. Tensioning devices using a screw thread, known as 'steamboat ratchets', are still widely used in pushing operations among the 'towboat community' in the USA for the same purpose.

The height of the barges being pushed and the length of the tow stretching out ahead of the tug present a problem of visibility for all tugmasters involved in

The Rijn, *operated by Smit Transport Europe, is typical of many small pushers in use in Europe and elsewhere. Clearly visible are the twin push knees, high wheelhouse and gangways to give access to the barges.* Rijn *is a twin-screw vessel of 17.11 m in length powered by General Motors main engines of 720 bhp (total).* (Author)

pushing operations. A good field of view forward over the barges is essential, bearing in mind that the bow of the first barge may be many metres away from the tug. This demands a wheelhouse mounted at a suitable height. In some areas the provision of a very high wheelhouse presents no difficulty, in others it conflicts with the need to pass under low bridges or through tunnels. Various forms of retractable wheelhouse are used to combat this problem. Most are hydraulically operated and can be readily varied in height to suit operating conditions while the vessel is under way.

The propulsion system is invariably of the conventional screw type with the number of propellers dependent on the size of the vessel and power output

Arjos, *owned by Bevi & Co, is pictured pushing loaded coal barges between Belgium and Holland. Built in 1981, the 16.33 m pusher has two Detroit diesel engines rated at 1,120 bhp (total). Note the stern anchors, elevating wheelhouse, and the car and motorcycle on the bridge deck ready to be hoisted ashore by the small crane.* (Author)

required. A twin-screw arrangement is most common but triple and quadruple installations are by no means rare. Multiple rudders astern and additional flanking rudders located ahead of the propellers are frequently used to enhance the vessel's handling characteristics. A triple-screw tug may well have a rudder system comprising at least nine rudders, one aft and two ahead of each propeller. Fixed propulsion nozzles are often used to improve performance and in very shallow-draft tugs the propellers may be located in tunnels beneath the hull. In some of the smaller tugs azimuthing propulsion units are used instead of normal propellers to enhance their manoeuvrability. The power output of the engines will depend on the size of tug but can vary from 120 bhp in the smallest canal pusher to more than 8,000 bhp in a very large 'towboat'. Unlike most other tugs, inland waterways craft often have completely self-contained engine cooling systems to avoid the possibility of picking up debris and foreign matter, a common source of trouble in shallow waters. A great curse of the conventional cooling system is the discarded plastic bag which can cause havoc once sucked into the tug's hull inlet. Instead of drawing cooling water from outside the vessel, the skin of the vessel or tubes under the hull are used to dissipate heat from the engine systems.

There are occasions when the pusher tug will need to anchor. Most have one or two anchors, located at the stern and controlled by a windlass in the normal way. These anchors are generally larger than those normally found on inland vessels to ensure that they are capable of holding not only the tug but also a heavy tow, should an emergency arise. In many areas the size and type of the anchoring system is laid down in local regulations. A towing hook may also be fitted at the after end of some pusher tugs and used to handle individual craft when the tug is preparing barges for a journey.

Small Pushers

The smallest pusher tugs of all are relatively simple vessels, consisting of little more than a hull, engines, and a wheelhouse. There is often no requirement for more than rudimentary accommodation. Measuring between 5 and 15 metres in length, with engines of 200–600 bhp, they have many uses. In most parts of the world, where large-scale push-towing is carried out, small pusher tugs are employed to assemble strings of barges in readiness for the larger tugs. This entails collecting barges from loading and discharging wharves, one or two at a time, and travelling short distances to and from the assembly point.

Similar pushers are also used in some areas by shipyards and marine civil engineers to move work barges, floating cranes and similar pieces of engineering plant from one site to another. Small pusher tugs may also be used in conjunction with specially constructed pontoon ferries to carry passenger and vehicular traffic.

In the United Kingdom a limited amount of stone, coal, fertilizers, paper products, and animal feedstuffs are transported by barge on the very narrow inland waterways. Motive power is provided by small pusher tugs or small conventional tugs equipped for pushing. Operating with barges of only 80–100

The twin-screw pusher tug Pile Express *of Grady Marine Construction of Fort Lauderdale, Florida, is typical of many very basic pushers owned by construction companies, shipyards, barge operators and even ferry operators. This simple vessel is 12.05 m long, with main engines producing a total of 636 bhp. (Author)*

tons they require engines of no more than 120–250 bhp. The size of barges and their attendant tugs is limited by the dimensions of the canals, and their lock systems, originally designed for self-propelled or even horse-drawn traditional 'narrow boats'. With much of the British Waterways canal and river system being developed for leisure use there remains the need for efficient maintenance plant. In recent years a whole new fleet of maintenance craft has been introduced, including work barges, spoil barges and dredging equipment. This fleet operates on a flexible modular principle using a standard pusher tug design as motive power for all of the craft.

In 2004 British Waterways, responsible for the inland waterways of the UK, took delivery of the first of 23 tiny pusher tugs to be used with a new fleet of barges, dredgers and other floating plant. The 6 m long, 2.07 m wide, vessels are powered by a single Beta Marine diesel engine giving only 39 bhp, with a hydraulic drive and single rudder. (Author)

European Pushers

Several hundred pusher tugs are employed throughout Europe on the inland waterways systems. Of these many are medium-sized pusher tugs or conventional tugs fitted with push knees, serving the shorter routes and feeder services. Large well-equipped pusher tugs undertake the longer-distance tows with up to six large barges. A large proportion of the barges are standardised – with those designated Europa Class 1 carrying up to 1,500 tonnes, and Europa Class 2 accommodating 2,800 tonnes of bulk cargo. There is considerable heavy traffic using the latter, which can be made up in trains of up to six craft. Larger barges of up to 5,000 tonnes are also in use, along with more specialised craft used to transport containers, vehicles and petroleum products.

Franz Haniel 15, of Haniel Reederei, is one of the larger long-range pusher tugs operating on the inland waterways of Europe, transporting bulk cargoes of ore and coal from Rotterdam to Germany. The triple-screw vessel is 34.98 m in length and powered by three Deutz main engines producing a total of 4,500 bhp. (Author)

The configuration chosen by European owners is determined very much by the regular routes on which the vessel will be used. The size of the waterway, its locks and bridge heights and the regulations applying to the particular waterway are all factors to be considered. Power requirements are governed by the size of the barges and likely tidal and current conditions. The result is likely to be a vessel of between 15 and 40 metres in length and up to 6,000 bhp. Twin or triple screws are the most common arrangement, with propulsion nozzles and multiple rudder systems. Flanking rudders are used in conjunction with the normal steering and propeller controls in some vessels to achieve a high degree of manoeuvrability. A vessel of similar size in use on the major rivers of America would be regarded as a medium-sized craft and employed on the shorter routes.

As previously mentioned, wheelhouse height can be critical and even on the larger vessels some form of variable height structure may be fitted. This may take the form of a straightforward vertical lifting wheelhouse or one incorporating a more complex mechanism. Most are hydraulically operated and in the lowered position blend with the superstructure. The vessel's radar antennae and masts are also capable of being raised and lowered. One or two high definition river radars are common in pusher tugs, enabling operations to continue in poor weather.

A feature of this larger type of vessel is the high standard of accommodation provided. Many of the European inland waterways tugs, and indeed many self-propelled craft, are operated and manned by family concerns and become a mobile home to those on board. As a result there are often signs of domestic accoutrements and family life on board. Small boats may be carried to act as

Among the many traditional pusher tugs operating on the European waterways is the Maasstroom 9, a 27.6 m vessel built in 1957 and now powered by a single Cummins-Wärtsilä diesel of 900 bhp. Note the large elevating wheelhouse and characteristically immaculate condition of the vessel – operated by Dutch company Vos Gebr of Ammerzoden. (Author)

tenders and workboats in the normal manner; in addition, it is not unusual to see a car parked on the afterdeck with a small crane or ramps provided for loading and unloading.

American Towboats

The origin of the large American towboat can be traced back to the days of the early stern-wheel paddle craft that plied the wide shallow waterways of the southern states. Their modern counterparts are an important part of the transport network, moving many thousands of tons of cargo on rivers flowing through the heart of the country. Many old-established companies operate sophisticated modern towboats on the Mississippi, Missouri, Ohio, and Tennessee rivers and their tributaries.

The configuration of these giants is basically the same as their smaller European sisters, but again the main difference is in the scale of the entire operation. The towboats vary in size from the smaller types of vessel previously mentioned to very large craft of over 50 m in length and 14 m beam. Such vessels may have a draft of less than 3 m. The power required to handle the very large tows undertaken by

The twin-screw towboat Kathy Ellen, *of Alter Barge Line Inc of Iowa, is shown pushing a string of barges on the Intracoastal Waterway in Texas.* Kathy Ellen *is a vessel of 42.72 m in length, fitted with two General Motors engines giving it a total of 3,800 bhp. Note the stern anchors.* (BMG Photos)

Ann Peters, *operated by the Ingram Barge Company of Kentucky, is a twin-screw towboat of 27.74 m in length powered by Cummins main engines of 3,000 bhp. Built in 1974,* Ann Peters *was reconstructed in 2008. The vessel is engaged mainly in the distribution of stone in the southern United States on the Ohio and Mississippi rivers.* (Cummins)

HMS America *is a small pusher typical of many in use on US waterways. Such tugs are used for the shorter distance tows and/or assembling tows for the larger towboats. HMS America, operated by Houston Marine Services, is 18.29 m long and powered by two General Motors diesels generating 1,600 bhp.* (B. Allen)

many tugs often exceeds 8,000 bhp. Twin-, triple-, and quadruple-screw propulsion arrangements are common. The most striking feature of the large towboat is the hotel-like accommodation, housed in a huge superstructure three or four decks high. The wheelhouse surmounts this massive structure, providing the master with an uninterrupted all-round view. A number of powerful search-lights are provided to illuminate the margins of the waterway when necessary and to inspect the tow.

The routes travelled can be many hundreds of miles long and the tow being pushed may contain over 30,000 tons of cargo and can comprise 15, 35 and even 50 barges. Individual barges on the Mississippi River system are standardised to some extent, with three main types: open hopper, covered dry cargo, and liquid cargo tank barges. Three main sizes also apply: small – with a cargo capacity of 1,000 tons; standard – 1,500 tons capacity; jumbo – 3,000 tons capacity. In any one tow the barges may contain a variety of cargoes and some will be empty. This presents its own problems. In order to make up a balanced manageable tow, the barges will be assembled with the heavier units in the centre and lighter ones around the sides. Also to be considered is the destination of each barge; some will be detached at intermediate ports and others picked up en route.

The use of large pushing towboats is not confined to the USA. Many other parts of the world have waterways equally suited to this form of transport. Several rivers in South America, Africa and Asia have similar systems in operation.

Double-Ended Tugs

A very small but notable minority of tugs, employed mainly in Europe, are designed as true double-ended vessels, being fully equipped for pushing and towing. The more modern double-ended tugs are vessels of 500–1,000 bhp and about 25 metres in length. A hull design with push knees at one end and a conventional bow at the other makes them unique. Tractor propulsion is used, generally with azimuthing propulsion units located beneath the bow. Such vessels are incredibly agile and have a wide range of uses.

Eerland 26 *was one of a very small number of true double-ended pusher tugs built in Europe and Britain in 1967. The 24.3 m vessel is a tractor tug with two azimuthing propulsion units, a normal bow and large push knees at the stern. Now owned by Smit Transport Europe, this vessel was rebuilt in 2004 with a pair of Mitsubishi main engines delivering 1,800 bhp (total) for a bollard pull of 20 tonnes. It is shown towing a barge loaded with a pontoon and equipment containers.* (H. Hoffmann)

When pushing, the vessel places its knees against the tow and is secured in the normal way. A tow hook or winch is fitted forward of the knees for use when towing astern. The towline emerges through an aperture between the knees and the vessel travels bow first. In most true double-ended vessels the controls in the wheelhouse and the vessel's towing and navigation lights are all designed to allow it to travel safely in both directions.

PUSHING WITH CONVENTIONAL TUGS

Conventional screw tugs are used in large numbers for push-towing on inland waterways and at sea. This form of operation offers great flexibility, often allowing the most suitable mode of operation, pushing or towing, to be chosen with little additional preparation. The main restrictions applying to a conventional tug push towing in exposed waters are related to weather and the state of the sea, restrictions that are overcome by some of the more sophisticated connection systems employed by articulated and integrated tug and barge units mentioned later in this chapter.

Small conventional tugs and tug/workboats are very popular for pushing operations on inshore waters in Europe and elsewhere. This means of providing motive power for single or small numbers of barges and items of construction plant is particularly economical when relatively short journeys are involved. The tugs used are either adapted for the work, or purpose-built. Many of those employed on inland waterways are comparatively elderly and have had very long working lives. Operating in fresh water reduces the effects of corrosion on hulls, slowing down the rate of deterioration significantly. It is not unusual for a vessel to be updated and a new engine fitted at intervals of twenty years or less. The tugs themselves are little different from those described in previous chapters. To adapt them for push-towing a single strengthened knee is built into the bow, or an alternative arrangement comprising a simple frame with fendering fitted, closely resembling the knees of a true pusher tug. Again, small hand winches are often used to tension the wires securing the tug to its barge. Pushing on a single knee demands great care in securing and tensioning the wires which run diagonally from the after corners of the barge to the winches on the tug's deck. In general the barges used have a flat transom stern. More elderly rounded barges are also adapted for pushing. As with the pushers previously mentioned, the height of the wheelhouse is of prime importance, to ensure good visibility forward over the barges. Additional flying bridges or ingenious variable height wheelhouses are used in much the same way.

Valk is a single-screw tug of 23.32 m operated by Dutch contractor E. Valkenburg and typical of many vessels that have changed hands and been re-engined several times. Built in 1928, the tug now has substantial push knees, an elevating wheelhouse and a 1,061 bhp Deutz main engine. (Author)

231

This method of towing is common in the USA on the smaller rivers and canals and in coastal waters. Many of the barges used have a shallow notch provided in the stern in which the bow of the tug is inserted, in much the same manner as larger seagoing craft. In smaller American tugs the securing wires are tensioned using the traditional 'steamboat ratchets' or by using wires from the towing winch.

All round the world conventional tugs are used to push barges using just a single bow fender and suitable means of tensioning the securing wires. The small Dutch tug Tender *is shown secured to a large pontoon barge using small hand winches to secure the tow.* Tender, *of Lekstroom Transport, is a tug of 18.66 m with a 260 bhp Brons engine.* (Author)

PUSH-TOWING AT SEA

Pushing rather than towing barges at sea is popular on many coastal and intercontinental routes. This method of operation, with a conventional screw tug pushing a barge at sea, was originally developed in North America and Canada where barges have been pushed on inshore waters for a great many years. More recently purpose-built barges, with notches built into the stern to accept the tug's bow, have become a well-established method of operation.

Tug and barge transport systems of this type have been adopted by companies in North America, Scandinavia, Northern Europe, the Middle East and the Pacific on coastal and deep-sea routes. The method is particularly suited to bulk cargoes, with coal, ore, stone, crude oil, and petroleum products being the most common. Specially constructed carriers are used to carry timber, forest products, cars, containers and cattle.

232

Teresa *is a twin-screw tug of 38.71 m operated by Penn Maritime in the USA and has two EMD main engines producing a total of 7,000 bhp. The tug is secured in a shallow notch to the 150 m petroleum barge* Acadia *by an Intercon coupler. Note the high-level wheelhouse used when pushing.* (BMG Photos)

Pushing at Sea with Conventional Tugs

The tugs engaged in this type of work are what may be described as medium-sized conventional screw vessels. Most have a twin-screw propulsion system, and the use of propulsion nozzles varies widely from owner to owner. The power required varies with the size of barge and the conditions it will operate in but vessels of 2,500–6,000 bhp are typical. In most respects they are equipped in exactly the same manner as a large ship-handling or coastal tug. As previously mentioned many American tugs regularly perform both ship-handling and barge-towing duties. The question of visibility forward over the barge is again an important one. Tugs regularly engaged in push-towing large barges can readily be identified by a high-level control position of some kind. A popular arrangement takes the form of a secondary wheelhouse mounted high above the normal one. Access to this 'crow's-nest' type of wheelhouse is via an external ladder or stairs inside the vertical column. Variable height wheelhouses, similar in design to those of inland vessels, are less common in seagoing tugs.

Suitable bow fendering is essential and often the shape of the bow is designed to match the notches of a particular series of barges. Unlike vessels involved in articulated or integrated tug/barge systems, the tugs employed are frequently required to operate with a wide range of barges. The techniques used to couple the tug and barge are a critical factor in the seagoing tug and barge operation and much effort has gone into developing suitable methods and equipment. The ideal form of coupling is one that allows the tug to be quickly and positively attached to the stern of the barge and automatically compensates for changes in draft of tug or barge. The most usual compromise is to have a moderately deep notch in the stern of the barge and a wire rope securing system using the tug's towing winch to provide the necessary tension. A common method of retaining the tug firmly in the notch of the barge uses two wires, one from each after quarter of the barge. The ends of the wires are secured aboard the barge and passed through heavy fairleads in the bulwarks of the tug, near the stern. The inner ends are then shackled to a

233

towline from the towing winch and tension applied, drawing the tug forward to engage firmly in the barge's notch.

The tug remains connected to the stern of the barge for the duration of its intended voyage, unless the weather conditions deteriorate beyond certain predetermined criteria. It is generally the state of the sea that limits the safety of the tug/barge combination in the pushing mode. The criteria laid down vary with the particular craft and type of coupling involved but a wave height of approximately 2–3 metres is likely to be the limit imposed on many tug/barge combinations using wire rope systems. Once this sea state is reached the tug will disengage from the notch in the barge to prevent damage to the connecting wires or to the vessels themselves. A normal towline will have been rigged on the barge in readiness for such an eventuality and arranged to enable the tug to take up a towing position ahead of the barge with a minimum of effort or lost time.

Ellen S. Bouchard *and its 122-metre, 80,000-barrel capacity tank barge* No 282 *form an ATB unit using an Intercon connecting system. The tug pushes in a deep notch and remains connected during seagoing voyages.* Ellen S. Bouchard *is a tug of 34.14 m in length with main engines of 3,900 bhp originally built in 1982 but refitted for its full ATB role in 2007.* (Intercon)

Articulated Tug and Barge Units

The 'articulated tug and barge' (ATB) unit takes the tug and barge principle previously described one stage further. By using specially designed or adapted tugs and barges with advanced coupling systems it is possible to produce an ATB unit which closely resembles a ship in performance, carrying capacity, and seakeeping qualities, yet can offer improved operational flexibility and substantial savings in crew costs. ATB combinations continue to grow rapidly in popularity, due mainly to developments in coupling technology – with the initiative emanating mainly from the USA. Bulk cargo barges, the majority designed to transport petroleum products, coal, cement, ore, sugar and grain, are available with capacities of between 10,000 and 45,000 deadweight tons. The ATB is currently proving particularly popular in the tank barge sector for transporting and distributing oil and petroleum products. American marine transport and towage specialist Crowley has a growing fleet of modern double-skinned barges, built to the latest standards and capable of carrying between 155,000 and 185,000 barrels of oil. The same owner has plans for a further series with a capacity of 330,000 barrels.

*Crowley Petroleum &
Chemical Transportation's
ATB tug* Resolve, *is seen
shortly after completion in
2007. A twin-screw vessel
of 41.15 m in length and
12.6 m beam,* Resolve *has
two Wärtsilä main engines
optimised to burn heavy
fuel oil and developing a
total of 9,280 bhp. Note
one of the 1.27 m
diameter Intercon
connecting pins, visible on
the side of the hull, used
to couple the tug to its
170 m tank barge.*
(V. T. Halter)

A tug used as part of an ATB unit is very similar to those used for push-towing at sea in tug/barge combinations using wires to secure the barge. The tug fits into a very deep notch in the stern of the barge to a depth of approximately half its length and is secured by one of a number of proprietary coupling devices. In general a modern ATB tug will be a vessel of between 36 and 45 metres in length with a high forecastle. A twin-screw propulsion system will be powered by engines of 3,500–10,000 bhp to drive conventional propellers, with or without nozzles.

At the heart of every successful ATB unit is the coupling between the tug and barge. A number of manufacturers and designers supply these highly specialised coupling devices. The most common systems are known as Artubar, Bludworth, and Intercon, manufactured in the USA, and Articouple from a Japanese company. In each case the tug is positively located on the centre-line of the barge but allowed some pitching movement. The tug therefore rolls and heaves with the barge and is 'articulated' about a horizontal pivot point.

With the Bludworth system a substantial vertical steel bar is fitted at the forward end of the barge's notch and is gripped by powerful hydraulic pads fitted on the tug's bow. The tug can pitch vertically about this connection but yawing and rolling motion is restrained by hydraulically adjusted side pads on the tug, which interface with surfaces on either side of the notch. The Intercon system comprises two very large horizontal pins that move outwards from the tug's hull to engage toothed racks on either side of the barge notch. In both cases the tug's vertical position in relation to the barge can be adjusted, to compensate for the differing drafts of either vessel. The Artubar and Articouple systems operate on similar principles, with both using horizontal securing pins. Although many tugs are fitted with the coupling systems described they may only be used with barges of the same type and with precisely matching couplings.

The ATB unit Sea Reliance *and its 27,000 tons deadweight tank barge is capable of carrying 185,000 barrels of petroleum products on seagoing voyages. The vessels are coupled using the Intercon system.* (Crowley)

ATB systems have the advantage of being quick to operate and offer good performance at sea. Although the tug has the ability to withdraw from the barge notch, should sea conditions become unacceptable, and tow on an emergency towline, most major operators report that this rarely happens in modern articulated systems.

Once the tug is secured in position at the after end of the barge, the ATB unit performs in much the same way as a small ship. A high wheelhouse gives the tugmaster excellent forward visibility over the barge and can normally be accessed internally. Remote controls are provided to enable the tugmaster to lower and raise the barge's anchors, control the various lights, stop and start auxiliary engines, and in some cases operate a bow thrust unit. These remote controls may be operated via an umbilical cable when the tug is pushing the barge and by a radio link when it is streamed astern on a towline.

New York *is a rigid integrated tug/barge unit, one of a number operated by the Amerada Hess Corporation out of US mainland ports. Built in 1983, the tug is a twin-screw vessel of 40.75 m in length with a catamaran configuration. The tug is rigidly connected to a 'ship-shaped' oil tank barge of 22,331 gross tons bearing the same name, and is only normally separated for maintenance.* (Author)

Integrated Tug and Barge Units

A number of rigid 'integrated tug and barge' (ITB) units are also in use around the seaboard of the USA and elsewhere in the world. The rigid ITB commonly comprises a relatively large 'ship-shaped' barge of approximately 18,000–22,000 tons deadweight pushed by a tug that is rigidly connected at the stern, and at first sight is almost indistinguishable from a small ship. The hull of the tug is of a twin-screw catamaran configuration designed to fit around the specially shaped stern of the barge. Hydraulically operated locking mechanisms are used to keep the two portions firmly attached to each other. A fully integrated tug and barge unit of this type is designed to operate exclusively as a transport system in its own right and is rarely separated. Once at sea, there is no provision for the tug to be released from the barge to tow on a towline. The tug is no longer a readily adaptable workhorse, but a dedicated power unit for a particular barge, with each vessel bearing the same name. Once assembled the tug and barge is for all intents and purposes a ship, albeit with some important savings in terms of manpower and other costs.

Index